Who Will Take Care of Me When I'm Old?

Also by Joy Loverde

The Complete Eldercare Planner: Where to Start,
Which Questions to Ask, and How to Find Help

Who Will Take Care of Me When I'm Old?

Plan Now to Safeguard Your
Health and Happiness in Old Age

JOY LOVERDE

Da Capo
LIFE
LONG

Da Capo Press
Hachette Book Group
1290 Avenue of the Americas, New York, NY 10104
www.dacapopress.com
@DaCapoPress; @DaCapoPR

Printed in the United States of America
First Edition: October 2017

Published by Da Capo Press, an imprint of Perseus Books, LLC, a subsidiary of Hachette Book Group, Inc.
The publisher is not responsible for websites (or their content) that are not owned by the publisher.

Library of Congress Control Number: 2017951374

ISBNs: 978-0-7382-1963-9 (paperback), 978-0-7382-1964-6 (ebook)

LSC-C

10 9 8 7 6 5 4 3

This book is dedicated to YOU—
who has decided to do something courageous today,
for which your future self will be extremely grateful.

Contents

Part Two
Where You Live Matters

Part Three
Ties That Bind And Unwind

Part Four
Safety Nets

Get Real

Almost every day—barring overextended itineraries (mine) and medical emergencies (his)—I log into my computer in the wee hours of the morning to video chat with Martin K. Bayne, my dear and longtime friend. He is an MIT graduate, journalist, and former Buddhist monk. He is also unmarried and childless.

At the peak of his professional career, Marty was diagnosed with early-onset Parkinson's disease. He was fifty-three. With no other choice but to move into an assisted living community, he knew that this housing decision would challenge him every waking moment to stay alive, let alone remain vital.

For the past sixteen years, he has been at the mercy of a call button that is answered by complete strangers. His fellow residents are on average aged eighty-five years and older, the majority of whom are living with the symptoms of dementia. As his chronic conditions worsen, so goes the freedom to come and go where he wants when he wants. To date, Marty has been "evicted" from three different assisted-living facilities when they can no longer care for him at the level he requires. He is trying desperately to avoid moving into a nursing home.

As a resident of assisted living, what he hadn't calculated is the depth of the daily, relentless exposure to despair, disease, dementia, dying, and death. That's where I come in. Marty tells me that he would have given up on living long ago if it were not for our friendship. When we are not talking about what is happening in his world, I do my best to balance the relationship by bringing what is happening on the "outside" to him. By way of my smartphone, Marty and I often take virtual walking excursions to my favorite local attractions. After one such visit to Chicago's Lincoln Park Zoo where I paused to greet a gathering of gorillas, he nicknamed me "Fear Swallower." When I see people walking and playing in the park, I stop and ask them to say hi to Marty. They love it, and of course, their enthusiastic, "Hi, Marty!" greetings make his day. We enjoy these outdoor adventures immensely. I depend on Marty every bit as much as he depends on me. While I offer him companionship and insights into my world of family and work, he is my teacher and voice of reality when it comes to aging alone. "You can't possibly understand, Joy, what my life is like." As a relatively younger assisted-living housing "insider," he says these words to me frequently when he is trying to make a point. He's right: I can't possibly understand what his life is like. I have never been that sick and that alone.

"I have no voice," Marty said to me one morning. I asked him to explain. The night before, he and the administrator of the assisted-living community had a difference of opinion about a particular resident policy. Marty challenged him, saying, "That's not fair. You get to go home every day at five o'clock, but this is my home." The administrator stood up, pointed his finger at him, and roared, "This is *not* your home. You just lease an apartment here like everybody else." At that moment, Marty realized he was alone, ill, and without the comfort and support of an on-site advocate. His spirit was broken.

Marty never fails to keep me grounded in the realities of aging alone. The essence of each conversation is not the subject matter, but rather the sharing of experiences with someone who genuinely cares about the big and little things in life that you wouldn't share with just anyone. I know now that if I have a friend like Marty in my life when I am old and alone, I will be able to get through anything that life dishes out. Marty is my trusted lifeline and shows me just how important our relationships are as we age—and how many challenges there can be to sustaining them.

Whether you have a "Marty" in your life right now or not, you have chosen this book for good reason. Perhaps, like Marty, you don't have children to call upon for help; perhaps you're like me, married now, and also wondering who will be available, able, or even willing to step in when necessary. But no matter what your situation, you have questions on how your life will change as you grow older. Are you ready for what the upcoming years have in store?

Join the Club

If you are living solo, you are not alone in this trend. One in three baby boomers falls into the category of separated, divorced, widowed, or never married.[1] As the numbers continue to escalate, millions of people over the age of sixty-five will require greater assistance because they are aging alone with no known family member or surrogate to act on their behalf.

Committed couples, you aren't out of the woods, either. If one partner suffers from a chronic illness, the other partner typically represents the first line of defense. However, when both need care simultaneously, all bets are off. As people make their way from adulthood through elderhood, the unmarried category will grow as individuals continue to experience divorce and widowhood.

Nor is being a parent a guarantee that adult children will care for you as you age. Children may choose to move away from parents (even a half-world away) to pursue dreams of their own; and they are also known to return home with little to no resources.

Simply put, you have no idea whether anyone you love and trust *today* will accompany you on your aging journey or be by your side up to and until you take your final breath. If you currently have a close network of family and trusted friends, and feel confident that they will be there for you any time of the day and night, then count your blessings. As your personal network evolves due to death or other extenuating circumstances, you can continue to use your relationship-building skills to develop new and rewarding alliances. If you prefer a more insular and solitary lifestyle, you may unknowingly be choosing to go it alone during uncertain times.

Let me be clear from the get-go—marriage is *not* the goal of this book by any means. Aging solo is the conscious choice of many and deserves its rightful status in society. If marriage (and partnering) is not, and has never been, a desire of yours, this would be a good time to update your language when referring to your preferred living situation. The use of the word *single* implies the state of not being married. To proclaim you live solo is more straightforward and powerful. No matter what you choose, the purpose of this book is to get you ready for old age and help you put your own plans in place so you can live as *you* want, for as long as possible.

Why This Book?

Who Will Take Care of Me When I'm Old? will change the course of your life, solo or with family. You need not be alone in old age unless you want to be. Also, be open to learning how to anticipate the challenges you'll face and prepare to meet them early on.

When people ask me when old age begins, I prefer to use the age of ninety as a starting point (you may have other ideas for when old age begins). With diet and exercise, along with medical advances, the idea of living to ninety is not a stretch anymore. By the time we reach our ninth decade, worn-out body parts may subject us to chronic medical conditions, which in turn will affect where and how we live on a day-to-day basis. We can also expect to outlive people in our inner circle of family and friends. When do you think old age begins? Do you believe that it is never too late to plan for a quality old age?

I learned the ropes of planning for old age by spending almost every waking moment of my life surrounded by old people. "You have to fight for what you want," they tell me. And fight they do. Witnessing the aging of thousands of older adults, I have heard their incredible stories—the good, bad, and sad. I have spent many hours with the dying. The memory of these encounters is what led me to write this book and fill it with the old people's advice.

I have been a family caregiver most of my adult life, and in 1993 published my first book, *The Complete Eldercare Planner*, now in its sixth edition. Thousands of readers have told me that my practical tips on looking ahead while managing complex relationships changed the course of their caregiving experience for the better. Since publishing that book, my research and writing on eldercare has evolved beyond caregiving to focus on how people can prepare to care for themselves as they age. I participate in as many webinars, workshops, group discussions, studies, expert panels, and conferences on aging as time allows. I am embedded in a social web that connects me with an expansive and diverse network of industry thought-leaders and mature-market business owners, continually seeking their advice and picking their brains. Extensive travel also allows me to compare experiences as I observe the cultures and traditions of old people worldwide. Above all, I am curious and inquisitive, and have a reputation for seeking ways of pushing the envelope. This includes a daily practice of reading books and any material that expands my outlook on old age. I want to know what others are saying—and doing—at all times about their own aging.

Inevitably, after every one of my keynote presentations, people approach me and express how worried and afraid they are about aging alone in old age. I am in the same boat; but when I think about the old people in my life who are aging alone, and how they know themselves inside and out, and how they flaunt their unshakable confidence when making important decisions, I believe that in my old age, I will have what they have—but it is up to me to put in the effort *now*. And I believe the same is true for you. You may not have chosen to age solo, but you must *own* it to succeed at planning for a quality old age.

I have spent years accumulating advice, tried-and-true tips, "secret formulas," and guiding principles from experts in the aging industry—the old people themselves. They are my truth detectors. Following in their footsteps, I make note of what works when solving the problems associated with aging alone in old age. On that note, here is a brief preview of what you gain from reading this book:

Real solutions for creating a support network
Critical questions you don't know to ask
Strategies to foster smarter decision-making
Alternative ways to think about old age
Insights for end-of-life planning
Accessibility to innovative products and services

To make this book possible, I have never stopped listening and observing old people. They are the teachers to where we are all headed. To be old is a complicated process; aging is an intricate web of interdependent physical, emotional, financial, and social factors. The willingness to be a lifelong student of the teachings of old age is what keeps me grounded in reality.

The Deal-Breaker

You must promise that from this moment on you will be completely honest with yourself about the fact that you are getting older. Sixty is *not* the new thirty. Sixty is sixty. Every time you make light of or even deny aging, you create an alternate reality; and subsequently, you are forced to live a life in two different worlds: the one you are fantasizing about and the actual one in which you are living.

Acceptance of your own aging paves the way for breakthroughs of all kinds—lying and deceiving yourself about growing old leads to the exact opposite. Instead of feeling powerless and a victim of circumstance, choose to face old age with self-respect and dignity. Plan ahead. Doing so will serve you in gaining better control of the situation at hand. *You* are the one and only person you can forever count on.

The aging process can be extremely unkind. Over the years, you may have known people who suffered terribly with chronic and emotional pain. Perhaps you watched helplessly when someone you loved plummeted into the darkness of depression or dementia. Witnessing the aging and dying process changes you.

You Are Here

The old people in my life often tell me how peaceful they feel in the moment. They tell me their work is done. They have accomplished what hopefully you are about to do: remain true to the realities of old age. They are honest with themselves. They ask for and accept help. They know what is important and what is a waste of time. They feel fear and take action anyway. Above all, they do not wait for a crisis.

Now It's Your Turn

Everything I have learned from my wise elder friends is what I wish for you today—that ailments do not depress you, that you are quick to laugh and even quicker to forgive, and that you are happiest of all when you are on the receiving end of tokens of love and kindness from others who genuinely care about you. You've got a friend in me.

—*Joy Loverde*

Don't Read This Book.
Work It.

This book was born of the unsettling question . . . *who will take care of me when I am old?*
    "Downright terrified" and "scared of being old and alone" is how thousands of people describe their endgame. No doubt, this book will stir similar emotions. Catch your breath, and then move on. There is a light at the end of the tunnel.

You alone know the truth as to why you are holding this book in your hands in the first place. You alone will have to find ways to keep yourself motivated—to read this book from cover to cover, to face the realities of aging alone in old age, to explore solutions to your unique problems, to create action steps, then to respond to new and unexpected circumstances that force you to go back and adjust your plans. I promise not to waste your time with unnecessary busywork. Everything about this book is purpose-driven.

How you read this book matters not. Whether you choose to cozy up for hours on your favorite reading chair, catch a paragraph or two on the run, or download the electronic version, keep in mind that *Who Will Take Care of Me When I'm Old?* is not a book to read once and put aside. The messiness of the aging process will demand that you continuously revisit the book's content as your circumstances evolve.

The book is divided into five main categories:

Part One: Personal Readiness
Part Two: Where You Live Matters
Part Three: Ties That Bind and Unwind
Part Four: Safety Nets
Part Five: No Tomorrow

Read the chapters in any order that works for you. To make it easy on what you can expect to read and accomplish, review the "Objectives" list offered at the beginning of each chapter. The end of each chapter offers a list of Insights and Inspiration. These are books, movies, songs, and TED Talks that go beyond the resources offered within each chapter. I've shared these with you to offer other perspectives and fresh takes on each chapter's theme.

Planning requires staying organized. Make good use of the worksheets and checklists recommended throughout the book. Suggested action plans will also contribute to your ability to stay on track. Downloading forms from my website—www.elderindustry.com—allows you to customize the content. The index at the back of the book makes it easy for you to find and refer to the desired content again and again.

As a reader of this book, you will benefit greatly by being computer and Internet savvy. This allows you to take full advantage of the online resources offered throughout. If you currently are not a home computer user, seek assistance at your local public library where free computers and basic computer instructions are available or, consider hiring a home-based "computer tutor."

Social media are a comprehensive source for support and information. Use the suggested keywords to search topic-related blogs, Twitter (www.twitter.com), and Pinterest (www.pinterest.com). Facebook (www.facebook.com) connects you to others who are experiencing similar situations. Specialty Facebook groups may be posted as "closed" due to privacy needs, but ask to join anyway. Requests to join are typically recognized quickly. My own social media accounts may be a great place for you to start:

Facebook: www.facebook.com/joy.loverde
Instagram: www.instagram.com/joyloverde
LinkedIn: www.linkedin.com/in/joyloverde
Pinterest: http://pinterest.com/joyloverde
Twitter: https://twitter.com/joyloverde
Website: www.elderindustry.com

The last section of the book, "Cross It Off Your List," will help you pull it all together. As you complete tasks, check off the boxes. Doing this will give you greater peace of mind that you are making progress toward accomplishing your personal goals.

Finally, everybody ages differently. Some of what is written in this book will apply to your situation and some will not. Take what works for you and leave the rest. There is something here for everyone. *You* ultimately decide how to go about integrating the action steps into your life. Do not take the content offered in this book at face value. When necessary, tweak the information to customize your unique life plan.

Part One

Personal Readiness

Meet Your Future Self

Discovering who you have yet to become

1

....
Objectives
....

After completing this chapter, "Meet Your Future Self," you will be able to:

• Use time travel as a strategy to plan ahead
• Face the truth of family and friends coming to your rescue
• Explore your readiness for taking action
• Connect with your future self

If I could, I would hand you a crystal ball so you can see how your life ultimately pans out. You would know if all of your dreams come true. You would know if you have no regrets at the end of your life. You would know how and when you die. You would know the destiny of the people you care about. You would know if you have enough money to sustain you for the rest of your life. And best of all, you would have the knowledge and wherewithal to do things differently right now to make everything turns out the way you would like.

Surviving uncertainty is something you and I do every day. We never know from one day to the next what surprise lurks around the corner. No more clinging to illusions of safety and security, because there are none. In spite of how real life continues to play out, we can bank on putting our innate skills and talents to use to weather disorienting storms of any kind. But I have much higher hopes for us all than mere survival. Thriving is the ultimate goal.

With old friends by my side teaching me the ropes along the way, all things are possible. What I am most looking forward to in my old age is looking back and saying, "It's been a great ride." How about you? Are you ready to start planning?

Crank Up the Time Machine

"For a quality of life, plan ahead," suggest the experts. That has always been my mantra. For the longest time, my process of planning would include reading books, making notes, establishing action plans, prioritizing challenges, and checking the boxes when tasks were complete. Whenever answers are black and white, that formula still holds true. However, when I need answers to more complex situations, I use an entirely different approach. Here is an invaluable planning lesson that was taught to me years ago by one of my most cherished elder friends.

I had spent twenty years working in the advertising industry. The time was right for me to take my career in another direction. I wanted to focus my attention to causes that offered more meaning and purpose in my life. Not knowing which way to turn, I sought the advice of one of my favorite elders. We made a date to meet *in person*.

During our time together, I explained that I was at a crossroads in my career and my life in general. My elder adviser listened patiently up to a point; then, she interrupted me and her unstoppable line of questioning began: *What were you like as a teenager? What did you learn about the advertising business? When did you know that you wanted to be in business for yourself? Did you have a childhood pet? What makes you sad? Where do you want to be one year from now? What do your parents do for a living? Who do you care about? What's the problem you are trying to solve?*

The room started spinning. My heart was beating faster and faster. I started squirming and couldn't sit still. What is going on? What do *these* questions have to do with anything? Where is this all going? Then something interesting began to happen. I quit fighting the process, and began to trust her. The more I answered her questions the calmer I became—layers of invisible mental barriers began falling by the wayside. By looking back and imagining the future simultaneously, I was slowly revealing myself to *me*. Everything that I had experienced so far in life—personally and professionally—was leading me to where I needed to go next. And so it was that I came to write my first book about eldercare and family caregiving.

What I learned that day is that everyone has in his or her possession at all times an invaluable planning tool—time travel. While you may be familiar with the concept of "time travel" as a literary and cinematic plot device, my version is a visualization technique you can use to steer in the right direction when you are unsure of which path to take.

At first, you may not realize the power of this slow and steady process. You may even brush off time travel as trivial. Impatience, and fear of the unknown, may drive you to want to come up with answers quickly especially when questions of money, housing, and health weigh heavily on your mind. We'll get there, but for now, bear with me—this is a process that will help you to get in touch with the bigger picture of where you want to go as you grow older, and better prepare you to make decisions that stay true to your unique wants, needs, and goals.

Remember This. Imagine That.

What fundamental decisions have you made in the past that are impacting the quality of your life today? Can you pinpoint the cause and effect of something that happened earlier in your life that is positively and/or negatively manifesting itself today? Pay close attention. Through time travel you will uncover clues that will ultimately lead you to advocate for your true self in old age.

Looking ahead is not an easy task—there are many unknowns. The process of remembering, on the other hand, is less of an effort. Try the following simple exercise:

Focus on what your life looked like ten years ago. Start by recalling the year, and then answering the questions (it may help you to write down your answers):

What year was it?
Were you working? If yes, where?
Where did you live?
Who lived with you?
What did you value the most?
What brought you the most joy?

Now answer the same questions as you envision your life ten years from today:

What year is it?
Are you working? If yes, where?
Where do you live?
Are you living alone or with others?
What are you valuing the most?
What is bringing you the most joy?

Were you able to answer these questions for yourself in the future? Or do you feel there are too many unknowns to bring the picture into focus? This is where your personal time machine comes into play.

Envisioning ten years from now is difficult, but not impossible. Use your observation skills to draw possibilities from the world around you: this is the time-travel approach. Many possible outcomes are already being played out around you; take the time to watch what is happening to others, and consider whether that could be you. If you see something that you don't like about where you are headed, commit to make a plan that can change outcomes.

Look for Living Answers

Surround yourself with as many elders as possible (people who appear to be at least ten years older than you are now). As you observe, pay close attention to what you are witnessing. Old people are everywhere. You will find them:

Strolling through the park or zoo
Visiting friends in a nursing home
Attending church services
Riding bikes
Pushing baby strollers
Jogging and working out at the gym
Playing slots at the casino
Socializing at the local senior center

Today's old people are *you* later on. Your future self is hiding in plain sight. As simple as this time-travel approach is, it may make you feel uncomfortable at times, like it does me—especially when I see elders walking down the street who can barely walk, not using canes or walkers, and refusing to let anyone help them when support is clearly needed. (I see old people rejecting help so often that I am beginning to wonder whether the phenomenon of resistance and/or denial is a given in old age. If it is, will I even know that I am traveling down the path of defiance by emphatically insisting that all is well?)

Are you feeling uneasy about old age right now? That discomfort can be your guide. Real-life examples of what it is like to be old can be warning signs just as much as positive role models for active aging can offer you what's possible for you to achieve in old age. The more you use the time-travel technique, the more it will help bring into focus what you want to happen ten, twenty, and thirty years down the road, and beyond. Are you willing to open your eyes into your future?

Stay Grounded

Over the years, my daily ritual of paying close attention to elders has changed my life. What I envision as my future self is evidence-based. The more I observe, the more I learn, and the less fearful I am of what is in store. An important result is that I am learning to take better care of my present self. Education is powerful and allows us to plan accordingly. Your future self is not a stranger—the signs of who you will become are there, if you choose to stop and take a look.

The past and present shape the person you are today. Consequently, nobody has a deeper understanding of your needs and wants better than *you*. By now you know:

What you like and what you tend to avoid

Interests, hobbies, and favorite activities

What makes you happy, sad, or angry

Strengths and weaknesses

Values and principles

Your unique style and signature traits

Who your friends are, and how to keep enemies at bay

Innate talents and skills

Where you fit in and where you don't

Different roles you play

As you proceed to make plans for later life, it helps to remember who *you* are in the process. Although your likes, dislikes, values, and roles will evolve over time, you can always count on your core self to be a predictable factor as you journey toward your unknown future into old age.

Who am I now? is the unavoidable question you will face each time a major change rains down upon you—the highs and lows of living and aging shape the essence of who you already are, and will lay the groundwork for who you have yet to become. You are already skilled at being you. You are a survivor and have the physical and psychological scars to prove it. Your morals and values have served you well so far; but as the years fly by, you are going to be challenged like never before.

The rate of change will accelerate and be especially hard-hitting when it comes out of nowhere. When the going gets rough (and it will) you will most likely yearn for someone to lean on. You will face making choices you do not want to make. The difficulties of aging are inescapable.

The following questions will help you to gain a clearer perspective of who you are today, both in your reactions to change and in your relationships with others. Give the following questions serious consideration; they may reveal what you need to work on to live well in your later years.

Do You Like People? Do People Like You?

It is natural not to like everyone, and vice versa. People vary in how social they are. If you do not currently have a circle of friends that you can count on or are not likely to call upon anyone if a need arises, and you have no intention of cultivating new friendships, then hiring professional caregivers and care-related service providers may be a possible long-term care option for you—*that is, if you can afford it.* However, even hiring care workers includes interacting and connecting, requiring you to develop a relationship with them on *some* level. Do you like to spend a lot of time alone and gravitate toward solo activities rather than group-type experiences? Do you seek out connections? How easy is it for you to make new friends?

Will Family Come to Your Rescue?

Just because you have access to people in your life you call "family," doesn't mean they will be there for you when you need them. You are living a dream if you are counting solely on family to have the time, desire, skills, and motivation to help solve your problems. Not everyone is willing or able to make major adjustments in his or her life to accommodate your care needs. When was the last time you spent quality time with family? Do you get along with family members when you gather together? Do you live far from one another? What is going on in your children's lives right now? Do they already have their hands full? Are your adult children financially secure? Does a daughter- or son-in-law shun you? Are you a respected—or rejected—grandparent?

Do You Justify Bad Decisions?

No one ages in a void—bad decisions have a domino effect. Failure to prevent a crisis that causes hardship on others has serious consequences. You will be held 100 percent responsible for your decisions and outcomes. Do you envision refusing to relocate out of your current residence when personal safety dictates otherwise? Might you insist on driving long past it is safe to do so? Do you have a habit of refusing to listen to others' ideas and observations? Do you have difficulty owning up to mistakes?

Are You Uncomfortable Asking for and Receiving Help from Others?

There is no getting around this one. Learning how to ask for and accept help is a critical life skill. Assistance and advice of every kind imaginable are available 24/7. Rather than wait for someone to offer assistance, are you willing to muster up the courage to ask for help? Are you willing to say yes when someone asks whether you need help? Will you consider being open to the possibility that people around you may want to be helpful? Are you willing to let new people into your life?

Are You Open to Advice from Others?

Understandably, it may be hard to imagine that one day you may have a support network of trusted friends, care partners, and advocates. Social workers, advisers, and coaches are ready to assist you. Are you willing to engage in seeking out their guidance now? Are you intent on connecting with others but not sure how to go about it? Are you willing to seek professional counseling to iron out the challenges that will get in the way of your goal to be socially available?

Frozen in Fear

I acknowledge and respect how you may be feeling right now about getting older; fears may have started long before this, perhaps at the first signs of physical change. You may also be thinking about the "neediness" of old age, or no longer fitting in and being overlooked by a generally younger crowd. The question I have for you is this: *Are you one to sit idly by when something is bothering you?*

Age is not a disease to be cured and eradicated. Instead of shuddering when every new wrinkle appears on your face, you can choose to celebrate age and life experiences. You have a wide range of choices to make to stay ahead of the game; and I am banking on you to be proactive and productive as you begin to consciously journey toward old age.

• • •

When I first heard about the standing-desk concept, I had no idea that I would take to it as much as I have. In fact, I wrote this book standing the entire time. No more sitting for hours at a time. Standing while writing has changed my life: My legs are stronger, I stay focused longer, and I get more exercise because I pace around the room when I am at a standstill as to what to write. Everybody who stops by for a visit gets a kick out of seeing my new method of working.

Best yet, my standing desk did not cost me a penny. I created it out of heavy-duty cardboard boxes, an unused shoe-storing shelf, plastic containers, leftover slabs of wood, and other materials I had lying around the house. The desk surely won't win any design awards, but it provides me a healthful and mindful way to spend my working hours.

Telling you about my standing desk is meant to inspire you to think about your old age in a way that you never have before. You have already picked up this book—that's a great start. Keep moving forward. Never stop exploring whatever it is that you may find scary or unacceptable about old age (if that is the case for you).

This chapter may have revealed to you that you need to work on your relationships or daily rituals so as to live well in old age. I also recognize that you may be feeling discouraged. But what you have at this very moment is an opportunity of a lifetime. You will *never* get this time back. You can positively change your personal history. Be brave.

Just for Fun

Talking about the future is intriguing. It's hard for any of us to imagine being ten and twenty years older than we are today, let alone establishing a relationship with that person. So, here is something fun to do as you contemplate life as your older self:

Buy one large manila envelope—the kind you can seal at the top.
Take a picture of yourself and put it in the envelope.
Prepare to write yourself a letter or record a video.
Start by describing your current reality—name, where you live, working or retired, people and pets in your life.

Discuss the following:

What do I value most?
What do I admire most about people and why?
What special moment in my life do I cherish most?
What is my greatest achievement?
Which later-life transition do I fear the most and why?
What are the unanswered questions currently occupying my thoughts?
What am I looking forward to?
What am I feeling remorseful about?
What was the biggest surprise in life so far?
What is the greatest lesson I have learned so far in my life?
What is my overall feeling about where I am today?

For additional insights on what to write, visit Values (www.values.com). The purpose of this website is to inspire people to live good values, seek out positive role models, and lead better lives.

Put your answers in the envelope, then seal it shut. Store it in a safe place. If you like, tell someone else where the envelope can be found if something happens to you and you would like him or her to know about it.

Make a date with yourself to open the envelope in the future—five years from now, ten years from now. You decide.

On the day you decide to open the envelope, keep in mind that the person reading the letter or watching the video is no longer the person who created the questions and answers. When you reconnect, here are a few reflective questions to ask yourself:

Did you make choices you wish you had not?
Does your life remain centered on the things you said you once valued?
What lessons did you learn?
Are you worried about the same things?

Did you do what you wanted to do?

Do you have advice for your past self?

When you are finished, decide if you want to share the outcomes with someone in your life. It will certainly be an interesting conversation.

Meet the Old Person You Are Meant to Be

Are you ready to be inspired about old age? Make good use of these invaluable resources to help move you in directions you never thought possible:

Aging 2.0: www.aging2.com.　A powerhouse organization that accelerates innovation to improve the lives of older adults around the world. Events and startup programs connect you with a "robust ecosystem" of entrepreneurs, technologists, designers, care providers, and older adults themselves.

Blue Zones: www.bluezones.com.　Want to add ten years to your life? Start here. Sign up for the Blue Zones Newsletter to access exclusive interviews and fresh tips for living longer—better.

The Center for Conscious Eldering: www.centerforconsciouseldering.com.　Through the process of workshops, retreats, and personal coaching, the center is dedicated to helping people envision their elder years as a time of purpose, growth and passion.

Encore: www.encore.org.　This is a movement of millions of people who are using their passions, skills, and decades of experience to make a difference in their community and the world.

Inventure—The Purpose Company: http://richardleider.com.　Read, watch, and listen to tips on unlocking the power of purposeful living.

Karen Sands, GeroFuturist: www.karensands.com.　Calling all visionary leaders, conscious social entrepreneurs, audacious world shakers, and change-makers-to-be. Your ageless story starts here.

Life Reimagined: https://lifereimagined.aarp.org.　World-class experts developed the transformational processes, methodologies, and insights that are the foundation of a life reimagined. Start where you are in your life, and see where the possibilities lead you.

The Longevity Project: www.howardsfriedman.com/longevityproject.   The Longevity Project uses one of the most famous studies in psychology to answer the question of who lives longest—and why. The answers may surprise you.

Over 60: www.over60.com.au.   This website inspires visitors to share ideas, experiences, and support one another through this exciting stage in life.

Sixty and Me: http://sixtyandme.com.   An online magazine and global community of over 500,000 women. The website's mission is to empower and motivate women to find their own voice and value in a transitional time of life that offers many new opportunities.

Insights and Inspiration

Recommended Reading: *The Complete Eldercare Planner: Where to Start, Which Questions to Ask, and How to Find Help*, updated and revised edition (2009) by Joy Loverde

Recommended YouTube: *100 Years of Beauty: Aging Cut Has a Field Day*, published May 14, 2015

Recommended Movie: *The Big Chill* (1983)

Recommended Song: "My Way," performed by Frank Sinatra, written by Thibault, Anka, Revaux, and François

Recommended TED Talk: "The Psychology of Your Future Self," presented by Dan Gilbert, psychologist and happiness expert, filmed March 2014

Good-bye Change, Hello Transition

Meeting the unknowns of old age head on

2

Our experience of change is different today. With daily 24/7 access to worldwide news about catastrophic events, our lives are propelled into ever-deeper levels of uncertainties. Change in this century means *constant* change—a flood of overlapping and accelerating transitions that occur rapidly one after another. The pace of change is intense with no end in sight.

Not only the constant threat of homeland terrorist attacks and chemical warfare, not only the chronic erosion of our planet, not only the constant worry of aging alone, not only the ongoing struggles with managing and saving money, not only the continuous loss of loved ones, not only the relentless constraints of time, but *all* of the above on top of other uncertainties, *all* the time.

In my own life, change is taking place at such a quick pace that I take a deep breath and steady myself each time the phone rings—another someone I love has died, a neighbor is diagnosed with dementia, a close friend is moving across country to be with her daughter.

Upon hearing the news, at once I feel unsettled, disturbed, and vulnerable, but I am not paralyzed or confused. After all, I have already weathered quite a few major changes in my life, and am confident knowing that I will land on solid ground once again. There is nowhere to hide. There is no getting comfortable with being uncomfortable. It is normal to be afraid of an unsettled, disruptive, and

Objectives

After completing this chapter, "Good-bye Change, Hello Transition," you will be able to:

- Define and manage a current unwanted change
- Be more open to the advice of others
- Manage fear of the unknown
- Learn to effectively take more risks
- Gain resources to sleep more soundly

unreliable world—and yet we are never more alive than when things get turned upside down. Uncertainty awakens us and keeps us on our toes.

As we age, none of us can count on "business as usual." This fact is especially hard hitting when it comes to being cared for in old age. People will come and go throughout our life. As we remain vigilant to this and other truths about aging, we can be better prepared to face any challenge that crosses our path.

Change and Transition Are Not the Same

Change is a situation or an event that happens or you make happen. Types of change include:

Self-imposed: You stop coloring your hair; you change jobs; you move to a new city.

Self-advancement: You learn a new way to do something you already do; for example, now you text instead of making a phone call.

Self-awareness: You choose to end a longtime bad habit, such as smoking or sitting too much; you stop associating with negative people.

Beliefs: You change how you think about something or someone; for example, you no longer drink diet soda because you have learned that artificial sweeteners are unhealthy.

Externally imposed change: Your cat dies; you are informed that your position at work has been eliminated.

Transition, on the other hand, is the psychological path one takes to adjust to the change; this process is explained in the wise book *Transitions* by William Bridges. Transition is what is happening *now.* The extreme ups and downs of divorce are a prime example.

In my case, I was a twenty-something, full-time mother of a four-year-old. At the time, there was no need for me to be working outside the home—my then husband provided for us financially and otherwise. The house, the dog, the car, and the extravagant social events with his co-workers were also part of the package. Life was good—or so I thought. As our relationship began to crumble, so did everything else. Poof! Dream over. And there I was—no money, no job, no house, no car, no work experience, and a daughter who depended on me for everything.

I recall seeking the advice of a divorce coach as my first step. "I really think he and I can work things out," I would say. I wanted so desperately to see my marriage as repairable rather than the damaged union it had become. She helped me separate fact from fiction.

Managing the variety of difficult transitions went on for over a decade. As one phase ended, another began. I rode an extreme emotional roller coaster that required an entire team of professionals, family, and close friends to pull me through. With their guidance and a lot of hard work, I eventually accepted the truth, including my role in the failed marriage, and moved on. Getting back on my feet required stamina, discipline, and the inner confidence that I could handle this life-changing event, and any other challenge that would come my way.

What I learned from the professionals who guided me throughout my divorce is that people who consistently flourish and prosper during times of unwanted change put *all* of their efforts in the *transition* process. Transitions are alive, ever-evolving, and filled with potential. In William Bridges's model, the stages of transition include the following:

Step One: Acknowledge the end of a situation.

Step Two: Responsibly manage the period of confusion, the unknown, and undefined— what Bridges calls "the neutral zone."

Step Three: Remain true to lessons learned and personal growth experiences to create new direction.

Putting your thoughts in writing about traumatic events is helpful. An increasing number of studies have demonstrated that when individuals write about emotional experiences, significant physical and mental health improvements follow.[1]

If the idea of writing about your experiences appeals to you, the Manage Change Worksheet on page 16 may help you gain clarity and insight during your own transition processes.

Keep Moving Forward

With every change comes the reality of living life in the "neutral zone." This happens when you find yourself between knowing and not knowing what to do next. As you age, this may happen with greater frequency. Stay positive by *turning inward*. Here are a few things to think about when nothing seems to make sense in the moment:

MANAGE CHANGE WORKSHEET
This worksheet is available to download and customize at www.elderindustry.com.

Changes—big and small—can happen at any time. Use this guide to get clearer about the big picture and ease into the transition process. In time, what you write about today will serve as a stepping stone to managing future challenges. Let your answers to the questions sink in. These are tough questions. Be kind to yourself. You deserve time and space to heal.

The Situation

Define life before the change

_____

Define life after the change

_____

What am I saying good-bye to?

_____

What am I saying hello to?

_____

How will the change negatively impact me?

_____

How will the change positively impact me?

_____

Who besides me is affected by this change?

_____

How will the change affect me a year from now?

_____

In what way has this change altered my assumptions?

_____

What were the clues that this change was inevitable?

_____

The Transition

How am I feeling right now?

_____

What can I not control right now?

_____

What don't I understand or am I confused about?

_____

What am I impatient and anxious about?

_____

What are my greatest fears regarding this change?

_____

What am I resisting and resenting about this change?

_____

What lost opportunities am I ashamed, angry, sad, or remorseful about?

_____

What are the positive effects of this change?

_____

Launch of Growth and Learning

What was my role in why this change took place?

_____

Which personal relationships are doing me more harm than good right now?

_____

Which professional relationships are doing me more harm than good right now?

_____

What advice would I give a good friend who is going through a similar situation?

_____

Who was I before this change occurred?

_____

What are some creative ways to say good-bye to the "old me"?

_____

What will it take for me to accept that I may never completely understand the change?

_____

What did I learn?

_____

How will I grow from this experience?

_____

What new opportunities are available to me now?

_____

What is one thing I can realistically do right now during this stage of the transition?

_____

Who can I lean on during this transition?

_____

I will not be in limbo forever. This is a temporary situation.

I have survived tough times before and I am determined to make it through this one, too.

I am not a slave to life's ups and downs. I have the power to work through them.

I accept that nothing stays the same or lasts forever; settling into a "permanent" state of *anything* is unrealistic.

I may continue to feel the range of this emotional experience, but I will not let my negative emotions dictate my every action.

I have no idea how I will survive this ordeal, but I choose to be positive anyway.

Here are a few additional suggestions on using your time constructively while you wait it out:

Engage in quality recharging activities—take a class, volunteer, take up a sport, sit on a beach and listen to the crashing waves.

Commit to eat right, exercise, rest, and take walks, and resist partaking in self-destructive behaviors.

Remove items from your life that no longer serve you—go through your clothes closet.

Empty your basement and attic. Feel the freedom of letting unused and unwanted objects go.

Their Two Cents

Have you ever said the words, "If I were you . . . " to someone? There is something fun and liberating about dishing out advice—whether it is asked for or not.

You are a fresh set of eyes and ears. You have not invested a lot of time and energy agonizing over the other person's decisions and choices. You hear the story for the first time and you know *exactly* what to do—not to mention you have nothing to lose. You think highly of yourself and are compelled to share your opinion.

Now turn the tables. *You* are the person who is in transition and struggling with choices and making important decisions. Instead of brushing off unsolicited advice, why not listen to what other people have to offer—bad, good, and risky—then decide whether their ideas are worth pursuing.

If no one comes forward with advice, you might ask someone whose opinion you respect, "What would you do if you were me?" Doesn't it make sense to hear what other people have to say?

Invest in People Who Invest in You

The journey toward old age consists of unexpected twists and turns, increasingly challenging our ability to stay physically, intellectually, and socially engaged. Depression seems right around the corner if we are not careful. Anything can and will set us off. Plus, it is not always easy to come up with answers to introspective questions like—Is there more to life than this? Will the choices I make today serve me in the long run?

When you feel like giving up and giving in, or when you are stuck in limbo and having difficulty moving forward, partnering with a transition coach may be the answer.

Transition coaches are not social workers, therapists, psychologists, or career planners. Coaching is not consulting, counseling, or therapy that analyzes emotional situations from your past. Transitional coaching offers a confidential, nonjudgmental relationship built on trust and respect over time with the purpose of helping you create a vision for your future.

Here are a few questions to ask yourself before you go to the next step of engaging a coach:

Am I determined to learn what's keeping me from moving forward?
Am I ready to invest in myself?
Am I willing to be completely honest with myself to get what I want?

If you are ready to get to work, here is a list of kinds of coaches that are available to you:

Abundance	Dementia	Life purpose
Active aging	Divorce	Relationship
Business	End of life	Resume
Cancer	Grief	Sleep
Coming out	Leadership	Spiritual
Couples	Legacy	Wellness

Working with a coach is a step-by-step process. Here is the typical action plan:

Establish a clear picture of the desired transition.
Identify opportunities and strengths.
Define a new vision.

Plan for obstacles and challenges.

Develop short- and long-term plans.

Define specific tasks.

Commit to weekly goals.

Make decisions for action.

Identify successes—big and small.

Before you commit to hiring a coach, it is wise to interview several candidates. The following list of questions will guide you in finding the coach that's right for you and your current situation:

What is your area of expertise?

What was your career before getting your coaching credentials?

What are your education degrees and coaching certifications?

How many years have you been coaching?

What is your proudest coaching accomplishment?

What proof of client successes can you offer me?

Would any former or current clients be willing to talk with me about their experiences of working with you?

What tools do you offer in your coaching practice? (books, notebooks, outlines, etc.)

When it comes to paying for services, coaches vary in terms of pricing. Typically, they offer a free consultation (at least 15 minutes), then charge hourly after the first session.

At the conclusion of your first free session, the coach should be able to define your general concerns and briefly outline a strategy for a future partnership. If this does not happen between the two of you during your initial consultation, keep looking.

Hourly coaching fees usually start at $50 per hour and up. Costs depend on length of sessions, frequency of sessions, duration of the commitment, and communications outside of sessions. Ask for package pricing if the project is long term.

To find the right coach for you, start by asking for references from trusted resources. You can also find coaches by typing "transition coach" into your Internet search engine.

You may also find the following websites of interest:

International Association of Professional Life Coaches: www.iaplifecoaches.org

International Coach Federation: www.coachfederation.org/ICF

Fear Factor

Bring up the subject of change, and conversations about fear typically follow closely behind. Being afraid on some level is one of the consequences of living in this unpredictable world. Feeling a little afraid is essential to being prepared for anything to happen. *Clinging* to fears is another matter altogether.

I can recall feeling nothing less than petrified when I was hired to give my first keynote presentation. My book *The Complete Eldercare Planner* had just been published, and a book-signing event was to be held at a well-known prestigious hospital. In the audience would be doctors, nurses, administrators, public officials, hospice professionals, and family caregivers. Since I had never given a keynote before, a flood of worrisome thoughts began to challenge my self-worth. *What if I don't do a good job? What if they think I'm stupid? What if my words don't make sense? What if they don't like me?*

With every question, I dug myself deeper into a pit of self-sabotage. My fears became overwhelming. Whenever I envisioned myself on stage at the podium my heart started to race, and I felt dizzy. I recall reading that public speaking is one of the top common fears. Was that reason enough for me to be afraid of the task at hand? I concluded the answer was no. My fear was holding immense power over me—as if it *owned* me. I decided then and there to change my self-talk: *I have effective communication skills; I know how to write; I know how to be entertaining and deliver a joke; I know how to dress appropriately for any occasion; I deserve this opportunity to speak to this astute audience as much as anyone else.*

I began visualizing myself on the stage and experiencing the keynote *without* the presence of fear. I accomplished this by watching other professional speakers in action. As they delivered their presentations, I would say to myself—*I can do what they do*. By shadowing other presenters, my self-imposed roadblocks slowly fell by the wayside and I began to believe what I was telling myself.

The day finally arrived for me to give the keynote. I walked up to the stage and took my place behind the microphone, grabbing both sides of the podium as though I was on a sinking ship and hanging on for dear life. As I looked out at the sea of faces staring back at me, my knees started shaking uncontrollably. Upon speaking my first words, my mouth went completely dry. I forged on. And even though I never felt comfortable throughout that speech, somehow I got through it in one piece. Afterward, people approached the stage and told me how I positively impacted their thoughts about family caregiving. Hundreds of presentations and keynotes later, my initial fears about public speaking have all but disappeared, but that is not to say that I do not get nervous before each and every one of my presentations. The difference now is my prespeech anxieties are healthy signals that I want to do a good job.

Cutting Through Fear

We all have fears, and while you may not be afraid of giving a speech, there are plenty of other challenges in life to keep you up at night: you might stay home alone because you are afraid you might not fit in with new people; you are afraid of running out of money; you don't ask your doctor about what is happening with your memory because you are afraid of what she will say; you work twice as hard at your job so your employer doesn't let you go or eliminate your position.

As frightening as these situations feel in the moment, people survive their personal dilemmas. Just as I was paralyzed at the thought of giving a keynote, I took on the challenge of managing fear, and not letting it run my life. It took every ounce of energy to break away from its powerful grip. What I eventually overcame was being afraid of fear itself.

You go to the gym to get fit, so why not do the same to strengthen your "fear muscle"? The antidote to fear is curiosity. With that in mind, follow this formula when your fears are getting the best of you:

1. Pick one fear that is currently weighing heavily on your mind. Write it down.
2. Define the power that fear has over your mind and your behavior.
3. Imagine the problem solved and pay attention to how you feel.
4. Separate fact from fiction—what are the real dangers in your situation versus what you are making up in your head?
5. Recognize that other people have solved this problem. Seek out people who have successfully accomplished or overcome what you fear.
6. Capture the opportunity this fear is presenting to you.

At one time in my life I feared running out of money. Here is what my fear-management process looked like when I followed this formula:

1. Pick one fear that is currently weighing heavily on your mind. Write it down. Fear of running out of money.

2. Define the power that fear has over your mind and your behavior. Fear of running out of money filled my head with nonstop worry, so much so that I had difficulty sleeping and concentrating. I was extremely cautious about spending money. I hid my feelings and did not talk about my financial situation with anyone since I felt that it was no one else's business. I was not fun to be around. I avoided socializing with friends because that usually meant spending money I didn't have on drinks or dinner. My fearing about money went on for over a year.

3. Imagine the problem solved. Pay attention to how you feel. When I took a step back and imagined that the problem was solved, my breathing changed. I felt more at peace. I could feel myself being a kinder, more compassionate person.

4. Separate fact from fiction. It took a while for me to tear myself away from false beliefs and the imaginary story I was creating in my head about my finances. Although it is true that anybody can run out of money, I finally realized that the possibility of it happening to me was far from fact: I was resourceful, and even if I lost my current income, I was employable somewhere else; I was good at planning and researching employment options; and I had elder role models in my life who were making ends meet on Social Security.

5. Recognize that other people have solved this problem. When I started investigating different financial strategies, benefits programs, housing options, and income possibilities, I felt as though I was making progress. I also stopped the harmful practice of not talking with others about my money fear. The more I confided in people close to me, the more we helped each other. Even fear of setbacks no longer scared me. Almost everyone around me had gone through a setback or two, and they lived to share how they rose above their situation.

6. Capture the opportunity this fear is presenting to you. Fear is here to stay. By following this formula repeatedly, my ability to face the unknown, and my confidence in solving problems, gets stronger. Conquering fear also means asking for help. The groundbreaking MacArthur Foundation study on aging suggests doing something that scares us—*every day.*[2] These days, I take on this sage advice with a passion. Whether it's going to a party unaccompanied or traveling alone to a foreign country, I have learned that reality isn't nearly as bad as my wild imagination.

You Must Take Risks

In the business world, risk taking is a given. "High risk, high reward" is not just an expression. These are words to live by. Seek the same in your personal life: taking risks is a critical life-skill.

RISKY BUSINESS WORKSHEET

This worksheet is available to download and customize at www.elderindustry.com.

Today's Date:_____Desired Decision Date:_____
The decision I am attempting to make:

_____

Every decision has its pros and cons. Fill in the following "Pros" and "Cons" columns as best you can. Making a list of what works and what doesn't will help you gain a clearer perspective of the situation. Consider the following when composing your lists:

> The effects of the decision on physical and emotional health
> Whether the decision puts others at risk, and the extent of those risks
> Whether the decision is irreversible or can be modified later on
> The potential consequences of the decision
> If the timing is right to be making the decision
> Whether existing resources are adequate
> The financial implications of the decision
> How much the decision will matter in a year from now

Pros	Cons

How did the pros and cons stack up? Did other concerns surface that require your immediate attention before you can make a final decision? If yes, create a plan of action to get those challenges resolved.

There is one more task before you make your decision, and that is to let your body weigh in. Put up a "do not disturb" sign. Take fifteen minutes. Close your laptop, silence your phone, close your eyes, and turn inward. Is your body calling out a warning or is it telling you that you are going in the right direction? What are you sensing? What are you visualizing? What are you feeling?

When you are ready to make your final decision, write it down. My decision is:

_____

Nothing about the transition phase of a change in circumstances is fixed. It is fluid and always in motion. Go with what is happening in the present moment and choose to engage in the game of life, no matter how you are feeling.

As time goes by, you can expect changes related to health, finances, relationships, and housing. During times of uncertainty, use the Risky Business Worksheet on page 24 as your guide.

Catch Up on Sleep

If you are currently in the transition stage after a major unwanted change and feeling tired most of your waking hours, psychologist Stephanie A. Silberman, PhD, reminds us that sleep is a daily requirement for both physical and emotional well-being. "Good quality sleep is restorative to the mind, allowing us to consolidate memories and maintain good cognitive functioning throughout our lives. Our bodies require a much-needed break from daily stressors."[3]

Also, look to the National Sleep Foundation (https://sleepfoundation.org) for a wealth of information and assistance.

Insights and Inspiration

Recommended Reading: *Transitions: Making Sense of Life's Changes,* Revised 25th Anniversary Edition (2004) by William Bridges

Recommended YouTube: Eckhart Tolle, *I'm Aware of Fear That Is Almost Continually in Me*, published May 10, 2016

Recommended Movie: *Life Is Beautiful* (1997)

Recommended Song: "Does Anybody Really Know What Time It Is?" by Chicago

Recommended TED Talk: "The Art of Being Yourself," presented by Caroline McHugh, chief idologist, February 18, 2013

Think Like a Strategist

Mastering critical thinking

Are there any absolute truths? Take the subject of coffee, for instance. Over the years, renowned universities and laboratories have conducted research on the topic of coffee and caffeine. To this day, scientific studies deliver a mixed bag of results:

Caffeine contributes to heart disease.
Caffeine helps alleviate heart disease symptoms.
Coffee lowers risk of prostate cancer.
Coffee may protect against Alzheimer's disease.
Caffeine raises cholesterol levels.
Caffeine lowers cholesterol levels.
Caffeine does not alter cholesterol levels.

Which is it? Is coffee good or bad? If you have changed your mind about drinking coffee, it is easy to understand why. You buy into the results of one research project as truth. The next study completely overturns what was considered fact the day before.

The choice to drink coffee, or not, pales in comparison to the make-or-break decisions you will be required to make going forward—*Should I age in place or move out of my house? Is this a wise financial investment? Which adviser should I trust? Should I go through with this medical procedure?* Figuring out answers to complex questions goes beyond the basics of planning—the who, what, when, where, and how. Making decisions in a world filled with uncertainty

Objectives

After completing this chapter, "Think Like a Strategist," you will be able to:

- Pay greater attention to *how* you think
- Prioritize and tackle planning tasks
- Challenge self-sabotaging thoughts about aging
- Rely on critical thinking skills to make decisions
- Use the power of visualization to lessen anxieties about the future
- Resist the temptation to procrastinate
- Think out loud as an effective planning strategy

becomes even more difficult where there can be multiple ways of dealing with the same situation. And we still need to get things done.

To complicate matters, if you followed up on my suggestion to mindfully observe old people (see "Look for Living Answers" on page 6), you saw firsthand that they are quite a diverse population:

Some are frail. Others are weight-trainers and marathon runners.

Some minds are sharp as a tack. Others suffer from dementia.

Some endure chronic diseases. Others are clear of maladies.

Some work every day. Others retired long ago.

Some take a daily dose of prescription drugs. Others thrive drug-free.

Some are joyful. Others are clinically depressed.

Making the time to observe groups of old people reveals the results of their years of decision making. Some got it right and are pleased with their choices. Others did not. If ever there was evidence of the importance of making smarter choices, it is when we are looking at our future head on.

According to the American Philosophical Association (www.apaonline.org), critical thinking is "the process of purposeful, self-regulatory judgment." Forging into old age requires critical thinking—in other words, evidence over emotion. "I just don't feel like taking a walk today," versus "I choose to walk to keep me healthier in the long run." The critical thinking process relies on clarity of personal values and logical reasoning. Even in extremely stressful situations we can remain calm and rely on our ability to think rationally. Developing critical-thinking skills now is time well spent.

The Stakes Are Even Higher

Do you believe that the next ten years of your life will look like the past ten years? Of course, you don't. What you *can* expect in the years ahead is destined to be even more eventful—relationships, money, responsibilities, and health-care needs have the potential to evolve into something altogether different than what you might expect.

You are a work in progress. The one constant in your life is change, and change related to your aging process is a force to reckon with. Classic crossroads—such as taking on the role of caregiver, becoming widowed, full-time retirement, the onset of a chronic illness—continuously force you to make sound decisions whether you feel up to it or not. Thanks to modern science, longevity is a real possibility. Unlike past generations, you have the advantage of approaching old age, and all its implications, with eyes wide open.

Thinking strategically about your aging process has never been more important. The problem is, *how* you learned to think in the first place may not serve you well now. Early on, traditional schooling teaches a linear approach to thinking:

1. Here is the question.
2. Figure out the answer.
3. Once the correct answer is revealed, remember it.
4. Repeat.

The education style of thinking that most of us grew up on was effective when attending schools that graded students for knowing the correct answers. Within these environments, creative thinking tendencies we may have had as children were driven out of us by this direct instruction method. In fact, the more creative we were, the less tolerant our teachers became—nonconformists were often punished one way or another for "being disruptive." I should know. I was one of those children. Somehow we survived, and moved on.

You Have Been Here Before

Think of a time when it was necessary for you to make an important decision and you had no way of knowing how the outcome would ultimately pan out. You may have found yourself in a few of the following situations:

Picking a college major
Deciding on a career
Figuring out where to live
Choosing to marry, or not
Having children, or not
Stopping a bad habit

With a bit of luck, your choices turned out pretty much how you wanted them to, and when they did not, you had the advantage of time to adjust, switch gears, and right wrongs.

As you plan for the future, the decision-making environment becomes increasingly complex and has more of a sense of urgency about it, since the time frame for making adjustments may be much shorter. Here are a few of the situations you can expect to deal with now:

Possibility of running out of money

Deciding to move out of your current home or stay put

Creating a care team when illness strikes

Designating decision-making powers to trusted individuals

Putting your end-of-life wishes in writing

As you can see, you are in the position of having to make choices in spite of having only partial and/or possibly inaccurate information.

Take a moment to assess *how* you think. How well is your current thinking process serving you? Look at the following list and see how your answer stacks up to thinking strategically:

Small Think ➔	**Strategic Think**
Reactive	Proactive
Independent	Interdependent
Short-term	Long-term
Age-based	Ageless
Denial	Acceptance
Status quo	Unchartered territory
Resistance	Readiness
Declarations	Questions
Dismiss	Observe
Impulsive	Deliberate
Rush	Patience
Details	Big picture
Teacher	Student
Fear-driven	Curious
Biased	Tolerant
Rigid	Flexible

Remaining calm and rational in the decision-making process is the goal. Strategic thinking gets you there. The following suggestions will fine-tune your thinking skills:

Anticipate. Exploring what you do not know requires investigating game-changing information. For example, when I have questions about my health, the doctor is not my only resource. I seek the wisdom of friends who have had the same or a similar medical condition. I ask them, "What is it that you wish you knew, and did not plan for, early on?" The doctor cannot tell me this important information.

Seek diversity. When you surround yourself with people who think as you do, you get the answers you want to hear. To gain new perspectives, seek advisers who come from different backgrounds and cultures. Tap into the life experiences of people who are much younger and older than you. You know you are on the right track when you say to the person you are speaking with, "I wasn't thinking of that. Thank you for opening my eyes."

Concentrate on quality questions. Questions with *is*, *are*, *do you think*, and *would*, lead to yes or no answers and may not offer you any new information. Questions with *who*, *what*, *when*, *where*, and *why* often provide a foundation for more thought and insights. Dig deeper by asking, "Why do you think that?" or "What do you base your answer on?"

Failure is an option. Addressing the hardest parts of a situation first and learning from failure can make you smarter about your next decision. For example: You move to a new city and spend the first month trying unsuccessfully to work your way into a social circle. Discovering a flaw in your approach may consume your heart for a while, but it doesn't necessarily mean packing up again and relocating. Oftentimes failure leads you to redirect your thinking process in another direction.

Stay true to yourself. When the going gets rough, you may be tempted to resort to wishful thinking. The truth can be hard to swallow at times (the diagnosis of a chronic illness, for example). Strategic thinking requires discipline and complete truthfulness in the face of uncomfortable facts. Be stellar in the true sense of the word. *Truth* or *comfort?* You decide.

Daydream. Lie back on the soft grass and watch the clouds pass overhead. Relax into the steam of a hot shower. Tune out the world. Let your mind roam. Mental meandering provides fertile ground for creative solutions to life challenges.

Decide. Problem solving typically incorporates not one, but a variety of potential solutions. When you arrive at a "good enough" position, pull the trigger and make a decision. Keep in mind there is no such thing as failure. There is only feedback.

Three excellent resources come to mind when it comes to learning more about making decisions and thinking strategically:

While the emphasis of the Mind Tools website (www.mindtools.com) is to increase productivity, improve leadership skills, and support organizational development initiatives in the workplace, I also use it for personal development. Click on the "decision-making" tab on the home page.

In a world of accelerating change, intensifying complexity, and increasing interdependence, critical thinking is now a requirement for economic and social survival. Join the Foundation and Center for Critical Thinking (www.criticalthinking.org) as it strives to make critical thinking a core social value and a key organizing concept for all educational reform. In its own words: "Critical thinking is essential if we are to get to the root of our problems and develop reasonable solutions. After all, the quality of everything we do is determined by the quality of our thinking."

An independent nonprofit organization, FrameWorks Institute (www.frameworksinstitute .org) designs, conducts, and publishes multimethod, multidisciplinary communications research. The institute offers professional learning opportunities for advocates, scientists, policymakers, and nonprofit leaders. For example, an initiative titled "Reframing Aging" is leading eight national aging organizations and fund developers to develop a more evolved narrative about aging. Priorities include: redefining aging, being aware that age discrimination exists, and knowing the consequences of not addressing the needs of an aging population affects individuals, families, and society.

Plan for an Uncertain Future

Review the following list. Although the details of what the future holds are unknown, these concerns are front and center as you journey to old age:

Financing a longer life
Creating a care team
Caring for dependents
Working
Retiring
Estate planning
Where to live
Physical fitness
Mental well-being
Purposeful living

Managing chronic illness
Estate planning
Advance directives
End of life

Now, take another look at the list. Rearrange the topics according to your priorities. If you feel as though every one of its topics is equally important, here are the top three needs (in this order):

1. Financing a longer life: Review the chapter of this book titled "The Fierce Urgency of Money," which begins on page 57.
2. Housing: Review the chapters in the part titled "Where You Live Matters," which begins on page 85.
3. Estate planning/Advance directives: Review the chapter of this book titled "'Just Shoot Me' Is Not a Plan," which begins on page 227.

Let the Planning Begin

In a perfect world, we would have all of our paperwork, including an inventory of all of our possessions, neatly documented and filed away in a perfectly orderly fashion. But let's face it: We are all susceptible to slacking off when it comes to completing organizing tasks. Please do not skip over this important step. How do you expect others to assist you if they have difficulty knowing what you want and where to find answers?

The first decision you will make is one of choosing to maintain hard copies and/or storing documents online. Keep in mind that filing "in the cloud" is not necessarily easier. The digital storage method also requires you to organize electronic information in e-mail messages, online, and within apps on your smartphone. If an online filing system is what you are planning to use, be sure to check the capacity and duration issues, among other limitations.

My personal preference is to store hard copies of all important documents in one place in my home office, and use such online storage systems as Google Drive (www.google.com /drive) and Dropbox (www.dropbox.com) as a backup. I scan the originals, then post the scanned documents online. I also update and back up my computer files weekly to an external hard drive.

A systematic approach for storing hard copies of important papers saves hours of anxious searching. Follow these suggestions:

Store all paperwork in one, 24/7 accessible place.

File papers in labeled folders. Many people prefer the hanging style of file folder that can be suspended in file drawers, rolling filing baskets, or various plastic or cardboard banker's boxes available at office supply stores.

You don't have to use a fire-resistant filing cabinet (consider the inside of the refrigerator), but you may want to use one if your paperwork cannot easily be replaced.

Next, organize files for each of the following categories:

Emergency contacts

Service providers

Medical history, including current medications

Home maintenance records

Warranties and manuals

Real estate investments and proof of ownership

Insurance policies

Vehicles—titles and registration

Driver's license or state identification

Pets—license, papers, medical history

Finances—bank statements

Credit cards

Loan documents

Safe-deposit box

Storage facilities

Powers of attorney—for health care and finances

Personal home inventory, including appraisals, valuables, and photographs

Business inventory

Tax documents

Monthly bills and receipts

Automatic bill-paying accounts

Memberships

Subscriptions

Employment, including employee benefit information

Employment history

Retirement and pensions

Military discharge papers

Proof of citizenship

Medicare, Medicare-supplement, and Medicare-prescription documents

Medicaid documents

Social Security documents

Passports

Vital records—birth, marriage, death, divorce, adoption

Education and diplomas

Estate planning—will, living trust

End-of-life advance directives

Religious and spiritual practices and preferences

Passwords, PINs, lock combinations, and access codes

The final step in getting organized is to provide instructions to your emergency contacts on where important documentation is stored, including websites and related log-in password instructions. The quality of your care will depend on the people you have designated ahead of time to help you, especially in an emergency situation.

But First, a Word About Procrastination

When I tell people that planning and making decisions are requirements for thriving in old age, many come up with a variety of excuses: "How can I plan when I have no idea where I will be and what I will need?" "My plans are bound to change anyway." And this is exactly the kind of mind-set that can and will sabotage your ability to stay in control of what you want in the long run.

I agree that preparing for an unknowable future is a daunting task. Consequently, you may be tempted to avoid the hard work altogether and let life simply unfold. Keep in mind that when you fly by the seat of your pants, life is bound to get messy; there is no planning when you are smack dab in the middle of a life crisis—you are not only out of time, you have limited choices, if any. Worse yet, someone else may end up making all of your decisions in your behalf—whether you like it or not.

You may have heard sons and daughters tell horrific stories about taking matters into their own hands when their parents neglected to make plans, with undesirable results, or about the difficulty of learning the personal arrangements or desires of independent-living friends who suddenly need help. When push comes to shove, any one of us can easily find ourselves in the same situation unless we become proactive about planning for our future. Researching care and living options, and related costs among other critical details pays off and keeps you in the driver's seat.

I urge you to think twice about a do-nothing "plan." Once you create some momentum, you will start to find relief knowing that you are making some progress. The more you plan, the greater your peace of mind and ability to control your destiny. If you are a procrastinator by nature, consider the following tips as a way to jump-start yourself into action:

If not knowing where to begin the planning process is holding you back, start anywhere. Devote fifteen minutes to one task—for example, conduct research on the Internet about housing options, make an appointment with a financial adviser or elder law attorney, create an emergency contact list and post it on your refrigerator, research work options if you are thinking about getting a part-time job, purchase a planner to get you organized. Slowly chip away at something, anything—every day.

When I dread certain time-consuming tasks, I ask advice. Here's an example of how this strategy works for me. Not long ago, I was in the market to buy a smartphone. My head was spinning with questions: Which brand is best? What makes one model better than another? Why are the prices all over the map? What features should I be looking for? Instead of relying on sales people to give me the answers, I called upon a colleague who has his act together when it comes to technology. Another reason I chose him to ask for advice: his home and work lives mimic mine—he has family caregiving responsibilities and has a business to run. Because of our similarities, he was the best person to advise me on which phone to buy. Fifteen minutes on the phone with him saved me hours of clueless and agonizing shopping and comparing.

Sometimes it feels as though the timing is not right to make plans or decisions—and you may well be right. Lack of information is a good reason to hold off. Allow time for more details to reveal themselves to you before moving forward.

If you are overwhelmed at the thought of planning for the distant future, make plans for a shorter period of time—six months from now, or next year, for instance.

Whatever plans you make, you always have the option of changing your mind. Life takes its course and reveals itself over time—giving you updated and perhaps new information to process. Learn the art of adjusting. As you take action, revise plans as needed, then act again.

Ditch sticky note reminders if you tend to ignore them. Instead, think about automation as a way to live more effectively. For example: If you dislike the thought of spending valuable time paying bills or saving money, prearrange for direct-deposit systems, bank alerts, and bill paying. In old age, automating as many processes as possible simplifies and streamlines your life—and can prevent necessary tasks from falling into the cracks. You can set up automatic systems for overdraft notices, membership renewals, pharmacy refills, house maintenance reminders, pet care, grocery orders, delivery of meals, and a host of other tasks.

When it comes to completing a major planning project, I reward myself—new shoes, a day at the spa, a trip with a grandchild—keeping my eye on the prize works for me. Commit to one task related to planning for your old age that you are putting off. What can you promise to yourself at the completion of the task? Imagine the possibilities.

Do you procrastinate by trying to solve a problem you don't have? What I mean by asking this question is that it is easy to waste time tweaking and adjusting what is already working in your life. This is an avoidance strategy. For example, let's say you already have plenty of money, and paying for your long-term care will not be a problem, but you have no friends or social life. The smart move is to stop focusing on adding money to your bank account (something you already know how to do quite well). Get out in the real world and start mingling with people who could eventually become your friends and be there for you in old age.

Picture This

Strategic thinking can be a visual process. "Brain science teaches us that a picture is worth a 1000 words because it serves as an attentional guide, motivator, and map to the brain to help you navigate your way to come from behind to reach or exceed your goals," writes Srini Pillay, MD, assistant clinical professor of psychiatry (part-time) at Harvard Medical School and author of *Tinker Dabble Doodle Try: Unlock the Power of the Unfocused Mind*.[1]

Dr. Pillay has researched the human brain for more than seventeen years. He says, "When you program your car's navigator with your destination, your car figures out how to take you to your destination. Similarly, your brain has the ability to map out your course to your goal once you clearly communicate to yourself what this goal is. In addition, imagining your journey also helps to keep your brain on track as it will constantly refer to this image and update your journey with greater ease than if you did not provide this information to it."

Bottom line: If you can picture yourself achieving a goal, chances are you will. The more vivid you can get, the better. Powerful visualization tools, such as collages of artwork, photographs, words and phrases, and quotations, can be used to represent what you would like to experience more of in life.

Get as detailed as possible. Picture in your mind what you will do once your goal is reached. How amazing does that feel? Envision your ideal future with the use of some of the following visualization tools:

Vision board: A vision board (also known as a dream board) is a reminder of your future intentions. Literally, it is any sort of surface (magnetic board, bulletin board, or notebook) used to display images that represent and reinforce whatever it is that you intend to want, do, be, and have in your life. Create a title for your board—for example, My Peaceful Home, My Dream Retirement, My Well Body, My Best Life, and so on. Also, post a specific date whereby you will have achieved you goal. An invaluable resource for you to consider is Make a Vision Board (http://makeavisionboard.com). You might also want to create an online vision board. Check out Pinterest (www.pinterest.com). The format is easy to use and highly inspirational.

Mind movie: A mind movie is a vision board "slide show" of a certain aspect of your life that you intend to improve upon or create. When your "movie" is completed, you can watch it online or download it on your computer or mobile device. Watching the slide show throughout the day reinforces clarity about your vision. Add music to stir even greater emotions. Your computer and smartphone most likely come equipped with a picture frame "slide show" feature. After you download your photographs to a designated file, go to your settings to turn on this function.

Positive list: Create a list of the things you like most about yourself. Post your list somewhere that you can look at it while you are getting dressed for the day. Promote as much positivity into your life as you possibly can.

Written entries: You learned earlier in this book about the documented benefits of writing about traumatic experiences. Keeping a diary opens yet other possibilities. According to studies conducted by Dr. Teresa Amabile, a director of research at Harvard Business School, and coauthor of *The Progress Principle* (http://progressprinciple.com), capturing small wins and big wins, writing down things that are important to your inner work life and will probably be forgotten, recalling concerns and problems, recording things you are grateful for, tracking things to do the next day that will help catalyze your progress, or anything else you want to remember could have a substantial impact on your motivation pertaining to creative tasks. Dr. Amabile suggests sitting down at the end of the day and jotting down your thoughts before switching off the light and going to sleep.

Gratitude board: A gratitude board is a vison tool used to capture information about people, experiences, and things in your life that make you feel grateful and appreciative. Take a few minutes to contemplate the following questions, then make a list of all the things in your life for which you are grateful: When are you most at peace? What makes you feel happy and alive? What or who do you appreciate? Create visuals to go with your list. You'll be amazed at how uplifting it is to simply turn your attention to the positive aspects of your life. Use this approach to override any negative assumptions in your belief system.

Law of Attraction

Studies reveal that we can attract whatever we think about—good and bad. "The ability to construct a hypothetical situation in one's imagination prior to it actually occurring may afford greater accuracy in predicting its eventual outcome."[2]

Every time we praise something, every time we appreciate something, every time we feel good about something, we are telling the universe, "More of this, please." On the other hand, worry is negative goal-setting—thinking about, talking about, and envisioning exactly what we *don't* want to happen.

The law of attraction also instructs us to act as if we have already achieved our goal to attract the people and circumstances that are in tune with our vision. Before I start out on any new venture, I take a moment to "see" it and "feel" it. I do this by sitting in a quiet place, shutting my eyes, taking deep breaths, and experiencing the fruits of my labor. Once my vision is strong, I am inspired by insights that pop into my mind. I act boldly.

I also take notice that all of the good that comes to me is not pushed or forced. It is meant to be, and simply unravels effortlessly before me. It is important that I am sensitively aware of each small bit of good that comes my way. I am grateful.

The first thing I do every morning is I choose to feel good; then, I decide from that mindset what to do next. This practice is about me feeling good habitually. Nothing can make me feel good every moment of the day; I must consistently *choose* a better feeling.

I have been practicing the law of attraction for years. It takes hard work and strong conviction to expect and attract positive results. Yes, bad things happen to good people, and good things happen to bad people. That's life, and I have learned to live with that reality as well.

To learn more about the Law of Attraction, visit the Abraham-Hicks website (www.abraham-hicks.com).

Of Course, I Talk to Myself. Who Else Can I Trust?

If there is one commonality that all people share in the aging process it is facing a variety of new and complex uncertainties. What lurks around the corner is anybody's guess. When the going gets rough, people do a lot of different things to ease tensions—exercise, eat, and play games, among others. They also talk out loud to themselves as a thinking strategy. I do it. You do it. It seems as if everybody does it. Whether you are testing a melon for ripeness at the grocery store, trying to stay calm when you are angry, or searching for your misplaced phone—when you are merrily speaking to an audience of no one, and answering your own questions, you are in good company.

Is thinking out loud something to be ashamed of? Is it a warning sign of dementia? Is self-talk madness or a form of high intelligence? Is it a normal part of aging?

Researchers call thinking out loud "private speech," and it is a common phenomenon, starting as soon as infants learn to talk—between eighteen and twenty-four months. The behavior serves children in several ways:

Practicing language skills
Reflecting on experiences
Learning new tasks
Dealing with stress

If saying our thoughts out loud when we are children is perfectly natural and normal, what leads us to want to stop this behavior in the first place?

In many households, well-meaning grown-ups stifled the instinctual impulse for children to talk to themselves. "Be quiet. Mommy's napping!" "No talking during the television program!" "Read quietly to yourself!" In response, we mutter, whisper, or move our lips with no sound, until eventually we learn that it is far better to keep our mouths shut than cause trouble with an adult. Over time, this conditioning is pretty much how many of us end up believing that talking to yourself in private or public is inappropriate, embarrassing, and socially unacceptable.

Returning to present day, and what we are all up against in our daily routines, it certainly appears as though there are multiple occasions and situations when private speech is quite beneficial and therapeutic. According to author Linda Sapadin, PhD, a psychologist and success coach (www.PsychWisdom.com) who specializes in helping people overcome procrastination (and other self-defeating patterns of behavior), talking with yourself not only relieves loneliness, it may also make you smarter. She writes, "It helps you clarify your thoughts, tend to what's important, and firms up any decisions you're contemplating. There's just one proviso: You become smarter only if you speak respectfully to yourself."[3]

Here are a few additional suggestions when self-talk will suffice as your own personal coaching tool:

Pep talk: Words of encouragement get you through tough times and keep dreams alive. "I can do this. Things will work out." "I don't need this cookie."

Feedback: Self-talk can be motivating while giving you immediate, unfiltered commentary about yourself. "I am absolutely fabulous! Pat myself on the back."

Evaluation: Asking certain questions offers valuable insights. "Where did I go wrong?" "How am I doing so far?"

Teacher: Hearing yourself say what you want to learn allows it to sink in. "*Io parlo Italiano.*" "*I* before *e* except after *c*."

Outburst: Giving people on television a piece of your mind is an outlet for all kinds of emotions. "You don't know what you're talking about!" "I can't believe you just did that! What the heck are you thinking?"

Release: Venting frustrations can calm you down. "Why can't I get this !&%$#!! thing to work!" "This sucks!"

Action: Realizing that something must be done when you listen hard enough. "I hate this job. I am so unhappy." "I never seem to have enough money."

Replay: Feeding yourself a play-by-play of your every move helps you get organized. "Now let's see, I had the house keys in my hand a minute ago. Where's the best place for me to start looking for them?"

Perspective: Processing events and putting things in perspective grounds you. "When I look back, I can see how I was as much at fault as the other guy."

Emotion: Grieving takes on many forms, including saying out loud what you are feeling inside. "I feel so sad, and have every right to feel this way."

Solution: Thinking out loud through a challenging situation may result in finding resolution. "What is the worst that can happen to me?"

Rehearsal: When feelings are hurt, speaking aloud the actions you may never follow through on may rationalize what happened and plan a response. "That so-and-so can't get away with this. Wait till I see him again; then, I'll really let him have it."

Airtime: Talking aloud, especially if you live alone, is a way to hear the sound of your own voice and fill in gaps of silence. If you have pets, they get to learn your language well. "It's going to be a beautiful day, Fluffy." "Come on, Spike. Let's go for a walk."

Presence: Even if no one else seems to appreciate you in the moment, you are always there for you. "At least *I* love me."

Be Conscious of the Dark Side

If you can say positive things about yourself to yourself, you also have the free will to be your own worst critic. Thinking out loud "I am an idiot!" or "I am so stupid!" is not helpful, nor is it kind. If you tend to lean toward negative self-talk, here are a few suggestions to keep your perspective in balance:

Explore the roots. In your formative years, did you often hear other people in your past speak this way about themselves? Did their negativity rub off on you?

Challenge. Remember that you can counter with positive feedback at any time. Your reaction to a mistake might be, "I can never do anything right." Instead of exaggerating and overgeneralizing, your response can be, "Aren't you exaggerating a bit?"

Appreciate. Notice and savor simple and precious life experiences wherever and whenever they occur. "The sun is shining." "This coffee tastes great."

Acknowledge. Recognize both the good and the bad, but favor the good. You might say, "I am working on this situation now and thank goodness I don't have that other problem at the same time," or "I'm sad about this and grateful about that."

Override. Replace negative programming with conscious, positive new direction. "Even if the rain continues I am *still* going to have a good day."

Go for the gray. Life is not black and white; there is plenty of gray to consider. Do you tend to only think and speak in terms of good and bad? Are you prone to using the words *never* and *always*? Practice adopting more self-forgiving words, such as *sometimes*.

Pivot. The mind can't think two thoughts at the same time. When you are aware of expressing the negative version of your thought, say "Stop it" to yourself; then, turn your words into saying something more pleasant.

Overcome. Slipping up and making mistakes is human. When that happens, use the word *but* to avoid judging yourself for not acting better. "I am overweight and out of shape, but I will go to the gym today." "I made a mistake, but everybody fails sometime. I can do better next time.

Think Before Taking Action

Sometimes when you least expect it, the demand for you to make a major life decision can come out of nowhere. Ready or not, as conflicts and problems surface, immediate decisions demand your attention. Even if you are proactive by nature you are not immune to dealing with unexpected life events.

To avert the possibility of spending a lot of time coming up with solutions to the wrong problem, or a problem that does not exist, use the What Should I Do Worksheet on page 43 whenever you find yourself in a challenging situation:

WHAT SHOULD I DO? WORKSHEET

This worksheet is available to download and customize at www.elderindustry.com.

Life happens, and now you have no choice but to make a decision. Keep in mind that problem solving and decision making are two separate and distinct processes. The goal is to get better at both. Strategic thinking takes practice. In time, confidence increases and you are less likely to rush to the first solution—which may not necessarily be the best one in the long run.

Begin by writing down the answers to the following questions on a separate sheet of paper:

What is the decision that must be made?

By when must the decision be made?

What is making this decision problematic?

What proof do I have that a problem exists?

What about this situation is within my control?

What about this situation is not within my control?

Based on your answers to these questions, conduct your own research on the problem and possible solutions.

Next, identify three trusted and diverse sources for advice regarding your situation. Seek out people you know both personally and professionally. Make a date to connect with them.

Before connecting with advisers, be prepared to take notes or ask for permission to record the meeting. Also come prepared to discuss in detail the decision that must be made and related challenges.

During your meeting with advisers, take notes. Write down *their* questions as well. Ask:

What is your perspective?

Why do you think this way?

What is your evidence for your beliefs?

What are the short- and long-term impacts of the problem?

What are the worse- and best-case scenarios?

After consulting with advisers, ask yourself the following questions:

Are there similarities in my advisers' answers?

Are there any significant differences of opinion or approach?

Are there multiple alternative solutions to the problem?

Do I have a new and different perspective on the problem and the decision?

Do I need to redefine the problem?

Before you decide what to do, also consider these questions:

Is *this* the right time to make this decision?

What are the likely consequences if I decide to delay the decision?

Who else is affected by my decision? Must they be consulted before or after I decide?

What are the needs of those who will be affected by this decision?

Will this decision have a negative effect on my physical or emotional well-being?

Will this decision alter my personal or professional relationships?

Have I researched all costs and who pays for what?

Am I being honest with myself or am I engaging in wishful thinking?

Do I have time to make adjustments if things don't work out?

What is my gut instinct telling me to do?

When you are ready or at a "good enough" position, make a decision.

This is what I will do, and why:

_____

Make a plan that defines a sequence of events and action steps necessary for completion.

Evaluate the results. Is the problem solved?

Insights and Inspiration

Recommended Reading: *Leadership Simple: Leading People to Lead Themselves* (2003) by Steve Morris and Jill Morris

Recommended YouTube: *5 Tips to Improve Your Critical Thinking* by Samantha Agoos, published March 15, 2016

Recommended Movie: *Inside Out* (2015)

Recommended Song: "Ironic" by Alanis Morissette

Recommended TED Talk: "The Surprising Habits of Original Thinkers," presented by Adam Grant, filmed February 2016

You Are Tougher
Than You Look

Thriving in times of uncertainty

"All is not lost. Everything happens for a reason." "There is no such thing as an accident." "What has happened is part of a great and mighty plan."

I have never for a moment believed in these philosophies—they are nothing more than platitudes. The greatest offense I find in statements of this nature is the invalidation of peoples' real life experiences and the right of every individual to be human, frail, and vulnerable.

Think of the traumas and life stories of the elders you know personally. They may have endured the devastations of war crimes, deaths of loved ones including children, painful childhood experiences, shattered opportunities, poverty, accidents, betrayal of friends and family, and natural disasters. Is it necessary that people suffer horribly and go through so much pain so as to gain perspective? Absolutely not. To state that a particular tragedy or loss *had* to happen for someone to learn a lesson is categorically untrue, not to mention, demeaning.

My mentally tough old friends wrestle with the same questions we all face when life turns upside down: Who am I now? What are my beliefs now? How should I proceed knowing what I know now? No matter what bad happens, many of them are naturally resilient—they forgive quickly, don't sweat the small stuff, stop and smell the roses, regularly express gratitude, and tend to inject humor into most situations. "Get back on that horse as soon as you can," they advise.

Objectives

After completing this chapter, "You Are Tougher Than You Look," you will be able to:

- Capture the essence of savoring
- Stay motivated to accomplish goals
- Create a sense of agency over what you can control
- Establish trusting relationships
- Steer the direction of difficult conversations
- Get a handle on guilt and grief
- Prepare for shifting responsibilities and roles

What is your typical mind-set and course of action when trauma, tragedy, personal crises, and simple everyday problems and annoyances interrupt your otherwise peaceful existence? Developmental psychologist Sybil Wolin, PhD, and psychiatrist Steven Wolin, MD (www .projectresilience.com) define *resiliency* as the capacity to rise above adversity—sometimes the terrible adversity of outright violence, molestation, or war—and forge lasting strengths in the struggle. The resiliency model honors the power of the potential to bounce back from hardship.

There is more to reaching old age in one piece than having friends and money in the bank. The need to be resilient resides side by side with the other essential life skills, such as critical thinking. When you are in school, for example, you need study skills. Buying a house requires negotiation skills. In the journey toward old age, it is necessary to be resilient. Are you ready to live well no matter what challenges lie ahead?

Savor the Good—*While It Lasts*

As they say, nothing good (or bad) lasts forever: You and your close friend spend years enjoying each other's company. You laugh and cry together. You support each other through the ups and downs of life. Out of the blue, she decides to relocate to Costa Rica. And just like that, she is out of your life forever. Or, since the day he was born, your grandson is the center of your universe. For the first decade of his life, you do many fun and memorable things together. He loves being with you. When he enters high school, he is consumed with sports and girls, and now he rarely makes time to see you. Your heart aches.

"Don't be afraid to love with your whole heart," advise my elder friends. They tell me this to make a point about what happens after a relationship ends. They explain that I can choose to be depressed long after the person is gone, or I can keep the memories of the good times alive in my heart, and move on. I hear their words, but what they suggest is easier said than done.

They suggest that I try to think about relationships in this way: You don't love a book that you are currently enjoying any less because you know that eventually you will finish reading it, do you? The same holds true for people and happy times. "Appreciate every good thing about your relationship *while it lasts.*" My elder friends remind me that pleasure lasts but a moment. Pain can last a lifetime—if you let it.

The elders in my life who are naturally resilient are quick to deliberately maximize the positive events in their lives—they are skilled at "savoring" whatever good they can wring out in the moment. Here are some of the ways they do this:

They share good feelings with others. Whether they are enjoying the flight of a butterfly or hearing the band play "The Star-Spangled Banner," they verbalize to the person nearby their positive feelings about an event that is happening in the moment.

They take mental photographs. When they feel particularly blessed, I have heard them say out loud, "This is wonderful. I have to remember this."

They are quick to congratulate themselves. For example, after two months of agonizing over a 500-piece puzzle, upon completion, my mom was ecstatic. She even asked me to take a photograph and share with others on social media. Her happiness was contagious.

They don't rush through everyday experiences. They sip their wine. They allow the chocolate to melt in their mouth. They make time to smell the aroma of food cooking on the stove.

With the help of my elder friends, I have learned to adjust my tendency to want to speed through life and instead practice savoring ordinary moments.

Keep Your Eye on the Prize

Do you recall learning how to tell time? In your youth, it was something you probably looked forward to. After you mastered the basics, you copied everybody else and started to track time according to what was important to you: How many minutes until I can watch my favorite television show? What time is dinner? How many days until school is out for the summer?

As you continue to assign time concepts to bring order to your life, you face the realization that the forward motion of the ticking clock stops for no one. Every day, you are handed the same 24 hours as everybody else. If you had all the money in the world, you could not buy extra hours.

It is a well-documented fact that although everyone's life story is unique, specific recurring regrets are voiced by people who are on their deathbed. They recall things they did that they wish they hadn't. They recall things they wish they had done, but didn't.

The following statements reflect what many people express on their deathbed:

People who are dying wish that they had been kinder.

People who are dying wish they had the courage to stay true to their wants and not other's expectations.

People who are dying regret not being a better parent, partner, or friend.

People who are dying are sorry for spending too much time working and not making enough time for fun.

People who are dying regret not expressing their true feelings when given the opportunity to do so.

We don't have to be on our deathbed to admit we all make mistakes and dumb decisions. The pain of regret stings like no other. (If you have ever experienced the intense emotional range of regret after accidently hitting the Reply All tab to an e-mail and destroying a relationship, then you know what I'm talking about.)

People have regrets over many different decisions—from getting tattoos to how time was spent (read: wasted) in school, career choices, and buyer's remorse over a financial investment that went south.

Are you carrying around a deep regret? Acknowledging that in this moment in time you are experiencing an emotional meltdown over a missed opportunity or disappointment, or you are beating yourself up—"How could I have done that? What was I thinking?"—is not a good use of your precious time. When my old friends offer advice about feeling the pain and exposure of regret, they say that life is messy business. They also lovingly remind me that I am human, with faults, suggesting I try to do better next time. They also tell me to take a moment to laugh at myself. That statement alone often makes me laugh.

Yes, we could all be better off or happier if we had done some things differently in our past, but somehow we have gotten to where we are in life right now. Learning to live with regrets, and the emotional pain that lingers, is a choice.

Whoever Said, "The Problem Is You Think You Have Time," Is Right

"I can't get everything done that I need to." This is a common complaint, and the standard response from time-management experts is, "Make a to-do list. Prioritize your list; then, hack away at the tasks. You will get it done eventually."

The challenges of clock time are unsolvable. No matter how much you want to stick to a to-do list, it won't be long before you are distracted. Plus, checking off one task on the list requires that you follow it up with another task. It can't be helped. It is a shortcoming of a flawed formula.

There are few schedules, deadlines, or ticking clocks old people deem worthier of their attention than the real-time life that continues to unfold before them. They do not tend to live in time frames as we may know them; my old friends live in a mental state where they are either having fun or grieving or at peace or in pain or thinking about dinner. At some point in their lives they choose to remove self-limitations associated with "not having enough time." They turn their efforts toward immediate desires, meaningful conversations, and purpose-driven relationships.

The sage advice I receive from the old people in my life spares me countless wasted hours and years of needless anxiety—they are my virtual reality without the headset. Because they live in real time, and have paid their dues many times over, they get to the core of difficult matters quickly. For example, in my dating years, if I wondered aloud whether a love-interest would turn into something more serious, my elder friends would say, "He doesn't love you, honey. If he did he would be banging down your door right now. Move on."

Now that I am inching toward old age and aging alone, I am acutely aware of how I spend my time. For years, I was completely unbalanced—putting work and making money ahead of everything else. What changed my focus was seeing how many of the old people in my life have friends who never let them down. Making time to cultivate friendships of all ages paid off. If I wanted the same for myself in old age, I came to the realization that I must change my thoughts, and my behavior. To surround myself with trusting and dependable people, I had to be one myself.

How do you prioritize your time? If you tend to struggle with time management as I do, perhaps the use of a written reminder system will help shift your thinking. Instead of work/career as your one and only priority, you might add such categories to your daily to-do list categories as social and creative endeavors, a spiritual practice, and physical and mental fitness activities.

You might also ask yourself who is in your life currently that deserves more face time. If it means getting on an airplane—so be it. You are making an invaluable investment of your time. The list of people that you love wholeheartedly today is ever evolving. It is a sad day when their name is removed from your address book after they die.

Spiritual director and author Kathryn Cunningham (www.atravelersview.org) writes, "If you assume the title of 'friend,' that carries with it great responsibility. Do you understand that your constant intercession for them can bring life or healing when they no longer can manage for themselves? Do you know that it's your job to carry them when they can no longer move forward? Do you know that when a friend has lost their vision for the future, that your vision can sustain them? These are the responsibilities of friendship."

It also comes down to trust. If you are my friend, my "trust detector" goes something like this:

When you say you will do something, you do it.

When I need something, you offer to get it for me if you can.

When you make a promise, you fulfill your agreement.

You keep secrets.

You speak from a place of goodness and tell me the truth.

Making small requests at first, I know early on in a friendship who will be there for me and who will not when I need them most. After all, I hold myself to these standards. Why shouldn't I expect the same from others? There have been occasional failures to follow through on both sides, but those incidents between me and my friends are extremely rare. In the meantime, I have carefully weeded out the people in my life that I do not trust.

From the point of view of establishing trusting and dependable relationships, such statements as "I don't have enough time" are meaningless. As you contemplate the realities of old age and living alone, decide today how you might reprioritize how you spend your time, and with whom.

Motivate Yourself

Which one of the following is your mantra? "When I really want something, nothing can stop me from getting it," or "I can always come up with a good excuse for not pursuing what I want." Whereas some people find strategies to constantly feel plugged in and invigorated, others simply change their mind, roll over, and hit the snooze button.

The excitement of taking on a new project or personal goal can easily go by the wayside. When you are tired or in pain or "not feeling up to it," you can talk yourself out of almost anything, but the sheer act of making an important promise to yourself is worth fighting for.

What is helpful is to come up with a plan ahead of time when you know that staying on track to meet your goals will be challenging. For example, perhaps you can think of a special person in your life to dedicate the rough spots to. This simple strategy may help catapult you to the finish line.

How you sustain the self-discipline and willpower necessary to create a quality old age, among other long-term goals, is up to you. The journey will not be easy. To keep up your momentum, do you know self-motivating and self-disciplined people you can buddy up with? If yes, when you are in their presence, make note of the following:

What are their perspectives?

How do they express their thoughts and feelings?

What kind of questions do they ask?

What kind of people do they regularly hang out with?

How do they know what they want?

Who do they go to for advice?

What do these self-motivators care about?

Be flexible. Try different approaches to manage the challenges of staying on track. I recommend the following resources for long-term motivation and inspiration:

Boomer Living: www.boomer-living.com. Offers connections to inspiring and active-aging individuals who use the power of community to stay focused and motivated.

Growing Bolder: www.growingbolder.com. Invites you to explore the concept of living full out. What is growing bolder? It's an attitude. A mission. A passion. A team of people who believe in the power of hope, inspiration, and possibility.

Lean Toward Learning Conversations

Saying no to paying for a grandchild's college education, disagreeing with a friend about loaning him money, hurting your neighbor's feelings and dreading apologizing: Talking about things you don't want to talk about cannot be avoided. Difficult conversations are risky—we either bring people closer to us or push them away. As time goes by we cannot afford to alienate people who are close to us.

Before you open your mouth, the question to ask yourself is: What is the purpose for having this conversation in the first place? It can take a lot of energy to redirect the impulse to get *your* message across, rather than making it your intention to *listen* to the other person. It also means finding a way to stop thinking that the other person is being controlling and irrational.

Years of practice of turning conversations around for the better have paid off for me. Relationships are healthy and intact even though there have been plenty of arguments along the way. I am to the point where I say, "Who cares who is right?" Learning about the other person's perspective is now my priority. Curiosity and silence gets me there.

Curiosity asks questions:

What information does the other person have that I don't?

What is this person's understanding of the situation?

What can I learn from this person?

When the other person starts talking, resist the temptation to interrupt. You can sip a glass of water slowly as a device to stop yourself from breaking into the conversation or losing control of your feelings. Resist filling in gaps of silence when there are pauses in the conversation. *Silence is a powerful communication tool.* When people feel confident that you are really listening and trying to better understand where they are coming from, more of what is on their mind may be revealed.

As an example, there were times when my mom and I would get into heated arguments about her choosing not to exercise. When I approached the conversation by saying that her inactivity worried me, and my steady stream of suggestions wore on her, she would cut me off in midstream and inform me that I was making her feel judged and foolish. I, in turn, felt frustrated. When I shifted my stance from persuading to learning, and limited myself to more listening and acknowledging her feelings, the process opened up a deeper understanding about her anxieties about being old. Making the adjustment from talker to listener also allowed a second benefit to occur: Mom is now a better listener when *I* speak. It's a natural consequence of both of us feeling heard.

Choose to Let It Go

Some situations simply do not make sense. Despite our best intentions and efforts sometimes, nothing works. I have learned that just because I am passionate (or obsessed) about a desire, I cannot force anyone to want what I want. We all have a specific way of doing things, but micromanaging situations and insisting on perfection kills relationships.

On the other hand, deciding *not* to have a conversation can also be a relationship strategy worth considering. As an example, I never talk politics or religion with anybody. If the other person brings up these subjects, I just listen. If I do respond, I say, "That's good to know." And then I change the subject.

Lessen the Grip of Guilt

Making a commitment to spend more time with people who are important to you will carry with it a constant emotional companion: guilt. No one can be in two places at once. The relentless struggle of this reality is not to be taken lightly. When you are with one person, you may grapple with how another person in your life equally deserves your time and attention simultaneously. You cannot win.

Guilt is such a powerful emotion that you can even feel guilty about *not* feeling guilty. But you can take action to get a handle on managing this powerful emotion. It takes practice, and lots of it. The result is worth it.

Think about a situation you are currently feeling guilty about. Once you have identified the situation, take a hard look at everything you have done so far to lessen guilty feelings. Ask yourself:

Has spending time agonizing over this situation served me well?

Has my feeling bad made a difference in the situation?

Has throwing money at the problem changed the situation?

Has saying "I'm sorry" changed the way I feel?

If you remain tormented about a specific situation, there is something else at play. When it comes to people you love and care about, *nothing* you do is ever going to be enough since there is always more to do. When you do your best in the moment, your best is good enough. Your best fluctuates—one day, you are tired and your actions show it; the next day, you are full of vim and vigor and you are unstoppable.

When you feel guilty about something, ask yourself: *Am I doing the best that I can right now?* If the answer is no, take one small step to change how you feel—make a phone call, send a text or an e-mail. However, if the answer is "Yes. This is all I've got in me right now," accept that truth as proof that you are not superhuman.

You Love. You Grieve.

Just as it is important to laugh and stay positive, it is equally significant to give yourself time to grieve. Death and divorce, accidents, and other traumatic events, we all must choose how to live going forward, but we do not choose *whether* to grieve.

In moments of rage, anger, despair, fear, and frailty, no one has the authority to deny your right to feel emotional pain. When there is grieving to do, there is nothing else to do, nothing to be responsible for, no figuring out how to feel better, and no pretending that you are "strong enough" to handle what happened. Just grieve.

Recovery from grief requires more than grieving. A Stanford University study revealed that the process of healthy grieving is more complicated than simply expressing your negative emotions.[1]

Marriage and family therapist, and radio host Cheryl Jones (www.weatheringgrief.com) asks, "Would you want to be someone who lost those you love but felt nothing? Loss and grief are inevitable outgrowths of living into old age as our parents, friends, and family die. Developing the capacity to grieve, then, becomes an invaluable tool in facing our own aging." Jones further explains that the relationship you had with the person you lost does not end and so, in some ways, grief doesn't end. "There will be moments, even after you have found a meaningful way through the most intense period of mourning, that you will once again feel the loss keenly. Over time, though, if you let yourself follow the stream of your grief, the sad or difficult feelings will be only one aspect of your continuing connection to your loved one. And often, the experience of grief can lead to some of the most meaningful and precious moments of your life."

As you grieve, if people give you any form of "get over it," "you can rise above it," "time for you to move on," or say, "there are no coincidences" or "you'll be better off because this happened," your first course of action is tune out their messages. Their inability or unwillingness to understand what you are experiencing is a form of choosing their own comfort over your pain.

During times of loss, the truly helpful people simply love you in silence, choosing to remain alongside you as you grieve. They listen patiently as you repeatedly express how much you are hurting. They ask if you are eating enough. They are present in the bad times to experience your loss *with* you. For example, when you have been diagnosed with a serious illness, and someone offers to accompany you to doctor appointments, that person loves you for better and for worse.

Grief is not an illness to heal, nor is it something to avoid, hide, or transform into something else. Choose to battle the isolation of grief and cross the barriers of insular instincts in your own way. Intimacy happens when you allow others into your life when you are suffering the most. If you find yourself struggling to find ways to cope or you do not have a strong and trusting support system, seek professional advice.

Who Am I Now?

It is *not* business as usual. You can't go back. What happened, happened. You are forever changed. What you once understood as reality no longer applies. Your setback has jolted you forward into another realm of possibilities. One day, you are working; the next day, you are unemployed. One day, you are a spouse; the next day, you are a widow. One day, you are healthy; the next day, you are diagnosed with a chronic physical condition.

First you grieve, but you have the capacity to do far more than just grieve. You have questions that, although they may not be immediately answerable, you ask anyway—What is truth now? How does what happened change me? What are the new rules and principles of this new reality?

Change happens; then, you practice resilience, or risk the possibility of spiraling down into a dark well of confusion and sadness. Before the setback, you may have achieved "success" in terms of health, profession, wealth, and power. After the setback, it becomes necessary to create new definitions—What are the new facts? What is my new reality? What does success mean to me now? Who do I aspire to be *now?* "One day at a time" is the advice I hear most often from my old friends.

Insights and Inspiration

Recommended Reading: *The Untethered Soul: The Journey Beyond Yourself* (2007) by Michael A. Singer

Recommended YouTube: Pharrell Williams, *Happy* (Official Music Video), published November 21, 2013

Recommended Movie: *Little Miss Sunshine* (2006)

Recommended Song: "I Hope You Dance" by Tia Sillers and Mark Sanders

Recommended TED Talk: "How to Stop Screwing Yourself Over," presented by Mel Robbins, career and relationship expert, filmed June 11, 2011

The Fierce Urgency of Money

Staying afloat financially

The subject of money and quality living in old age caught my attention several decades ago while attending Mass one Sunday morning. The congregation was buzzing with excitement emanating mostly from five elder ladies who had gone out on the town the night before. I knew these women on a first-name basis—all of them lived alone and relied solely on Social Security. None of them had money to burn.

The night before, they shared dinner and drinks at a local popular pizzeria followed by an evening performance at the Second City comedy club. A few weeks later I learned that the same group of women boarded a bus to the Wisconsin Dells for three days of food, fun, and entertainment. I began to wonder how they could afford these excursions. When I heard about their third outing to a performance of the Chicago Lyric Opera, I realized that these ladies were on to something that I needed to learn: living the good life on a tight budget.

Old age is expensive. And in many ways, so is retirement. Imagine a future when your paycheck comes to a complete halt. What will it take to sustain your current lifestyle? How will you afford housing, entertainment, travel, hobbies, and other expenses? Have you investigated establishing your long-term financial stability around the latest calculation of retirement funds per the experts?

Government entitlements are adjusted every time there is a changing of the guard in the White House; suddenly, we all become acutely aware of the headlines. Weathering the storm of policy change requires staying informed. When legislators talk about "rolling back" legislation, for example, beware. What is law or policy today might not exist tomorrow.

When the government speaks about Medicare and Medicaid, pay particular attention to any changes related to the following:

Medicare Part A (hospital insurance)
Medicare Part B (medical insurance)
Medicare RX (prescription coverage)
Eligibility requirements
Out-of-pocket costs
Flexibility to choose Medicare Supplement Plans
Privatization strategies

In the meantime, the cost of care in old age is off the charts. Here are the 2015 averages for long-term care services in the United States: $220 per day or $80,300 per year for a semi-private room in a nursing home, $250 per day or $91,250 per year for a private room in a nursing home, $3,600 per month or $43,200 per year for basic services in an assisted living facility, $20 per hour for a home health aide (typically with a four-hour minimum), and $59 per day for adult day services.[1] Who can afford these prices? Worse yet, much of the costs associated with long-term care are not covered by Medicare. Plus, if you are not yet age-qualified for Medicare, then what?

You want, you pay. Sticker shock takes on a whole new meaning when it comes to quality living and care. On the other end of the spectrum are those who are lucky enough to have deep pockets who can afford anything their heart desires.

What Is Your Relationship with Money?

Do you have a history of stretching yourself thin between fantasizing and wishful thinking? Take a look at the following money mind-sets:

Everyone else comes first.
Buying expensive gifts makes me feel good.
Financing a grandchild's education is a good investment.
Loaning money with no expectation to be paid back is okay with me.
Donating substantially to my favorite causes is worthwhile.
Sacrifices required of a frugal existence are not for me.

The government will take care of me when I am old and in need.

I am completely comfortable letting someone else manage my money.

What I have in terms of money is nobody else's business. I like my privacy.

Do you see versions of yourself in this list? Are you challenged with overspending, gambling, or credit card misuse? Changing a lifetime of self-sabotaging habits is not easy. Realistically, if you have never succeeded at being financial stable, it will likely take double the effort to get on track now.

We all know that money does not equate to happiness, nor does it insulate anyone from relationship conflicts, pain, and suffering. Money is simply the vehicle that allows the basics—a roof over your head, food on the table, and quality care when you need it the most. As you create your budget for old age, you can expect to spend your money on the following:

Housing

Helpers

Specialized care

Transportation

Insurance

Socializing

Fitness endeavors

Advisers

Medications

Food/special diets

Pet care

Taxes

End of life

Death-related services

Silence Hurts You

Do you believe that talking with others about your personal finances is taboo? Perhaps you feel uncomfortable broaching the subject with someone else because no one spoke about financial planning and budgeting when you were growing up. As an adult, you can work hard for years, and still end up with zero savings if you were never taught the ropes. Whatever your personal history, avoiding talking about money will work against you as you approach old age.

This is exactly what happened to a good friend of mine. She lived with her male companion, in his house, for twelve years. Both had been widowed. Both had adult children. They chose not to marry. As domestic partners, they never created any legal agreements between them; then suddenly, he died. *The day of his funeral*, her companion's adult children informed my friend that they were legally evicting her from their father's house. She had one week to vacate. And just like that, at the age of eighty-five, she had nowhere to live.

Get Thee to Advisers

If you think you may eventually run out of money; if you are the sole financial provider; if you are a candidate for a chronic illness, including dementia, have debt, have investments, have dependents, are in the middle of a divorce, are a grandparent, are going through a bankruptcy, are a homeowner, are at risk for loss of income, or are close to retirement—time is not on your side. Act now to put your financial affairs in order.

The term *wealth management* is not a reference to the rich and famous—it is a discipline that incorporates legal and financial planning, and the coordination of the following services:

Banking
Estate planning
Durable powers of attorney
Dependent-care planning
Postdeath social media management
Health-care planning
Medicare
Medicaid planning
Social Security
Contingency planning for loss of income
Retirement planning
Long-term care financial planning
Insurance products
Tax credits
Maximizing investments
Liquidating
Claiming benefits
Advance directives for incapacity

Estate planning is an essential component of financial stability. In addition to planning for orderly distribution of assets and paying death-related expenses, a key element of estate planning includes the preservation and distribution of funds *before* death. With the potential to live a long life, investigating strategies now with advisers is a wise move.

Money management and getting legal affairs in order is complicated. At the same time, do-it-yourself downloadable legal forms for documents, such as wills and promissory notes, among others, have become more common. Although these forms are based on the idea that a lawyer is not required, what you are signing off on may not be what you want, and more easily contested. As an alternative, seek professional advice for legal and financial matters. Before hiring advisers, discuss their fees and related costs:

Advisers

Elder law attorney
Real estate broker
Veteran's accredited advisers
Certified public accountant
Certified financial planner
Certified financial adviser
Certified financial gerontologist
Chartered financial consultant
Chartered strategic wealth professionals (Canada)
Chartered financial planners (UK)
Daily money manager

Legal Representation

Elder Law Answers: www.elderlawanswers.com
Justice in Aging: www.justiceinaging.org
LegalShield: www.legalshield.com
National Academy of Elder Law Attorneys: www.naela.org
National LGBT Legal Aid Forum: www.nclrights.org

Financial Organizations

American Association of Daily Money Managers: www.aadmm.com
American Institute of CPAs: www.aicpa.org
American Institute of Financial Gerontology: www.aifg.org
Canadian Securities Institute: www.csi.ca

Financial Industry Regulatory Authority: www.finra.org

Institute of Financial Planning (UK): www.financialplanning.org.uk

National Association of Personal Financial Advisors: www.napfa.org

National Association of Realtors: www.realtor.org

How to Obtain Professional Advice

Your adviser should be someone who is accredited and certified. Be cautious of "free" help and of organizations that you are not familiar with that have official-sounding names. Attorneys can be accredited, as well as people who are not attorneys. They are called accredited agents. Anyone who seeks accreditation must keep his or her training up to date so as to retain the accreditation status.

When considering veteran benefits (especially veteran pensions), you want advice from someone who oversees many such applications. Begin your search by visiting the Department of Veterans Affairs website (www.va.gov) and click the "For Veterans" tab on the home page.

If you cannot afford to hire a professional adviser, rest assured there are numerous ways for you to obtain professional advice without paying a dime for advisory services:

Begin your search for financial advice at your neighborhood bank. Many banking institutions employ financial advisers.

The Certified Financial Planner Board of Standards (www.cfp.net) offers free consultations in various cities. This organization hosts events called "Financial Planning Days." Visit its website to find out if an event is coming to your neck of the woods anytime soon.

Legal and financial advice is readily available on television, YouTube, the Internet, and mainstream newspapers and magazines. There are plenty of "dummies" books and blogs.

If your employer sponsors a retirement plan, contact the human resources department and ask how to obtain advice about a 401(k) and IRA, among other financial products. If you are over the age of fifty, you may be permitted extra contributions into your retirement programs.

Also seek advice on the process of taking penalty-free withdrawals from retirement accounts. There may be taxes due on such withdrawals, unless the account is a Roth IRA. In that case, taxes have already been paid. Be aware of the required minimum distribution (RMD). You must take distributions from your retirement accounts no later than the April 1 of the year after you reach age 70-1/2.

Social Security guidance is critical. You can begin receiving reduced benefits before "retirement age." But is that a wise move? Contact your local Social Security branch and make an appointment with a counselor. There is no charge for this service. Social Security is an important piece of the financial puzzle. Seek professional advice prior to making decisions. You might also want to pick up a copy of *Get What's Yours—Revised and Updated: The Secrets to Maxing Out Your Social Security* (2016) by Laurence J. Kotlikoff, Philip Moeller, and Paul Solman.

If you are a UK citizen, the Money Advice Service provides free and unbiased guidance on all money matters. Visit its website at: www.moneyadviceservice.org.uk.

AARP (American Association of Retired People) offers free legal, tax preparation, and financial advice to members. Check out its website: www.aarp.org/money.

Contact your local Area Agency on Aging to find out about free legal and financial seminars.

Public libraries, community centers, and senior centers often host free lectures.

The Long-Term Care Clearinghouse (www.longtermcare.gov), administered by US Department of Health and Human Services, is a reliable resource on long-term care planning.

Lower your tax bill. The federal government provides free tax advice for people aged sixty and older on a year-round basis. Well-trained volunteers from nonprofit organizations offer services through the federal Tax Counseling for the Elderly Program. The Internal Revenue Service website (www.irs.gov) can lead you to a location near you.

Type "volunteer legal services" into your Internet search engine to locate free legal advice. Many law schools offer free legal assistance to low-income older adults.

The following organizations offer guidance on a variety of financial-related topics:

Medicaid: www.medicaid.gov

Medicare: www.medicare.gov

Social Security: www.socialsecurity.gov

SAGE (Services and Advocacy for Gay, Lesbian, Bisexual, and Transgender Elders): www.sageusa.org

State Health Assistance Insurance Program: www.shiptacenter.org

Enroll in Medicare on Time

Coverage under Medicare begins at age sixty-five; however, your initial window to apply opens three months before the month of your sixty-fifth birthday and ends three months after the month you turn sixty-five. You pay a penalty in the form of an increase in your Medicare Part B premiums if you fail to sign up during your seven-month window. Part B includes doctor visits and diagnostic services. Signing up late for Medicare Part D, which covers prescription drugs, can also cost you. Arrange for Medicare during the appropriate timelines so you don't end up paying more than you need to. If you move out of state, you will be required to update your Medicare supplement and prescription coverage.

Enrolling for Medicare is only part of the equation. Shopping for an appropriate Medicare supplement is critical and it may take a significant amount of time to find one that is appropriate for you. Your health history is the key. Seek purchasing advice by contacting your local Area Agency on Aging or visit the Medicare website (www.medicare.gov).

Living Forever Online

An important consideration of financial and estate planning pertains to your digital footprint. Banking online and automatic bill-paying leave traces. So do social media. You will want to include instructions in your estate plans regarding closing e-mail accounts, bank accounts, investment accounts, personal websites, business websites, social media accounts, and clearing your browser history, among other online activities. After death, management of accounts is handled by the legally designated executor since digital assets fall under the umbrella of your estate.

Why wait? If you want to stay in control of your online activity, you can start shutting down and deleting online accounts far in advance of your death. If you choose to do nothing (not delete accounts or fail to make mention in a will), you are at the mercy of the website's terms of service (which can and will change over time).

Some websites have policies related to death. Others allow accounts to remain dormant until deleted due to inactivity (keep in mind people may keep on posting to your social media pages). Click the menu tab of your various online accounts; then, dictate per their instructions and settings what will happen to your online account after you die.

Do you have accounts on any of these and other popular websites? What is your plan to make them inactive?

AOL
Facebook
Google (Google+, Gmail, Google Apps, YouTube)
Instagram
LinkedIn
Outlook
Twitter

Pinterest
Yahoo!

Deputize Your Decision Makers

There may come a time when you designate another person (called the agent or attorney-in-fact) to make all money-related decisions—in specific financial matters or in all matters. Giving more than two people joint financial powers for the purpose of averting theft is unrealistic—most agents find the process of having to collaborate with other agents burdensome. Be aware that many banking institutions will not accept joint arrangements.

Giving someone durable power of attorney does not mean that you no longer have control over your money. You maintain the right to manage your money and property. However, you are also giving your agent access to your money—so be aware that naming someone your financial agent comes with serious risks.

The designated person must be someone you trust without reservation. He or she should also be one who has demonstrated financial responsibility in his or her own affairs, and who lives fairly close to you. *Giving broad authority to newcomers in your life is not advisable.* This person will have access to your bank accounts, your possessions, your valuables, your house—*everything.* If financial powers are granted within an estate-planning context, this person makes decisions when you are incapable of doing so.

Review your durable power of attorney documents periodically to make sure you remain in agreement with your choices. If your agent becomes incapacitated, untrustworthy, shows evidence of memory loss or dementia, develops a conflict of interest, or dies, choose another person to take his or her place. If you move, differing state laws require you to use the forms that match where you live. Most banks and investment institutions have their own forms to complete.

Financial powers can be canceled or revoked at any time. When you want to effect changes, ask your attorney to destroy the original document and prepare a new one for distribution. Also ask your attorney to inform all concerned that their durable power of attorney for finances is no longer a valid instrument.

If you do not have anyone in your life that you trust to protect your financial interests as durable power of attorney, or a person you ask to represent you refuses to take on the responsibility, you can give your attorney or accountant limited power of attorney for specific authority (e.g., sign a deed of sale for your house) or a much broader range of powers (for example, access your bank accounts). If the attorney accepts the task, expect a fee to be charged. For additional representative resources, type "public guardian" and "professional fiduciary" into your Internet search engine, followed by the name of your city and state.

Avoid Getting Ripped Off

Committed relationships are built on trust. Consequently, financial infidelity between two people goes undetected because, typically, trusting individuals do not look for it.

It is frighteningly easy for an individual to hijack someone else's money or property after having been designated the latter's durable power of attorney for finances. With one click online, the designated attorney can transfer funds into his or her own personal account. Have you established someone you trust as your durable power of attorney for finances? Are you aware of the potential for unintended consequences?

If you have already given another individual the responsibility of managing your money and/or paying your bills, continue to open all of your own mail and oversee your monthly bank and credit card statements for as long as you are able. Keep the communication channels wide open. STAY INVOLVED.

Memory Loss Puts You at Financial Risk

Your ability to think clearly when managing money and legal affairs may be compromised due to failing health. Unintended mismanagement of prescribed medications, alcohol and drug abuse, heavy cigarette smoking, head injuries, stroke, sleep deprivation, severe stress, vitamin deficiency, and illness are examples of conditions that can impair memory.

Watch for warning signs. Does it take more time than usual for you to complete financial tasks? Is sorting out bills and filling out forms confusing? Have you missed payments? Are basic math calculations more laborious? Have others reported errors in your calculations?

Set recurring invoices to come to you automatically online. Similarly, use online banking to pay recurring bills automatically to avoid late fees and overdraft charges.

Create agreements (also known as a letter of diminishing capacity) between you and your financial planner and legal counsel. The agreement states that if there are questions about your cognitive abilities, advisers are granted permission to notify a predesignated representative who is willing to step in and assist.

Arrange in-person meetings with your advisers, especially if you have been diagnosed with a chronic illness. Taking new action relative to existing powers of attorney for finances is driven by the progression of the disease. Meeting face-to-face allows advisers to see for themselves how you are doing—physically and mentally.

The Aftermath of No Paperwork

Not legally designating someone as your durable power of attorney for finances comes with serious consequences. In the event of incapacitation, a court appoints a guardian or conservator to manage your affairs. And just like that, your basic rights are stripped away. You cannot get married or divorced. You cannot vote. The guardian decides how your money is spent, where you will live, and who you are allowed to see, among other decisions.

A recent news article reveals a situation where the guardian, a lawyer appointed by the county, placed a forty-year-old incapacitated woman in a group home for seriously mentally ill adults. The woman was not mentally impaired, and she did what no one expected her to do: she recovered. In the interim, however, the court had granted permission for the guardian to sell the woman's home and its contents to pay outstanding debts. With the help of an advocate, and media attention, the woman fought the guardianship in court and won back her legal rights. She is one of the lucky ones.

It doesn't take much. While the evidence stating that you can't handle your own affairs is supposed to be "clear and convincing," the reality may consist of the judge taking the word of an adult child, other family members, and a doctor's affidavit or report over yours.

Despite a system that is in place to protect you and watch out for your best interests, hundreds of abuses—physical and financial—by guardians are reported every year. Courts, with limited staff and financial resources, are not set up to monitor guardians. Your best bet is to avoid the situation altogether. Get a durable power of attorney and a health-care advance directive. These documents will help keep you out of the courtroom.

If you are a victim of abuse, call your local adult protective services agency; you can find the appropriate contact for your area at the Eldercare Locator (www.eldercare.gov) or call 800-677-1116. Another resource for you to consider is the National Association to Stop Guardian Abuse (http://stopguardianabuse.org).

The Future of Banking Is No Banks

It feels like magic. With a click or a swipe on your computer or mobile device, your entire financial life is laid out before you. Stay current, keep organized, and track every aspect of your finances:

Categorize and track spending.
Create customized budgets.
Set financial goals.

Earn cash or accumulate reward points.

Organize multiple rewards programs.

Transfer funds.

Set up auto-pay systems.

Deposit checks.

Chat on-demand with roboadvisers.

Manage investment portfolios.

Compare prices.

Send instant invoices.

Sign and send financial documents.

Create financial charts and graphs.

Systematize saving.

Track stocks.

Download coupons.

File tax returns.

Obtain credit scores.

Arrange automated alerts.

Set overspending warnings.

Track bills and statements.

Order products for in-store pickup.

But online financial transactions can be a security nightmare. Although storing all of your data "in the cloud" to conducting business with robot investment advisers is certainly convenient, cybersecurity must be included in your financial planning.

Computer crashes, identity theft, cyber scams, forged messages, and computer viruses are not for the faint of heart. Companies continue to invest huge sums of money making sure websites and apps are safe and secure. In the meantime, take every necessary online precaution:

Use not-easily-guessed passwords for all accounts.

Change passwords every few months.

Use different user IDs and passwords for financial accounts.

Do not use your Social Security number as a password.

Ignore e-mails that request account information.

Be mindful of sharing personal information on social media.

Secure your smartphone with a screen lock and fingerprint access.

Keep sensitive information, account numbers, and passwords off your phone.

Continuously update the latest virus protection software.

Monitor all of your accounts regularly.

Make financial transactions from secure locations (never in cafés and airports).

Check web links for encryption: the URL should begin with *https*.

Working for a Living

There are various ways to stay afloat financially—you can work full-time, part-time, or on-demand; you may receive an inheritance or gift; secure a loan; take advantage of discounts and free offerings; sell your belongings and property; and curb your spending.

If staying on the job appeals to you, key drivers of the way people work these days has created three distinct job environments:

Traditional employer-employee relationships: a formal interview process leads to being hired and reporting for work at a specific location.

Peer-to-peer transactions: no experience or formal interviews; people who want goods and services connect with people who provide them for a price.

Crowd sourcing/crowd working: people perform specific tasks and work as part of a team from anywhere in the world, thanks to mobile phones, tablets, and laptops with Internet connectivity.

If the traditional work environment appeals to you, seek jobs in industries where the demand for workers is high and careers are aimed at your demographic. Target job-related websites that are geared for your specific age brackets. For example, type "jobs for people over 50" into your Internet search engine. Social media, such as Facebook and LinkedIn, are especially effective networking and advertising outlets for peer-to-peer opportunities. Update your online profile as needed, and sign up for job alerts.

Show Me the Money

How can you create an income stream? Let me count the many ways. Plus, if the idea appeals to you, working from home has never been easier. To locate specific websites and resources that advertise the job you seek, use the following list as a guide for Internet search engine keywords, followed by the keyword "jobs." Income-generating suggestions include:

Tutor (math, reading, computer, language)

Makeup, wardrobe, and color consultant for mature women

Interpreter/translator

Singing coach

Instrumentalist or singer in a wedding band

Sports coach

Driver/chauffeur

Handyman

Craftsman

Furniture restorer

Mystery shopper

Flight attendant

Travel companion

Care worker

Companion

Pet sitter

Dog walker

Plant sitter

Babysitter

Organizer

Product demonstrator

Customer service representative

Business consultant

Teacher

Tour guide

Crossing guard

Writer/ghost writer

Editor

Speech/comedy writer

Comedian

Model/actor

Mock juror

Keynote speaker

Instructor (musical instrument, card games, dance, cooking, craft)

Caricature artist

Telephone sales

Tailor/seamstress

Valet/housekeeper

Librarian

Virtual assistant

Web designer

PowerPoint designer

Computer programmer

Data specialist

Research assistant

Chore helper

Courier/messenger

Tax-return preparer

Bookkeeper

Receptionist

Clerical worker

Shop greeter

Temp assignments

Focus group participant/facilitator

Photographer

Retail sales

Cashier

Bagger (grocery store)

Home sales (e.g., accessories, clothing, cosmetics)

House sitter

Security guard

Chef/cook for busy families and religious communities

Consider going back to school for a refresher course or getting certified in a new career if you think it will land you a better-paying job. While you are in school, don't forget to make good use of student discounts. Popular certifications for people reentering the workforce include:

Virtual assistant: International Virtual Assistants Association (http://ivaa.org)
Coach: International Coach Federation (http://coachfederation.org)
In-home services: Research certification options at www.care.com
End-of-life doula: International End of Life Doula Association (www.inelda.org)
Celebrant: Celebrant Foundation and Institute (www.celebrantinstitute.org)

The US Department of Education (www.ed.gov) publishes a directory—available in local libraries—of postsecondary schools with occupational programs. Also, type "vocational schools" and "trade schools" into your Internet search engine for local school resources. Federal funds may also be available for continuing education and related services designed primarily for adult women.

AARP (www.aarp.org) is an invaluable resource for work training and job opportunities. Type "worksearch" into the website's search field. You might also consider volunteering your way into a job.

Job training and work opportunities for older adults can be found on these websites:

Senior Service America: www.seniorserviceamerica.org. Includes access to the following employment initiatives: the Senior Community Service Employment Program, the Senior Environmental Employment Program, and the Agriculture Conservation Experienced Services.

Easterseals: www.easterseals.com. Offers a range of training, placement, and job-related services that help people prepare for the workforce including veteran reintegration.

National Able Network: www.nationalable.org. Helps make careers happen. Career coaching, specialized training, and direct connections to the job market are offered. Programs assist jobseekers from all backgrounds, including the unemployed, career changers, veterans, and IT professionals. At this date, services are available to job seekers in Delaware, Illinois, Indiana, Maine, Massachusetts, and New Hampshire.

What Do You Think?

Your opinion matters. Get paid to contribute information about your experience with products and services. Investigate websites that offer this kind of work by using the following list of phrases as keywords to type into your Internet search engine:

Clinical trials

Focus groups
Paid surveys
Test apps and websites
Opinion outposts and polls
Buy and test products
Watch videos and complete offers

Consider Crowdfunding

Such sites as GoFundMe.com, GiveForward.com, and HelpHopeLive.org encourage fundraising for people to hit their financial targets. This approach can be challenging, but if you have an interesting story to tell, people may feel generous and support you.

Sell Stuff

It can take years to get rid of unwanted and unused items. Plus, if ill health sets in, you will regret having to pay someone to haul items away, or worse yet, discard items that could have brought you much-needed cash. Downsize a little bit at a time. If the process gets overwhelming, take a break and start up again in a few weeks. Is there a local church or inner-city school that can use some of your items and furnishings?

Sell your car. If on-demand transportation options are readily available, getting rid of your vehicle could save you thousands of dollars a year. Even if your car is fully paid off, there are expenses such as insurance, parking, repairs, and filling up the tank to deal with.

If you are paying for a storage unit to house unused items, and hurting financially, you are throwing money out the window. Review the items that are being stored, then decide to toss, give away, sell, or donate. If you can afford to do so, get valuables appraised. Donations can give you almost as much in tax deduction as a yard sale reaps in cash.

Here's a sad story as it relates to selling valuables. A close friend decided to auction an original painting given to him by a rich uncle. His cousins (the uncle's children) halted the auction by claiming that he had stolen the painting. Things got ugly and the family is torn apart.

Here are a few lessons to keep in mind as you go through your belongings:

Situation: You find yourself on the receiving end of potentially valuable artifacts.
Solution: Rule of thumb: leave tracks—if you don't, there is a strong possibility that feuds (including litigation) may ensue among the greedy or disgruntled. If you have been gifted a treasured heirloom, or even something of seemingly insignificant (at the time) economic

value, make sure you acknowledge receipt of the item with some form of written (or otherwise preserved) communication. To be on the safe side, ask the person who gives you the gift to put his or her intentions in writing.

Situation: You are on the giving side of a transaction. Your intention is to let someone have a particular item to enjoy during their lifetime—-but you want/expect to get it back. For example, you may lend your car to your granddaughter while she attends college.
Solution: The same rule as above applies. Put your intentions in writing.

When it comes time to selling items, consider the following sales outlets:

Online sales and auction outlets
Bulletin boards
Auctions houses
Garage sales
Consignment shops
Secondhand furniture outlets
Antique malls
Church bulletin notices
Pawnshops
Classified ads
Flea markets

Rent Desirables

Renting your belongings and property is a great way to bring in extra income. Post notices around town and online. Have a lawyer draw up a legal agreement between you and the renter. To find rental outlets online, type "rent my stuff websites" into your Internet search engine. Rentables include:

Power tools and yard equipment
Designer purses
Furs and diamonds
Costume jewelry
Vintage clothing and costumes
Vehicles, boats, and trailers

Medical equipment—wheelchairs, shower benches, etc.

Musical instruments

Home furnishings

Camping equipment

Sports equipment

Garage, shed, or storage area

Party ware—tablecloths, silver, stemware, punch bowls, coffee urns

Your house—for weddings, special events, and movie locations

Parking and garage space

A room in your house

Turning your house into a vacation rental

Renting your land

Put Your Money Where the House Is

Mortgages, property taxes, utilities, insurance, and home maintenance and repairs cost big money. If your home is your castle, make it work for you. Action plans include:

Sell the house for a profit.

Downsize to a smaller house or apartment.

Investigate reverse mortgage.

Cash in on an insurance policy.

Explore a home-equity loan.

Challenge property tax assessments.

Open up a bed-and-breakfast (if zoning laws permit).

Refinance to a lower interest rate.

Retire abroad to a place where the cost of living is substantially less.

Dig for Discounts

If you must spend money, why not get the best prices possible? Create keyword searches using the following words; then, type them into in your Internet search engine to locate specific websites, apps, and resources:

Rebates

E-bates

Coupons
Discounts
Cash back
Frugal living
Price compare
Group rate
Shopping days

Local churches, synagogues, and charities may be able to provide financial assistance. Trade schools are excellent sources of discounted services. For example, a barber college may offer free haircuts. A local dental college may also be a source for reduced-cost dental treatments and second opinions. The following resources offer additional guidance on discounted dental services: Tooth Wisdom (www.toothwisdom.org), Dental Lifeline Network (https://dentallifeline.org), and Free Medical Camps (www.freemedicalcamps.com).

Type "peer-to-peer companies" into your Internet search engine. These companies bring people and/or businesses together online and deal directly with each other—eliminating the expensive middle man. Here's an example: For a flat fee, Lemonade (www.lemonade.com) offers an insurance experience that is fast, affordable, and hassle free. Traditional insurance companies make money by keeping the money they don't pay out in claims. Lemonade handles and pays most claims instantly.

Pay less for health care, medical equipment, fitness programs, prescription drugs, food, home repair, utilities, and more. Type "Medicare discounts" into your Internet search engine. Also check the following resources for discounts:

Age UK: www.ageuk.org.uk
Benefits Checkup: www.benefits.gov
Christmas in April: www.christmasinapril.org
Eldercare Locator: www.eldercare.gov
Everything Zoomer: www.everythingzoomer.com
Medical Tourism Association: www.medicaltourismassociation.com
National Council on Aging: www.ncoa.org
Persons with Disabilities: www.disability.gov
Pharmaceutical Assistance Programs: www.medicare.gov/
    pharmaceutical-assistance-program
Programs4People: www.invisibledisabilities.org
Veterans Benefits Administration: www.benefits.va.gov

Help for Aging Veterans: www.helpforagingveterans.com

Aid and Attendance Veteran Pension: www.VeteranAid.org

PACE

If you are fifty-five or older, and live within the service area of a PACE organization, and you meet specific income and asset qualifications, I have good news for you. PACE (Program of All-inclusive Care for the Elderly) is a Medicare and Medicaid program that may keep you from going to a nursing home or other care facility.

A team of health-care professionals work with you to ensure that you get the coordinated care you need. If you qualify for PACE, you are provided the care and services covered by Medicare and Medicaid, including adult day services, dentistry, emergency services, home care, meals, and more. Best yet, with this arrangement you get to sleep in your own bed at night, with assistance nearby in case of emergency.

Some people who qualify say no to PACE because they may have to switch their physicians to those within the PACE network. Think twice about rejecting what PACE has to offer: if your doctor is offered a multimillion-dollar contract to run a high-tech medical business, do you think he or she will stick around for you? By the way, you can always leave the program and go back to your doctor of choice if you so desire.

Just say yes to PACE. Visit the Medicare website (www.medicare.gov) and type "PACE" into the website's search field, or call 800-633-4227.

Follow the Free

Do you recall the story at the beginning of this section about my church-lady friends who are living the good life on an extremely limited budget? They succeed for two reasons: (1) They have done their homework and know where to get products and services for free, and (2) they are never shy about asking for handouts or discounts. That's just who they are.

Like my elder lady friends, let the word *free* rule your world. Look for local free opportunities. Also check out swap opportunities. The Internet is a nearly limitless source for free everything. A keyword search in your Internet browser, using the following words (or words of your choosing) will lead you to a variety of resources:

Free medications

Free legal assistance

Free rides and reduced fares

Free clothes

Free books

Free classes

Free memberships

Free merchandise

Free samples

Free haircuts

Free food

Free dental work

Free eye exam

Free medical clinic

Free medical equipment

Free pet clinic

Free pet supplies

Free things to do in [name the city]

Free magazines

Free games

Free counseling

Free tax preparation

One of my all-time favorite websites for affordable and free resources is *Stuff Seniors Need* (http://stuffseniorsneed.com). Free cell phones, free financial assistance, free medic alert systems, free pull-ups—the list goes on and on. Check it out.

When you find what you are looking for, read the "fine print" on every agreement and on every website. Make sure that you are not signing up for something you will have to pay for once you accept the free item or service.

Lower Grocery Bills

Food budgets can easily get out of hand. Follow these tips and check out the resources that may keep spending to a minimum:

Eat at home.

Purchase generic brands.

Shop sales at different grocery stores.

Check the marked-down section for perishables.

Use coupons.

Grow your own vegetables and herbs.

Type "restaurant leftover food" into your Internet search engine.

Type "food bank," followed by your city and state, into your Internet search engine.

Take advantage of senior discount days or cards offered by local stores.

10,000 Steps

It is possible that averaging ten thousand steps per day can earn you discounts on health and life insurance premiums, and reward you with points, gift cards, and other prizes. Measured steps are also being monitored by some employers to encourage employees to stay fit. Everyone benefits when people get healthier—just by walking.

Find out whether wearing a fitness wristband can save you money: ask insurers and employers whether they are or intend to sponsor a step program.

Lessen Death-Related Expenses

Expenses incurred related to one's death run the gamut. Burial or cremation? Funeral or memorial service? Musicians, obituaries, printed materials, celebrant fees, death certificates—every little detail adds up.

Per the Federal Trade Commission, a casket often is the single most expensive item to purchase if you plan a "traditional" full-service funeral. Caskets vary widely in style and price, and are sold primarily for their visual appeal. Although an average casket costs slightly more than $2,000, some mahogany, bronze, or copper caskets sell for as much as $10,000.[2] For a basic cremation, which includes transportation of the body to the crematory, cremation procedure, and placement of the ashes (cremains) into a simple container for pickup, begin your calculations at around $700. Prices for identical products and services vary tremendously depending on who is selling the product and geographic location.

Type "cheap caskets" into your Internet search engine.

Buy trip insurance to cover the cost of transporting your body back home.

For guidance on lowering funeral and death-related expenses, check out these resources:

Funeral Consumer Alliance: www.funerals.org

The Funeral Site: www.thefuneralsite.com
I'm Sorry To Hear: www.imsorrytohear.com
Parting: www.parting.com
US Funerals Online: www.us-funerals.com

Parent: Once Again for the Last Time

What comes to mind when you think of the word *grandparent*? Probably not someone who is buying cribs and baby supplies, researching elementary schools, interviewing pediatricians, attending grade-school soccer games, hosting children's birthday parties, shelling out money for relief babysitters and daycare, and tucking emotionally distraught children into bed, night after night, trying to convince them that they are safe and loved.

If you are a grandparent and not currently raising school-age grandchildren who have been physically removed from their parents, you may be facing this common family crisis at some point later on. The number of children living in a grandparent's home has increased significantly over the past decade, according to data from the US Census Bureau.[3] What's behind all this? Any number of reasons including death of a parent, drug and alcohol addictions, mental illness, incarceration, divorce, overseas work assignments, military service, and poverty.

Raising a grandchild is challenging—emotionally, physically, and financially. There is, however, a silver lining. In the process of giving grandchildren a safe, stable, and nurturing home environment at this critical time in their life, you may also be carving a path for them to take care of *you* in old age.

Financing this unexpected family arrangement causes grandparents to worry about money, especially as the grandchild gets older and daily expenses escalate. Here are some suggestions on staying afloat financially:

Ask one or both parents to contribute financially if they can do so. Even if you have legal custody or guardianship, parents can be asked to pay a specific child support amount.

Offer to watch someone else's child in return for them watching yours. Meet other parents who are members of your church or synagogue. Playgrounds and the local public library storytime hours will also connect you to parents. You might also be able to locate "grandparent only" playgroups. Type "playgroup" into your Internet search engine.

Speak to the person in charge of special programming at your church or synagogue. If a holiday "family adoption" program is offered, ask to have your name added to the list.

Temporary Assistance for Needy Families (TANF) (www.benefits.gov) offers cash assistance for low-income families. Eligibility is determined by residency, income, and assets. Type "TANF" into the website's search field.

You may be eligible for utility-bill assistance, paying for prescription drugs, food stamps, and more. Visits the Benefits Checkup website (www.benefitscheckup.org).

Find out which local charitable organizations offer scholarships, programs, and financial aid; these may include Lions (www.lionsclubs.org), Rotary (www.rotary.org), and Kiwanis (www.kiwanis.org). Type "freemasonry" into your Internet search engine to locate the local Mason organization.

Contact the local Social Services Office and ask about any free or low-cost programs, including daycare.

Check with your specific health-care plan about health insurance for your grandchild. In many states, you must be the child's legal custodian or guardian to add them to your plan. If you are currently receiving Medicare, your options are limited.

Visit the Social Security (www.ssa.gov) website, and click on the "Benefits" tab. You can apply for benefits by calling the national toll-free service at 800-772-1213 (TTY 800-325-0778) or by visiting your local Social Security office.

The Supplemental Security Income (SSI) (www.ssa.gov) program pays monthly cash benefits to families with mentally or physically disabled children. To qualify, families need to have a limited income. Type "SSI" into the website's search field for more information.

Look into Medicaid (www.medicaid.gov). Even if your income is above limits, you may be able to enroll just your grandchild. Medicaid covers medical, dental, and mental health services. If grandchildren qualify for SSI, they automatically qualify for Medicaid, but you will still need to file an application for Medicaid coverage separately.

Contact Children's Health Insurance Program (CHIP) (www.healthcare.gov). If you earn too much to qualify for Medicaid, yet are having trouble affording private health insurance for your grandchildren, you may qualify for CHIP. The requirements and level of assistance varies from state to state, but in most cases CHIP covers checkups, vaccinations, prescriptions, and hospital visits. Type "CHIP" into the website's search field.

Feeding America (www.feedingamerica.org) offers access to nutritious food to feed yourself or your family. Local food banks and food assistance programs can provide free groceries for low-income families, emergency food assistance for at-risk populations, summer meals for children, and more.

Why Hunger (www.whyhunger.org) refers people across the United States to food pantries, soup kitchens, summer meals sites, government nutrition programs, and grassroots organizations. Call 1(800) 5-HUNGRY or use the form provided on the website to locate local food providers.

Your local Area Agency on Aging offers a wealth of information about local Grandparents Raising Grandchildren programs and financial assistance.

The local Health Department offers children immunizations, health care, and more. Ask about its WIC (Women, Infants, and Children) program.

Pediatricians are knowledgeable about affordable community resources that are available in your area.

Check to see whether your local youth community center and senior center offer free programs for grandparents raising grandchildren.

Visit the following websites for a wealth of information and support for grandparents raising grandchildren:

Michigan State University School of Social Work Kinship Care Resource Center: www .kinship.msu.edu

University of Florida Extension: http://edis.ifas.ufl.edu

University of Georgia Cooperative Extension Family and Consumer Sciences: www.fcs .uga.edu

University of Wisconsin–Extension Family Living Programs: http://fyi.uwex.edu

Western Michigan University: https://wmich.edu

Also check out the following grandparent-as-parent websites:

American Grandparents Association: https://aga.grandparents.com

Generations United: www.gu.org

Grandfamilies: www.grandfamilies.org

Grand Magazine: www.grandmagazine.com

The Grandparent Effect: www.grandparenteffect.com

The Grandparents Association: www.grandparents-association.org.uk

The Grandparents Rights Organization: www.grandparentsrights.org

Raising Your Grandchildren: www.raisingyourgrandchildren.com

Grandparents often say that their job as grandparents is exhausting at times, yet if all grandparents walked away from the scene, there would likely be no "home" at all for these children. While grandparents typically say that they neither wanted nor expected to become primary caregivers for their grandchildren, they often describe the relationship as one of the most rewarding experiences of their life.

Insights and Inspiration

Recommended Reading: *Affluence Intelligence: Earn More, Worry Less, and Live a Happy and Balanced Life* (2011) by Stephen Goldbart and Joan Indursky DiFuria

Recommended YouTube: Pink Floyd, *Money* (Official Music Video), published June 25, 2014

Recommended Movie: *The Pursuit of Happyness* (2006)

Recommended Song: "Spinning Wheel" by Blood, Sweat, and Tears

Recommended TED Talk: "How a Penny Made Me Feel like a Millionaire," presented by Tania Luna, surprisologist, filmed July 2012

Part Two

Where You Live Matters

Aging in Place Alone— What You Need to Know

Averting the risks of aging home alone

6

So, you want to remain in your own home, among your familiar surroundings, daily routines, and in the same neighborhood, up and until the moment you take your last breath—*did I get that right?* This idea of yours has a name—"aging in place." Bringing products and services into the home is the cornerstone of how it works.

Need a hand with grocery shopping and cooking? Is bathing or getting dressed in the morning becoming more difficult? Would you like someone to help manage your medications? These are not dire scenarios if people you trust volunteer or are paid to be of assistance to you, and their services are readily available. Plus, now that you can get anything you desire delivered to your home via drone, taxi, and courier, or you can print the item yourself on a 3-D printer—*why bother to move?*

As the previous chapters have shown, though, you need to be prepared for any number of changes in your later years. Simply put, aging in place may not be a safe or desirable option for you. Unexpected life events (the aftereffects of a fall, the diagnosis of a chronic condition, financial loss, and home disrepair, among others) are what may necessitate reevaluating your realistic ability to age at home. That said, aging in place alone need not scare you—as long as you plan ahead.

Objectives

After completing the chapter "Aging In Place Alone—What You Need to Know," you will be able to:

- Learn the value of asking for outside help
- Connect with certified aging-in-place professionals
- Gain knowledge of community-friendly concepts
- Size up and manage personal obstacles to aging in place alone

Age Alone with Others in Mind

People who choose to age in place alone may be unsuccessful, not because the goal is unachievable, but rather *something* gets in the way of asking and accepting help when assistance is needed. You may have heard about someone you know, or someone in your community, in these and similar situations:

> Calling the 911 emergency hotline to ask that someone buy and deliver groceries to his or her home
>
> Driving an automobile long past when it is safe to do so because there are no alternative ways to get around town
>
> Forgetting to turn off a burner on the stove, which results in a house fire
>
> Hoarding, and becoming a recluse to the extent that the police must break into the house, finding it uninhabitable with the homeowner curled up in bed in his or her own filth

You will most likely define your own terms for aging in place, including the right to choose to withdraw from social activities and face-to-face human interactions. Unfortunately, you may make choices that result in putting yourself, and others, in jeopardy. If you ever find yourself saying that you don't need or want help from anybody, and that you have everything under control, *that* mind-set alone is the beginning of your demise.

Consider This

In 1995, my hometown of Chicago experienced a social nightmare. On July 13, the heat index peaked at 119°F—a record high for the city—causing 465 people to lose their life due to the heat. Of the decedents for whom age could be determined, 51 percent were seventy-five years of age or older.[1]

It was devastating to watch the entire scenario unravel. Socially isolated older adults (many of them near poverty) remained terrified behind closed and locked doors and windows, their air conditioners off due to rising utility bills. Their fear of being robbed and of other criminal activity kept them from responding to "strangers" who continuously warned them of imminent danger. Refusing to leave their homes for city cooling centers cost the lives of hundreds of elders who, instead, died a slow and horrifying death.

I continue to feel deeply sad and angry when I think about what happened that summer. How is it that so many people were profoundly affected by something we would appear to have a handle on? How pervasive is social isolation? How might this trend of living alone end up ultimately costing anyone their life?

In another incident, the lonely death of George Bell[2] tells the story of a man who died days before his decomposed body was found in the living room, crumpled up on the mottled carpet. "He had lain there for a while, nothing to announce his departure to the world, while the hyperkinetic city around him hurried on with its business." No one collected his body. No one mourned the conclusion of his life. In the year 2014, George Bell, age seventy-two, was added to New York City's death table.

In 2007, forty-four-year-old Sandra Drummond left few possessions when she died. Police found a jar of Vaseline, a hot water bottle, a stuffed koala bear, a roll of cellophane tape, and a child's snow globe. Her body had lain undiscovered for almost twelve months. No living relatives could be traced. No mourners attended her funeral.[3]

Today, people continue to be at risk of being "left behind." People who have other choices.

Seek Advisers

You may be choosing to age where your roots are currently planted not only because it strikes an intensely personal preference, but because you think you have no other options. Before you settle in for good, seek the advice of the following professionals:

Aging Life Care Professionals (www.aginglifecare.org), formerly known as Geriatric Case Manager, offer insights on remaining in your home. They are also knowledgeable about alternative housing options if staying put does not work out.

Certified Senior Housing Professionals (www.seniorsrealestateinstitute.com) are instrumental in selling your house and transitioning you to a different location.

The National Aging in Place Council (www.naipc.org) is an alliance of in-home aging services providers, from builders, lenders, and businesses to aging-related organizations and government agencies. All members of local chapters are vetted and screened. They also agree to background checks and sign a Code of Conduct.

Talk to the staff at your local Life Plan Community (www.lifeplancommunity.org) and continuing care retirement community. Ask whether they offer home- and community-based services.

Focus your attention on advisers who have obtained Certified Senior Advisor (CSA) status through the Society of Certified Senior Advisors (SCSA) (www.csa.us). Certified professionals are trained to demonstrate their competence and knowledge of working with older adults.

Seek advisers who have completed training for Certified Aging in Place Specialist. Type "aging-in-place remodeling" and "certified aging-in-place specialist" into the National Association of Home Builders website's search field (www.nahb.org).

If you plan to hire in-home care professionals, ask workers whether they have obtained Certified Eden at Home Associate Training (www.edenalt.org). Eden at Home promotes a culture of meaningful care.

Size Up Your Obstacles

When you exercise your right to remain in your own home, you will "move" in other ways as old age and chronic medical conditions make its unique physical, emotional, and financial demands on you. Even if you reside in the same house, on the same street, in the same neighborhood, most of your life, you will *not* live as you did in the past.

While *aging in place* is the popular long-term care buzzword, it is not meant to be taken literally—the concept casts a net much wider than taking extra precautions for home safety and bringing in care services from the outside. There is no actual "place" to age; your aging process happens wherever you may be in the moment, including the attitude about aging that you carry with you always.

Feeling healthy and mentally alert is a good thing, but is it enough? In an age-friendly environment, you are given ample opportunities to deepen how you experience everyday life. Resources are plentiful and accessible, inclusivity and mobility are a given, you are recognized as a valuable member of the community by residents, work opportunities are abundant, growing and learning new things is a never-ending process, and the community affirms your efforts to live life on your terms without you ever having to move out of your home—unless you want to.

Ours is far from a perfect world. The reality is that numerous visible and invisible landmines stand between you and your desire to age in place. Limited eyesight and hearing, arthritis, memory problems, and side effects from medications, among other shortcomings, carry with them potentially dangerous consequences of your living home alone. To lessen the possibility of a visit to the emergency room, check out the Age-Friendly Home Checklist on page 89.

If you are currently experiencing a medical condition, ask the doctor how your illness will progress and consequently affect your long-term housing.

Consider the Big Picture

Planning for obstacles and challenges along the way is a must if your goal is to remain in your own home. Physical decline, for example, makes the dynamic interaction of your home

AGE-FRIENDLY HOME CHECKLIST

This checklist is available to download and customize at www.elderindustry.com.

With a strong desire to age in your current home, you may be tempted to review the following list under the illusion of wishful thinking. If that's the case, you are shooting yourself in the foot, not to mention risking living in a potentially hazardous home environment. Be truthful; then, decide to fix what needs adjusting. If you really want to age in place, the following information dictates what is necessary to make that happen.

SAFETY
Smoke and carbon monoxide detectors are installed and working properly.
Handrails and balance bars are installed in bathroom and both sides of long hallways.
Heat and air-conditioning systems are in working order and easy to operate.
Protective coverings from the sun are installed in outdoor seating areas.
A trusted neighbor has the keys to your home in the event of an emergency.

FLOORING
Area rugs and runners throughout the house are removed.
Low-pile carpeting (or no carpeting) averts falls.
Floor surfaces and stairways are slip-resistant.
Floors, hallways, and stairwells are clear of clutter.

LIGHTING
Bright, functional lighting is installed throughout the house and all entrances.
Nightlights are installed in hallways, bedrooms, bathrooms, and the kitchen.
Light switches (preferably flat-panel) are available at all room entrances.

FUNCTION
Lever handles replace knobs on doors and faucets.
Appliances and work-surface heights are adjusted for easy use.
Bathroom sink vanities and mirrors are easily accessible.
Walk-in shower and shower seating is installed.
Elevated toilet seat is installed.
Walk-in closet with clothes racks at reachable heights is available.
Remote-control window blinds and curtains installed.

COMMUNICATIONS
Telephone access is available throughout the house.
Wi-Fi access throughout the house.
Emergency medical alert system in place.

Interactive testing and medical diagnostic devices in use.
Telephone and online access to community support and social activities.

ACCESSIBILITY
Ample electric outlets and light switches are within easy reach.
No-step entry and thresholds installed at house entrances and interior doorways.
Steps to bedrooms, kitchen, bathrooms, laundry room, and living room are eliminated.
Wide corridors and doorways accommodate wheelchairs and motorized scooters.
Wheelchair-accessible rooms, especially bathrooms, are available.

environment—-cooking, cleaning, laundry, bathing, dressing, and negotiating stairs—much more difficult.

Your aging-in-place plan should also include giving thought to accommodating the special needs of visitors. For example, if you live in a third-floor walk-up apartment building, will friends continue to visit if they eventually find stair-climbing to be physically impossible? Bringing care into your home means that a revolving door of strangers (caregivers) will physically enter your home, leaving you vulnerable to all kinds of abuses—physical, emotional, and financial. Add dementia to the mix, and an extra layer of "scam security" is needed. You may also be challenged in other ways.

Financial Challenges

Who pays for in-home services? *You do.* When it comes to aging in place, the financial realities are as follows:

Read carefully. If you are hoping that Medicare (www.medicare.gov), the federally funded health insurance for Americans aged sixty-five years and over, will finance your personal care needs (bathing, dressing, continence care, medication management, etc.) and any tasks considered "custodial" in nature, unfortunately it will not. Under specific circumstances, Medicare *may* cover short-term skilled nursing, rehabilitation, and end-of-life care.

Be aware. Hospitals may classify people as "for observation" instead of "inpatient" as a means of excluding Medicare reimbursement for the skilled care that might follow.

Be even more aware. Medicaid (www.medicaid.gov), the federally funded health insurance for low-income people, covers long-term care for individuals who qualify as "medically needy"—a category under which some, but far from all, people fall. Those who qualify for Medicaid have limited care options. Not all states, for example, allow Medicaid to pay for assisted living. To determine one's Medicaid eligibility or to find a Medicaid adviser, use the free services provided by the American Council on Aging (www.medicaidplanningassistance .org/find-a-medicaid-planner).

If you can afford to do so, you may be inclined to integrate technology into your living space to enhance your safety—for example, webcams and wearables to alert others in case you fall or never get out of bed. Additional safety measures include the installation of ramps and bathroom/hallway balance bars. In the meantime, the cost of hearing aids, incontinence products, eyeglasses, motorized scooters, and other independent-living products continue to increase.

No matter where you reside, aging comes with a hefty price tag. To gain strategies about financing a longer life, read the chapter of this book titled "The Fierce Urgency of Money," starting on page 57.

Social Challenges

When it comes to aging in place, you may be challenged socially in the following ways:

Isolation, loneliness, and depression

Being "invisible" (people you encounter have no desire to acknowledge your presence)

Dealing with stigmas (dementia, chronic medical conditions, age, childlessness, and living alone)

Difficulty accepting and asking for help (leaning toward a self-sabotaging mind-set of independence rather than interdependence)

Intolerance (an "us" versus "them" mentality, such as young vs. old, straight vs. gay, well vs. sick, wealthy vs. middle class vs. poor, and old vs. old)

For additional insights, review the chapter of this book titled "You Are Tougher Than You Look," which begins on page 45. Also read the "Good-bye Change, Hello Transition," chapter beginning on page 13. Stay in the game as best you can.

Service Challenges

When it comes to aging in place, you may experience service challenges, including:

Dwindling pool of professional and/or qualified caregivers

Lack of geriatric-specialized medical workers

Finding a doctor who will take on new Medicare patients

Friends and/or family are not willing or unable to step in and help

Specialized medical care is unavailable in your area

Managing the hiring/firing process of in-home care workers

Long wait lists for preferred services, including assisted living and skilled nursing care

Bringing aging parents and other dependents into your home

Location Challenges

When it comes to aging in place, circumstances that you have very little control over may present all sorts of roadblocks, including:

Limited transportation

Few employment opportunities

Risky home environment

Unsafe neighborhood

Lack of affordable housing

Prohibitive zoning laws

Elephants in the Room

We knew years ago that a boom in the aging population was on the horizon, yet there is little social structure in place to advocate for adult solo dwellers. Collections of individuals who tend to keep to themselves, don't ask questions, or don't volunteer to come forward have displaced neighborhood sensibilities from a time when people used to make themselves available to others in need. Few Americans today say they know their neighbors' names, and far fewer report interacting with them on a daily basis. Pulling data from the General Social Survey, economist Joe Cortright wrote, "Only about 20 percent of Americans spent time regularly with the people living next to them. A third said they've never interacted with their neighbors. That's a significant decline from four decades ago, when a third of Americans hung out with their neighbors at least twice a week, and only a quarter reported no interaction at all."[4]

We could blame this phenomenon on cars, television, air-conditioning, technology, fenced-in yards, and even the government. It may be some or all of these, *but does it really matter how things got this way?*

Overall progress to foster aging-in-place practices in US cities is slow for many reasons—an abundance of red tape, outdated zoning laws, and a lack of direct involvement on the part of leadership, among other challenges, have been cited across the board. Consequently, entire neighborhoods have no choice but to pitch in to care for their residents, especially the ever-growing population of older adults—*but how?*

The World Health Organization (www.who.int) identifies eight domains of city life that might influence the health and quality of life of older people: (1) outdoor spaces and buildings, (2) transportation, (3) housing, (4) social participation, (5) respect and social inclusion, (6) civic participation and employment, (7) communication and information, and (8) community support and health services.[5]

Consequently, some cities and towns have big plans to improve the quality of life for its aging residents. *Is yours one of them?* The WHO Global Network for Age-Friendly Cities and Communities currently includes 314 cities and communities in 35 countries, covering over 124 million people worldwide. Alexandria, Minnesota; Chicago, Illinois; Portland, Oregon; New York City, New York; Barcelona, Spain; Belfast, United Kingdom; Berkeley, California; Bethel, Maine; Geneva, Switzerland; Calgary, Canada; Carlsbad, New Mexico; City of Suwon, Korea; Uppsala, Sweden; Columbus, Ohio; Clarence, Australia; Denver, Colorado; Dallas, Texas; Des Moines, Iowa; Dijon, France; and Guadalajara, Mexico, join a growing number of cities and communities worldwide that are striving to better meet the needs of residents of all ages. Cities who join the network commit to a five-year cycle of planning, implementation, and evaluation.

Find out about your community's plans for becoming age-friendly by visiting your city/town and local government websites. You may be pleasantly surprised to learn that aging-in-place initiatives are already in progress. If you discover that your community is doing nothing to further the cause to age in place, take action—one small step, such as exchanging emergency contact information with your neighbor, may one day save your life.

Not Just About Old People

Aging in place within your community is only problematic if that is how you view it. Whether the need is meeting the demands of the large numbers of solo residents or meeting the demands of the large number of cars on the highway, the goal now is for *all* generations of people to create solutions together.

The same work that is put into making cities business-friendly and culturally vibrant to attract younger professionals and new families can be applied to ensure that everyone, at every age, and every economic status, has an equal opportunity to age in place. The first step in achieving this goal is making it clear that aging is place is not only about old people. Most of the things that old people need and want are good for the rest of the community, too.

Misunderstandings and generalizations about people who are different from each other cloud visions of what is possible. To sustain a thriving age-in-place community requires adjusting attitudes and remaining open-minded—you never know who will come to your rescue when the tables are turned and *you* are the one who needs help.

With many people aging at home alone, we simply cannot afford to alienate one another. With this in mind, three specific community goals must be addressed: The age-friendly community, the dementia-friendly community, and the LGBTQ-friendly community.

The Age-Friendly Community

In the Western culture, few people understand the central purposes of old age. The consequence is a culture in crisis—ageism, elder abuse, antiaging campaigns, disability stigmas, and an increasing separation between the young and the old. *Who does these sorts of things?* We all do—professionals, family, marketing experts, and the old people themselves.

Blaming others for not respecting old people, for whatever reason, is part of the same attitude that keeps people oppressing other groups as well—women, toddlers, teenagers, poor and working class, people of color, people with disabilities, and homosexuals, among others.

Ageism is multifaceted and manifests itself in multiple ways, including cutting work lives short. *This Chair Rocks: A Manifesto Against Ageism*, by Ashton Applewhite, is an invaluable resource that guides readers through the landmines of ageism. In the book she writes, "Like racism and sexism, ageism serves a social and economic purpose: to legitimize and sustain inequalities between groups. It's not about how we look. It's about how people in power assign meaning to how we look."[6]

I welcome the day when old people are treated with respect and dignity; but until then, what is needed is an updated public conversation about people respecting people, period. Respect is *earned*, and not simply a by-product of an age number. There is no truth to the presumption that with age comes wisdom. This false belief leads many adults to disregard the perspective of the young, which in turn continues to divide the generations.

So often, old people complain of feeling "invisible." Trust me. If you attempted to walk out of a department store with a sweater under your arm without paying for it, you would be seen. No one is invisible. To receive positive attention from others, you must *give* it. To be relevant means sharing what you know and being genuinely concerned for the well-being of others.

In the meantime, the language of ageism is complex. People are often unaware that they are engaging in an ageist form of communication. As well, the person on the receiving end may also be unaware of the bias being communicated. Take a moment to reflect on how you might be talking and thinking about old age:

Addressing a mature woman as "young lady." This assumes that the recipient would rather be someone else, preferably someone younger.

Declaring, "I'm not going to live with a bunch of old fogeys." Intolerance among old people teaches society that rejection of the old is acceptable behavior.

Responding to a person who has revealed her age with, "Wow, you look great for your age." The underlying message is, "You don't just look great."

Refusing to use a walker or a hearing device when evidence shows that one is clearly needed relays messages of shame and self-loathing.

Indicating that you are "still" working or "still" playing tennis. The word *still* implies that old people are not expected to be doing well later in life and are in a continuous state of decline.

Zeroing in on an adult as "cute," "adorable," or "precious." Words typically used to describe babies, kittens, and puppies are diminutive and demeaning, relaying an expectation that old people have little to offer the world.

Purchasing products and services labeled as "antiaging." While the term in and of itself is politically correct, the message conveyed is old people are an embarrassment to the world.

Using a tone of voice normally applied to children. Speech patterns associated with being patronizing presume old people are not fully competent.

Stating that a "senior moment" is the cause of forgetfulness. People of every age suffer brain injury, disease, and other limitations on cognitive ability.

Labeling old women as "feisty" and "spunky." Inappropriately identifies women who do not behave as others expect them to behave in later years.

Age-Friendly Community Resources

There may be community initiatives happening in your town that are already operating in full force. To find them, the following keyword searches can help:

Age-friendly
Age-friendly workplace
Intergenerational programs
Life plan community

In addition, visit these websites:

Responding to Ageism

It is clear we need to speak up. The Old Women's Project (www.oldwomensproject.org) offers many examples of what to say when you are on the receiving end of ageist remarks. Here are a few tips to consider:

When people interject age into a conversation ("Well, at your age . . . "), you might say, "My age has no bearing on this particular conversation or situation. Please leave it out of the discussion."

"Compliments" about how young you look could be met with, "No. This *is* what fifty/sixty/seventy/eighty/ninety looks like."

Instead of publicly cringing at the mention of how long you have known someone, acknowledge the rich history that exists between the two of you.

Put the word *old* back in your vocabulary. Even though at first it may sound weird, and perhaps rude, say it anyway; for example, say outright, "I am eighty years old"—not coyly "eighty years young." Claim *old* as a statement of fact and pride, not shame or humiliation. Believe in age, not as a number, but as a positive energy that stands on its own.

"What do you mean?" is one of the most effective responses when someone speaks inappropriately. Said preferably with a tone of genuine puzzlement rather than hostility or sarcasm, this question places the burden squarely on the speaker to contemplate what was said and why it was said in the first place.

Strangers who call you "honey," "dear," or "sweetie" can be asked, "Oh, have we met before? Only people I know well use such endearing terms. My name is Ms. Jones. You may call me that."

AARP: www.aarp.org. Type "livable" and "age-friendly" into the website's search field.

The Age of No Retirement: www.ageofnoretirement.org. An organization whose goal is to create a world where our age does not define us, shattering age-related barriers and ageist stereotypes, and creating an age-inclusive future.

American Planning Association: www.planning.org. Type "age-friendly community" into the website's search field.

CityLab: www.citylab.com. Through original reporting, analysis, and visual storytelling, this organization informs and inspires people who are creating the cities of the future—and those who want to live there.

World Health Organization: www.who.int. Type "age-friendliness" into the website's search field.

The Dementia-Friendly Community

My experience has been that the general public has limited understanding of dementia. I say this because I have personally witnessed what happens when people publicly reveal that they have been diagnosed with early-onset Alzheimer's—they are likely to be treated differently from that moment on.

It is not uncommon for people who are living with the symptoms of dementia to be stigmatized and marginalized. At home, in public, and in the workplace, they are often on the receiving end of such statements as the following:

"I can no longer trust you."
"I've lost confidence in you."
"I'm sorry. I wish you hadn't told me. Now I have to fire you."
"Doesn't everybody lose their memory when they are old?"

Alzheimer's is a chronic disease, just like diabetes, Parkinson's, and cancer. Revised models of dementia care are emerging around the globe; slowly but surely, stereotypes and attitudes associated with dementia are shifting for the better. Let these paradigms be the goal moving forward:

A person first—who happens to live with a disability
A condition that is not the fault of the individual or caregiver
A focus on abilities, continued growth, and learning
Independence through enabling environments
Attention to each person's unique needs
Honoring the value of all communications and connection

The constellation of experiences called dementia affects *everyone* in a community on some level. Because of dementia's prevalence and effect on the world—at home, in your city, where you work, in the marketplace, and in health-care settings—you are wise to give this disease your immediate attention.

Dementia is an "invisible" disease. It's relatively easy to meet a person who has early-stage dementia and not realize the daily struggle he or she faces. On the outside everything may seem okay; but make no mistake, that is *not* the case. Here are some true stories to ponder:

A woman becomes frantic when she forgets how to get out of her locked car and well-intentioned bystanders yelling instructions is making her increasingly confused and scared.

Without knowing the patient is living with Alzheimer's, the surgical nurse enters incorrect information about allergies and medications into the pre-op chart.

A man is arrested because he forgot to pay his bill and left the restaurant.

We are all in this together. For further insights, review the "Early-Onset Alzheimer's: The Value of Knowing," chapter of this book, starting on page 211. If you are a candidate for dementia, there are advantages of getting tested early on.

Dementia: The Intentional Community

Imagine neighborhoods where police officers, sales clerks, bus drivers, crossing guards, bank tellers, clergy, employers, shop owners, and students are trained to recognize, interact, and assist people who are living with the symptoms of dementia. Now, compare the outcomes and costs of establishing a dementia-friendly community versus one that ignores the obvious presence of dementia among its citizens.

The forward-thinking community vision is that people living with dementia are "out of the closet" and *everyone* is actively engaged in solving the dementia-related needs of the community. This is not a pipe dream. Dementia-friendly cities already exist. To date, many have joined the Dementia Friendly America (www.dfamerica.org) network, including: Tempe, Arizona; Riverside, California; Denver, Colorado; Tallahassee, Florida; and Grand Rapids, Michigan.

Statewide dementia-friendly initiatives include the following:

Alabama	Maine	Ohio
Arizona	Maryland	Oklahoma
Arkansas	Massachusetts	Pennsylvania
California	Michigan	Texas
Colorado	Minnesota	Utah
Connecticut	Montana	Washington
Florida	Nebraska	West Virginia
Hawaii	Nevada	Wisconsin
Indiana	New York	Wyoming
Illinois	North Carolina	

Education: Training programs enhance community cultures that result in supporting people who are living with the symptoms of dementia, those who accompany them on their journey, and those who fear being afflicted with the disease.

Inclusive mind-set: Enlightened residents believe that the *person* comes before the illness. Stigmatized language is regarded as unacceptable.

Public acceptance: Residents, business owners, and workers who interact with the general public are trained to notice, understand, and assist people who are living with dementia and their caregivers.

Interdependence: The community culture values and respects people who live with dementia. In turn, all residents engage in everyday activities and are assisted by others who are trained to step in when everyday tasks become more difficult.

Dementia-friendly physical environments: The community offers a framework for the design of homes, workplaces, shops, public spaces, medical settings, and transportation systems that are user-friendly for people who are living with dementia and their caregivers.

Dementia-Friendly Community Resources

There may be initiatives that are already operating in full force in your community. The following keyword searches could help you locate them online:

> Alzheimer's-friendly business
> Dementia-friendly
> Dementia-friendly workplace

In addition, visit the following websites:

ACT on Alzheimer's: www.actonalz.org
Alzheimer's Association: www.alz.org
Alzheimer's Disease International: www.alz.co.uk
Alzheimer's Reading Room: www.alzheimersreadingroom.com
Alzheimer's Society: www.alzheimers.org.uk
Dementia Action Alliance: http://daanow.org
Dementia Friends USA: www.dementiafriendsusa.org

The LGBTQ-Friendly Community

In many respects, people who are lesbian, gay, bisexual, transgender, or questioning (LGBTQ) face the same dilemmas as everyone else—they are aging alone and they may be childless. Additional complications that put this population at risk include estrangement from family and friends, homophobia, and rejection in the form of harassment, discrimination, and abuse.

There is a vast difference in walking down a street that is gay-friendly and one that is not. Some communities are more progressive than others, scoring high for nondiscrimination: an abundance of LGBTQ social services, respectful medical practices, supportive workplace policies, and overall nonjudgmental relationships within the community. Forward-thinking communities are not *trying* to understand, but *do* understand.

Millions of LGBTQ older adults face profound housing challenges. In response, National LGBT Elder Housing (http://sageusa.org/lgbthousing) offers a five-key initiative: Building model housing and sharing SAGE's expertise from projects, training existing facilities to provide housing in a welcoming, non-discriminatory manner, changing public policies for additional housing and bar discrimination against LGBT older people, educating LGBT older people in how to find LGBT-friendly housing and how to exercise their rights, and expanding LGBT-friendly services in housing sites across the country.

LGBTQ–Friendly Community Resources

LGBTQ-friendly initiatives already may be operating in full force in your area. To find them online, type in the following keyword searches, plus the name of your city or town:

LGBTQ community center	LGBTQ financial planning
LGBTQ family	LGBTQ legal
LGBTQ-friendly	Transgender

For additional resources, type "LGBTQ" into the search engine of the following websites:

Alzheimer's Association: www.alz.org

Alzheimer's Australia National: www.fightdementia.org.au

American Seniors Housing Association: www.seniorshousing.org

Alzheimer's Society: www.alzheimers.org.uk

American Society on Aging: www.asaaging.org

Human Rights Campaign: www.hrc.org

LeadingAge: www.leadingage.org

National Center on Elder Abuse: www.ncea.aoa.gov

NextAvenue: www.nextavenue.org

Opening Doors London: http://openingdoorslondon.org.uk

Additional LGBTQ Resources

CenterLink: www.lgbtcenters.org

Gay and Lesbian Medical Association: www.glma.org

LGBT National Help Center: www.glbthotline.org

LGBTQ Aging Pinterest: www.pinterest.com/joyloverde

National Center for Lesbian Rights: www.nclrights.org

National Gay and Lesbian Chamber of Commerce: www.nglcc.org

National Resource Center on LGBT Aging: www.lgbtagingcenter.org

PrideNet: www.pridenet.com

SAGE: www.sageusa.org

Beat the Odds

Aging in place alone is doable, but not easy. You will be pushed outside your comfort zone especially when you have little to no control over outside influences. Use the Beat the Odds to Age in Place Checklist on page 102 to create a customized action plan. The idea is to stay *ahead* of the challenges that may get in the way of your goal to remain in your own home for the long haul.

Insights and Inspiration

Recommended Reading: *Going Solo: The Extraordinary Rise and Surprising Appeal of Living Alone* (2013) by Eric Klinenberg

Recommended YouTube: *How I Love My House* (from *The Wubbulous World of Dr. Seuss*)

Recommended Movie: *Wings of Desire* (1998)

Recommended Song: "What a Wonderful World," performed by Louis Armstrong, written by George David Weiss and Robert Thiele

Recommended TED Talk: "The Power of Introverts," presented by Susan Cain, filmed February 2012

BEAT THE ODDS TO AGE IN PLACE CHECKLIST

This checklist is available to download and customize at www.elderindustry.com.

List the following:

Financial challenges of aging in place:

_____

Social challenges of aging in place:

_____

Service challenges of aging in place:

_____

Location challenges of aging in place:

_____

Check off the following tasks upon completion:

_____ I have explored resources to manage the financial challenges.

_____ I have explored resources to manage the social challenges.

_____ I have explored resources to manage the service challenges.

_____ I have explored resources to manage the location challenges.

_____ Financial challenges are resolved.

_____ Social challenges are resolved.

_____ Services challenges are resolved.

_____ Location challenges are resolved.

_____ I have determined that I can age in place and have reviewed the chapter in this book called "Bring Livability Home," which begins on page 103.

_____ I understand that my current housing will not serve me in the long run, and have reviewed the chapter in this book titled "Moving On," which begins on page 119.

Bring Livability Home

Establishing equity, health, and safety for all

Objectives

After completing the chapter "Bring Livability Home," you will be able to:

- Explore livable city options
- Access home repair and remodel programs
- Implement home-safety precautions
- Expand your circle of support
- Obtain resources to access volunteers
- Consider alternative transportation options
- Upgrade to smart-home technologies

"I love my house," said a friend recently. "But my house doesn't love me back." Anna told me that she had gotten to the point where she could no longer take showers. Once she got into the bathtub, she couldn't get out. Anna prefers to live alone but her house is making it impossible for her to age alone.

That's only half the story. While the interior design of Anna's house made aging alone difficult, her car-dependent neighborhood makes it next to impossible to remain mobile—with her failing eyesight, it is simply a matter of time before she has to give up the car keys. After that, she has no idea how she will get around.

An age-friendly home environment and a pedestrian-first community are important goals of a livable community. When both mileposts are achieved, there are tangible benefits: residents feel safe and secure, have a sense of belonging, have access to fresh food and clean air and water, can bike and/or walk just about anywhere, are offered affordable housing options, enjoy quality education and health care, have employment opportunities, can liberally use accessible public transportation, and have ample access to affordable child care and eldercare services.

Do these neighborhoods really exist? The answer is yes. Livable ratings are based on thirty factors across five areas: stability, infrastructure, education, health care, and environment.[1] In 2016, Melbourne, Australia, ranked number one, followed by Vienna, Austria. Vancouver, Canada, came in third.

Conduct an Internet search on "livable cities" and you will be bombarded with lists that judge the best places to live, work, raise a family, and age.

To further explore your city's livability score, visit Area Vibes (www.areavibes.com) and Livability (www.livability.com). To read up on the community programs that put cities on the "Best Place to Live" list, visit the Milken Institute (http://aging.milkeninstitute.org).

Lucky are those who are either born into a livable city or who have the resources to pack up and move to greener pastures. In the meantime, threats to the quality of everyday living elsewhere remain; we have no choice but to fend for ourselves.

Don't Move. Improve.

The story about my friend Anna who could not take showers because of the bathtub barrier has a happy ending. I suggested that she contact the local Area Agency on Aging for guidance on obtaining affordable remodeling resources. Within two months, her bathroom was completely gutted—the bathtub was removed and an accessible no-threshold shower was installed.

Under certain financial circumstances, free and affordable home-modification assistance is available. The US Department of Housing and Urban Development (HUD), the US Department of Veterans Affairs, the US Department of Health and Human Services, and other federal agencies provide resources and expertise for home improvements. Find out if you qualify. Begin your search by visiting the Eldercare Locator website (www.eldercare.gov). Also visit the Benefits Checkup website (www.benefitscheckup.org).

Remodeling and retrofitting rooms and passageways to age in place can be expensive. The process may include hiring professionals to assess the home environment and make recommendations for installing stair lifts, ramps, and balance bars; building roll-in showers; widening doorways; lowering countertops; modifying room configurations for first-floor bathrooms, laundry room, and bedrooms; improving lighting; emergency response systems; adding nonslip strips to floors and smooth surfaces; upgrading climate-control systems; and improving wiring systems, among other modifications.

The ability of citizens to remain in their own home requires deliberate action by local governments, planners, and developers. At this writing, there is evidence that municipalities are starting to investigate how they can relieve some of the financial burden of home repair and remodeling either through tax credits, grants, or affordable loans. Rezoning and land-use discussions are also under way.

In the meantime, if you can afford to pay out of pocket to renovate your home, obtain additional home-design information by typing the following keywords into your Internet search engine: "universal design," "living in place professional," and "certified aging-in-place special-ist." You will find additional insights by visiting Aging in Place (http://aginginplace.com).

If your financial resources are limited, making small and more affordable upgrades will make a big difference. Download AARP's HomeFit Guide by visiting the AARP website (www.aarp.org); then, type "homefit" into the website's search field.

The good news is that home modifications that improve a homeowner's safety as well as some medical equipment may be covered by Medicare (www.medicare.gov). Find out if this is the case for you. Type "durable medical equipment" into the Medicare search engine.

Home Safety Is No Accident

There are books and blogs galore on the topic of home safety. To save you time, I have high-lighted some of my favorite tips:

Prevent falls: Falls are the leading cause of injury-related deaths in adults. Most falls occur in the home setting. Remove throw rugs, do not store items on stairways, know where small pets are at all times, do not wear floor-length skirts or robes, shorten hems on pajama bottoms, and use canes and walkers indoors and outdoors. The Falls Free Initiative is a national effort led by the National Council on Aging. Learn more by visiting www.ncoa.org.

Here's a quick story about falling: One morning, my mom took a tumble when she got out of bed and tripped over the bedding. Due to her tossing and turning in the night, the top sheet and blanket had separated from the bed and were lying on the floor next to the bed. The solution was to buy a wooden bed frame where the box spring and the mattress fit snugly inside the frame. Sheets and covers stay tucked in all night long. Problem solved.

Get steady: How do you get out of a chair? Do you grab on to the nearest table and hoist yourself up? Imagine what would happen if that table were to collapse. Is your furniture strong enough to hold you? Is there a better way to get up off a chair? Have you considered strengthening your leg muscles with a daily exercise routine?

Avoid slipping: Rubber bath mats in the tub and/or shower are helpful. Antislip footwear and socks are a must.

Turn on the lights: Make sure interiors and exteriors are well lit. Add nightlights through-out the house. Install light switches at the top and bottom of stairs, and room entrances.

Motion-sensor lighting systems might be useful. Never enter a dark room or hallway. Keep flashlights handy at several locations throughout your home.

Relocate the microwave: Is it getting more difficult for you to retrieve food from the microwave because of your reach limitations. Relocate the microwave to the kitchen counter or kitchen table.

For an extensive list on making your home a safer place to live, review the Age-Friendly Home Checklist on page 89.

Do It Yourself

If you are of the age to remember the Anacin commercial (circa 1960s), you'll recall how the nation latched on to the punchline: "Mother, please! I'd rather do it myself." If you're like me, that attitude holds true today. And why shouldn't it? My philosophy is to do it yourself as long as you are able and safety is not compromised.

Most people are used to getting themselves dressed, but what happens when physical ailments make that daily chore a major challenge? Impairments caused by arthritis, Parkinson's, Alzheimer's, diabetes, swollen feet, leg stiffness, and other conditions can be minimized by wearing adaptive clothing and footwear. Adaptive clothing is designed to make dressing easier and less painful, and works especially well if you are wheelchair bound. Visit Silvert's Adaptive Clothing and Footwear (www.silverts.com) for an extensive line of fashionable high-quality apparel.

Without a doubt, the use of independent-living products makes life at home safer. For example, using long-handled grippers to access lightweight items on a high shelf or washing hair with dry shampoo when instructed not to take a shower after a medical procedure. Visit The Wright Stuff (www.thewright-stuff.com) for everything you could possibly want when it comes to products that make it easier for you to complete certain tasks yourself.

It is also worth noting that the presence of stairs in a multistory residence is *not* a deal breaker for every homeowner. There are plenty of people who depend on daily stair-climbing to keep themselves in shape, strengthen leg muscles, and improve their balance—myself included. Many of my old friends tell me that stair climbing is every bit the "sport" that walking is. They "take the stairs" every chance they get. Having said this, living in a dwelling with stairs depends upon one's health, weight, the wear and tear of cartilage in hips and knees, and the onset of arthritis.

Neighbors Need Neighbors

Before technology was a household word, people got through life by talking with one an-other face-to-face. If there is one thing I have learned in the past sixty-plus years about old people who live alone, it is that they know the art of being neighborly—creating connections was simply a matter of knocking on someone's front door and introducing themselves.

Nobody I know, including me, would even think about doing something like that today. If someone knocked unexpectedly at my house, I would tip-toe to the front door and look through the peephole. If I did not know that person, I would stand quietly until he or she went away. But the fact remains, I need to connect with kind and trusting neighbors. After all, who will come to my rescue when I am home alone and need immediate assistance?

I am well aware that if *I* do not make the effort to introduce myself to people who live nearby, relationships will not cultivate themselves. There are only a handful of people I know personally who, like me, are willing to stick their neck out to meet their neighbors. It is un-comfortable at best, but I do it anyway.

To make connections, here's what you can do. Focus on the people in your immediate surroundings. Greet people you recognize as neighbors with a smile, a wave, or brief hello when you see them walking down the street, waiting for the elevator, or mowing their lawn. In no time, you will also become a familiar face to them. As you become more comfortable in their presence, initiate "small talk" conversations: "I love your boots." "Isn't this a beautiful time of year?" "What breed is your dog?" "How about those Cubbies!"

When you continuously run into the same people who seem friendly and willing to en-gage with you, make the effort to keep conversations alive and upbeat. If you like, you can step it up a notch by inviting them to have coffee with you at a local establishment. Or sug-gest that you meet for a power walk in the park. Give it time for the relationship to take its course.

The goal is to develop trust and dependability:

Phone numbers and e-mail addresses are exchanged.
Small acts of genuine kindness become routine. "I'm going to the grocery store. Need anything?"
You get together socially. "I'm having spaghetti and meatballs for dinner. Care to join me?"
Informal agreements are verbalized. "You can count on me. Can I count on you?"
Elevated levels of trust result in an exchange of house keys.
You are simultaneously on the watch for tell-tale signs that something is wrong next door.

You carry in your wallet an emergency-contact list that includes the name and phone number of your neighbor.

You can breathe a little easier for now knowing that at this time in your life you are not alone in this world.

Blueprint for Villages

The neighborly concept is expandable into the greater community. Imagine small groups of unrelated people meeting and discussing ways to think differently about being there for one another. The inclusive approach becomes the mind-set of every resident—young and old. Reciprocity pays big dividends. Groups can agree to create systems that result in people assisting each other with simple tasks.

What are the possibilities of you getting together with a few other people and forming a pact to help one another with the following tasks?

Housekeeping
Laundry
Pet sitting
Dog walking
Plant care
Grocery shopping
Cooking
Home repairs
Transportation
Fitness partners
Health-care advocacy
Yard work
Snow removal
Checking in

The Naturally Occurring Retirement Community (www.norc.org) and Village to Village Network (www.vtvnetwork.org) offer a template to start your own community-support program. You can volunteer to perform the tasks yourselves or hire service providers (at a discount).

You might also look to local organizations and businesses to provide grants for your efforts. Grantmakers in Aging (www.giaging.org) is an invaluable resource. The idea is to form strategic partnerships.

Here are a few examples of what happens when residents of a community contribute to the livability:

Several companies agree to sponsor the cost of adding a bike path on the main street.

A land-rich business owner makes several acres available for the city to build a playground for adults. To see what others have created, type "playgrounds for adults" into your Internet search engine. Also visit Never Leave the Playground (www.NeverLeavethePlayground.com).

Several apartment buildings hire a "lifestyle ambassador" who not only acts as a concierge but also as a liaison between residents and neighborhood businesses—for example, the ambassador connects residents to doctors who make house calls, arranges transportation to the airport, secures discounts at local restaurants, and steers residents in the direction of volunteer opportunities.

Local fitness centers, church groups, and businesses join forces and invite employees, members, residents, and neighbors to join them in recreational, or even competitive physical activities like walkathons.

Possibilities for collaborations and partnerships are endless. Find out whether your city planners, policy makers, and public managers are open to meeting and discussing livability initiatives.

You may also find the following resources extremely helpful in the process of making your community more livable:

Good Life Project: www.goodlifeproject.com. A global community of people from all walks of life who are on a quest to help each other live more meaningful, connected, and vital lives. This organization is about living in the real world, pursuing good lives in a way that is powerful and inspired, yet also sustainable and practical.

Life Planning Network: www.lifeplanningnetwork.org. A global community of professionals from diverse disciplines supporting other professionals. This organization offers national and international programs, conferences, collaborative projects, referrals, resources, purposeful planning, and access to best practices from leading thinkers and practitioners.

Pass It On Network: http://passitonnetwork.org. A place where innovative minds from around the world meet to explore, document, and spread creative insights and resources that are shaping a new way of talking and being as we adapt to a longer life span. How can we be useful to ourselves, to each other, and to our communities? How can we remain independent and self-sufficient? How can we keep on learning?

The Prevention Institute: www.preventioninstitute.org. Brings research, practice, and analysis to today's pressing health and safety concerns. Determined to achieve equity, health, and safety for all, to improve community environments equitably, and to serve as a focal point for primary prevention practice, Prevention Institute asks what can be done in the first place, before people get sick or injured.

Redstring: www.myredstring.com. A community-building technology and consulting company for retirement-housing communities, corporations, retail shops, hospitals, associations, municipalities, and service providers. One-click tools help web users of all ages explore, educate, plan, connect, organize, do business, help others, get results, and have fun.

Smart Growth Network: http://smartgrowth.org. Supports the development of vibrant, healthy communities. National programs, conferences, projects, communications, trends, events, funding, awards, and resources are included as the Network encourages community development that boosts the economy, enhances community vitality, and protects the environment.

No Neighbors to Count On? Not to Worry.

You live alone. You choose to keep to yourself. You are far too uncomfortable to initiate conversations with strangers. There is no possibility of asking or receiving help from neighbors. You are not interested in expanding your social circle. I understand; yet you need to be prepared in the event of an emergency. Here are a few suggestions for you to consider:

Be prepared for strangers to enter your home in the event of an emergency. Use the exterior of your refrigerator as the main message board. Post emergency contact information; doctors' information; allergies; and a list of current medications. If you have documentation for do not resuscitate (DNR), do not intubate (DNI), and do not hospitalize (DNH), post copies of the documents. The refrigerator is where first responders typically look for information about the dweller.

Your neighborhood letter carrier can be a lifeline. Delivering mail to the same residences day after day, letter carriers become familiar with a customer's habits and often notice changes in routine that signal something may be wrong. To find out whether there is a

Carrier Alert program operating in your neighborhood, contact your local post office or the local National Association of Letter Carriers (www.nalc.org).

Arrange daily contact. Volunteers for telephone reassurance programs call you each weekday to check on your well-being. Early intervention strategies like this can delay or sometimes even prevent nursing home placement, which is a far more cost-effective way to go. Here's how it works. Failure to answer the call brings a second call within minutes; no answer to the second call results in a visit from a designated person who physically goes to the home. Other programs may require you to phone in at a specified time of day. This service may also be offered through your local Area Agency on Aging. Type "telephone reassurance program" into your Internet search engine to access resources that provide this service.

TeleConnect Senior Services (www.teleconnect4seniors.com) is a US based call center that assists people with medication and appointment reminders, technical support, call reminders, and is there if you just feel like talking with someone. Services are 24/7/365 on a month-to-month subscription basis.

For people living in the United Kingdom, The Silver Line (www.thesilverline.org.uk) is a confidential, free helpline for isolated elders available every day and night of the year. The specially trained staff offers information, friendship, and advice.

If your plan is to receive Meals on Wheels America (www.mowaa.org), your delivery person will be an important point of contact. Be sure to let him or her know if you are experiencing any difficulties. For more information, call your local Area Agency on Aging. Be aware there may be a waiting list for meal delivery. Also, services may not be available in your area.

Contact your local retirement community, life plan community, as well as local assisted living communities. Ask how you might participate in social activities. Some communities allow nonresidents to engage in their programs and outings. Also inquire about their home and community-based services program for in-home care and medical support services. If you need a ride to and from the hospital, services may also be provided for a fee.

Your local senior center will offer a wealth of knowledge and resources for people who are aging home alone.

Explore health-care resources. Medicaid in-home programs serve a variety of targeted population groups, such as people living with mental illnesses, intellectual or developmental disabilities, and/or physical disabilities. Visit Medicaid (www.medicaid.gov), and type "home and community-based services" into the website's search field.

If you are in the market to hire professional caregivers, visit Home Healthcare Agencies (www.homehealthcareagencies.com) and Lifecare Innovations (www.lcius.com). These care agencies offer a wealth of information on their websites, including blogs and articles.

Doctors who make house calls are every bit as much a part of today's modern world as they were in the past. Do your homework about the availability of this service *before* you need it. Locate a provider when you visit the American Academy of Home Care Medicine website (www.aahcm.org).

Type "medical alert" into your Internet search engine to research costs and options for emergency response systems that keep you connected to first responders and health-care professionals.

Access Local Volunteers

Volunteers are available to assist when you need it. You just have to know where and how to look for them. Here are a few suggestions:

Visit your neighborhood or city website and type "volunteers" into the website's search field.

Masonic Orders, Rotary Clubs, Lions Clubs, Odd Fellows Lodges, Eagle's Clubs, veterans' organizations, unions, business clubs, and teachers' associations may provide special services and volunteers to members and nonmembers alike. Type the names of or descriptive terms for these organizations as keywords, followed by the name of your city, into your Internet search engine.

If you are a member of a religious congregation, ask how you might go about accessing volunteers to assist you.

Find out whether local high school students are looking for volunteer opportunities to enhance their community-service resumes.

Local community centers and senior centers often provide a multitude of volunteer services, ranging from transportation services to social functions and group-meal outings.

Find out whether your local university, college, or nursing school is looking for volunteers for geriatric-related school assignments. A friend of mine volunteered to be a tester for a technology project developed at a major university. The students installed a monitoring system that detected falls. Another friend was the subject of a nursing school study that measured the results of occupational therapy, nursing, and handyman visits.

Youth groups, Boy Scouts, and Girl Scouts may be seeking opportunities to volunteer to earn rewards and badges.

Reinvent the Wheel

On-demand, driverless electric cars and shuttle buses can't get here soon enough. (By the time you are reading this, they may already be operating on the streets where you live.) We will work in them, text in them, talk on the phone in them, relax in them, ride-share them, and best of all, we never have to park them. Soon enough, having a car or driver's license won't be a concern. You will summon a vehicle from your smartphone, and get in and say, "Take me to the grocery store."

As the need to personally own and operate an automobile goes by the wayside, it remains to be seen how benches and tables, street vendors, pop-up cafés, and kiosks replace curbside parking spaces. Increasing the possibility of people interaction will organically result in connection and community. Free outdoor curbside charging stations and Wi-Fi might not be far behind.

Your local Area Agency on Aging can provide information on community volunteer programs.

Contact the Corporation for National and Community Service (www.nationalservice.gov) and Volunteers of America (www.voa.org) and ask how you can qualify to receive their volunteer services.

Visit the Senior Care website (www.seniorcare.com/featured/volunteer-to-help-the-elderly). Volunteer opportunities are listed by state. Make contact with each of the organizations to find out how your name can be added to the list of individuals who are on the receiving end of care.

Be Realistic About Driving

Few people make plans to retire from driving. Trouble is brewing: driving too slowly, running red lights and stopping for green lights, forgetting how to get to familiar places or getting lost, experiencing near misses, hitting curbs, sideswiping other cars. In the meantime, the existing transportation network in most towns is not keeping up with the demands of our mobile aging population. Also, there are no national standards or systems to identify drivers who have physical and/or mental impairments.

Ideally, people voluntarily choose to hand over the car keys when driving skills become compromised. But many don't. In the meantime, here are some suggestions on what to do about driving and staying mobile:

Stay in Shape

Make an appointment for a physical exam, including a vision and hearing checkup.

Review medications with your doctor or pharmacist and discuss possible side effects.

Eat right, exercise, and stay fit.

Think Ahead

Plan trip routes ahead of time.

Get a smartphone with GPS.

Avoid left turns and parallel parking if they prove too difficult for you.

Avoid driving at night or in hazardous weather conditions.

Make the Car Safer

Purchase a wide rearview mirror.

Add a seat cushion if you need to gain height to see better when driving.

Keep a cell-phone charger in the car at all times.

Make sure the car is in excellent working condition.

Learn to Become a Passenger

Use on-demand ride-hailing services.

Get used to asking others for a lift.

Connect with a teenager who loves to drive. You pay for gas.

Ask the doctor whether transportation is available to medical appointments.

Explore public or other transit services.

Explore More Options

The Alzheimer's Association (www.alz.org) offers information about early-onset Alzheimer's and operating a vehicle.

Take a driver safety course. Type "roadwise" into the AAA (www.aaa.com) website's search field. Check out the AARP Driver Safety Program (www.aarpdriversafety.org).

Type the name of your city, followed by "transportation," "para-transit," "dial-a-ride," or "volunteer drivers," into your Internet search engine.

Contact your local Area Agency on Aging and ask about neighborhood transportation services, voucher programs, and door-though-door services. Also contact the Eldercare Locator (www.eldercare.gov).

Check out the Shared-Use Mobility Center (http://sharedusemobilitycenter.org), a public-interest organization working to foster collaboration in shared mobility (including bike sharing, car sharing, ride sharing, and more. The goal is to help connect the industry with transit agencies, cities, and communities across the nation.

Religious groups and other service-minded organizations may have volunteers who provide transportation.

Move out of a car-dependent neighborhood and into a housing setting where transportation is provided or easily accessed.

Transportation resources include:

American Public Transportation Association: www.apta.com

Canadian Automobile Association: www.caa.ca

Community Transportation Association of America: www.ctaa.org

GoGo Grandparent: https://gogograndparent.com

Independent Transportation Network of America: www.itnamerica.org

Keeping Us Safe: www.keepingussafe.org

National Aging and Disability Transportation Center: www.nadtc.org

Project Action: www.projectaction.com

Transportation for America: www.t4america.org

Age in Place with Smarter Technology

For starters, if you don't already have one, upgrade your phone to a smartphone model. I say this because besides the ability to talk with another human being in an emergency (including the use of face-to-face interaction applications), this phone model is a lifeline to the following critical tasks:

Accessing e-mail and text messages

Retrieving important and legal documents

Shopping for products and services

Touch screen 911 emergency access

Finding your way via GPS and public-transportation systems

Conducting banking transactions

Tracking the whereabouts of friends and family

Social-networking applications

Hailing on-demand drivers

Taking and exchanging photos and videos

Voice-controlled assistants

Step and calorie counters
Booking flights and appointments
Staying current with newsworthy events
Monitoring fitness and heart rates
Relaying real-time data to a medical team

If you would like to buy a smartphone, and money is tight, perhaps someone you know well will give you a phone that is no longer used or will lend you one. You can also save money on phone-related expenses by asking a friend to add you to his or her monthly plan. Type "buy a cheap smartphone" and "free smartphone" into your Internet search engine or visit your local phone service provider. But don't forget that besides the cost of the phone, there are monthly charges and yearly contracts to consider.

The price of smartphones keeps coming down. Buy last year's model and you are sure to get a better deal.

Another option is to purchase a smartphone that has no monthly charges. You buy the phone, then pay service fees and air time as needed. Check out the different models and programs at your local drug store and discount outlets. Also research GreatCall (www.greatcall .com) as a smartphone option.

If you are not willing to buy a smartphone, at least buy a cordless model for home use. They typically come in packages of two. While you roam about from room to room, keep one of the phones with you always. In an emergency, you have access to help immediately.

How Artificial Intelligence Can Work for You

Having no one to rely on when help is needed is a thing of the past. Relationship technology has advanced to a point where robot personal assistants can keep you company and provide any number of services, such as lifting you out of bed, helping you stand up, or relocating you to a wheelchair. Robots will even follow you around and chat with you.

Artificial intelligence, and voice and facial recognition, among other technologies, anticipate and evaluate your needs as well as your physical and mental status. "Facial recognition algorithms, for example, could detect the first signs of sadness or depression, which are major health concerns for people who live alone."[2] Recognizing faces also offers security advantages. When you have new people in your home, artificial intelligence software classifies visitors as friends, family, nurses, or helpers. People who are not known to you raise a red flag.

Type "robot personal assistant" and "intuition robotics" into your Internet search engine. Innovative robotic products are surfacing every day. To date, robots are extremely expensive. Inevitably, prices will become more realistic over time.

Stay Up to Date

Technology is advancing quickly, and electronic devices or their software may need periodic upgrades to stay fully functional. To learn more about what is in store for aging technology consumers, visit Age in Place Tech (www.ageinplacetech.com), Center for Research and Education on Aging and Technology Enhancement (www.create-center.org), and the Leading Age Center for Aging Services Technologies (www.leadingage.org/cast).

Of course, technology is not the answer to all of our connection and livability problems. Devices will never replace the need for human touch and companionship.

Insights and Inspiration

Recommended Reading: *The Berenstain Bears Lend a Helping Hand* (1998) by Stan and Jan Berenstain

Recommended YouTube: Gil Penalosa, *Mobility as a Force for Health, Wealth, and Happiness*, published December 12, 2014

Recommended Television: *Seinfeld* reruns

Recommended Movie: *St. Vincent* (2014)

Recommended Song: "Lean on Me" by Bill Withers

Recommended TED Talk: "The World's Largest Family Reunion. We're All Invited!" presented by AJ Jacobs, author, filmed June 9, 2011

Moving On

Determining optimal housing options

8

Objectives

After completing the chapter "Moving On," you will be able to:

- Think strategically about relocating or staying put
- Plan ahead to access affordable housing
- Review a variety of housing options
- Evaluate rural living options
- Begin the downsizing process

"I am not moving out of my house. You'll have to carry me out of here feet first!"

And that is exactly what happened when a beloved neighbor threw caution to the wind, and ignored pleas from friends to move out of her four-bedroom, multi-level house. (She had a housekeeper, but of course, nobody can clean a house like *she* can.) She was standing on a stool cleaning a light fixture and started to feel dizzy. She fell and broke a few bones, and landed in the hospital, then rehab, then assisted living—never to see the inside of her home again.

Do you love your house enough to put yourself at serious risk? Where you live now may not be the most desirable living arrangement and environment for growing old: but with adequate planning, you can control your housing destiny and prevent last-minute, regrettable decisions.

Where You Live Matters

Housing decisions take into account many factors—finances, personal preferences, social network, and proximity to quality health care, among others. As you journey toward old age, the "ideal" place to live changes over time, and sometimes overnight. Refusing to make an adjustment when real-life circumstances dictate otherwise will put you in an extremely vulnerable situation.

Your ongoing challenge is to stay real, or risk losing control of managing your own affairs—housing and otherwise. With a growing aging population coming to terms with housing needs simultaneously, long wait lists for the most desirable places are the norm. When you procrastinate regarding this critical life task, you lose out on getting what you want. Worse yet, doing nothing almost always guarantees that eventually you will be at the mercy of other people making decisions in your behalf—and that is the last thing you want to have happen.

Planning ahead is especially important when it comes to affordable housing. Finding a vacancy takes time and effort because there is an extremely limited supply of buildings. Signing up on several wait lists at the same time is a smart strategy. Contact your local Area Agency on Aging to obtain the most current list and information on how to qualify. Also visit Programs for Elderly (www.programsforelderly.com), an incredibly comprehensive website that is sure to steer you in the right direction no matter where you live.

Should you move or stay put? You are as capable as you will ever be to choose one path or another. Review the following list. If you check off any one of the boxes, it's time to take action—either decide to make minor or major adjustments related to where you live now, or you can start packing:

_____ I am struggling financially.

_____ I live in a house that needs repairs and maintenance.

_____ I live far from friends and family.

_____ I do not have a network of support.

_____ I am not in good physical health.

_____ I am experiencing memory loss.

_____ I am incontinent.

_____ I am unable to manage my medications.

_____ I am isolated and alone.

_____ I do not eat nutritious meals.

_____ I am in constant fear of falling.

_____ I do not have access to transportation.

If your desire is to remain in your current house for the rest of your life, read the chapter of this book titled "Aging in Place Alone—What You Need to Know," starting on page 85, to learn what the full spectrum of your decision realistically entails.

Investigate the housing page on the USA.gov website (www.usa.gov/housing). Type "housing" into the search engine of the Canada Seniors website (www.seniors.gc.ca). These comprehensive websites offer services with finding and keeping a home. Information includes affordable housing, foreclosure, housing scams, keeping your home safe, mortgages, and more.

If you are contemplating a move to a more supportive health-care environment (such as an assisted living community), gain additional insights by reading the chapter of this book titled, "Chronic Illness: The Game Changer," beginning on page 197.

Sometimes, not knowing *where* you want to move may stop you from making a housing decision. If this is the case for you right now, rent an executive, furnished apartment for a month in the area you are contemplating. This will give you a "feel" for what daily life would be like if you relocated there permanently.

If lack of money is the reason why you are staying put, read the chapter of this book titled "The Fierce Urgency of Money," starting on page 57, to begin the process of getting back on your feet financially. If lack of money is the reason you are considering living elsewhere, check out The Earth Awaits (www.theearthawaits.com), a website that allows you to learn, explore, and discover affordable places to live.

Homeward Bound

Housing options of today are a far cry from cookie-cutter models accepted by past generations—customization, technology, mobility, personal fulfillment, diversity, socializing, livability, and a host of other criteria provide the foundation for where and how you live.

Review the following comprehensive list of housing options. Perhaps one or several of these suggestions will appeal to you.

Shared Housing

Move in with strangers, aging parents or relatives, friends, siblings, or adult children. Or choose to remain in your own home and accept boarders and roommates—from grandchildren, university students, travelers, and others. Consider your room rental options by visiting Airbnb (www.airbnb.com). If you are so inclined, and zoning laws permit, open up a bed-and-breakfast. For additional resources, check out Bed and Breakfast.com (www.bedand breakfast.com).

The idea of sharing housing may work well, but it requires a lot of talking up front to avert potential conflicts—length of the stay, considerations of other household members, unresolved relationship conflicts, abiding by existing household rules, and much more. Find out whether city codes restrict the number of unrelated people living together in one residence.

Sharing a household stretches available dollars while providing added security and companionship. Financial arrangements, room access, expected household tasks, and caregiving responsibilities vary according to mutual verbal and/or written agreements.

Type "shared housing," "housemates," "roommates," and "living together" into your Internet search engine. Also check out the National Shared Housing Resource Center (http://nationalsharedhousing.org), Silvernest (www.silvernest.com), and Women Living in Community (www.womenlivingincommunity.com).

Living Smaller

The "tiny house" movement is testing the limits of small for those who embrace minimalism. For the rest of us who may simply want to scale down, downsizing to a smaller house or apartment may offer more affordable alternatives to maintaining a big house.

Accessory-dwelling units (also known as granny pods and mother-in-law suites) include backyard cottages, basement apartments, and converted garages. This type of dwelling exists on property that would normally have only one house on it. Prefabricated homes offer housing on idle land, such as unused parking lots, and can also be put in garages and on driveways. Zoning laws and permits dictate whether or not these concepts are feasible.

Co-Living

Co-living is a variation on the shared-housing concept. Move into a fully furnished bedroom, not as a renter but rather a member of a household who has access to all common areas (living room, kitchen, laundry room, and den). Members are encouraged to plan group activities and participate in social events, such as potluck dinners, movie nights, book clubs, and bowling.

Like co-working spaces that attract freelancers and entrepreneurs, the co-living concept resonates with people who are not served emotionally or culturally by the typical solo-resident apartment lifestyle. Members can always choose to be alone, but when they want company, they are never alone in this housing environment. Some co-living providers allow members to bounce among their various locations if members have not yet decided on a permanent location in which to settle down. Whether the sense of community and friendliness can be replicated for people with health issues or early-stage dementia remains to be seen. Co-living (http://coliving.org) is a great place to start your research.

Cohousing

You may also know this living arrangement by the term *commune*. The common characteristic of the cohousing concept is one where neighbors commit to being part of a community for everyone's mutual benefit. An intentional community of private homes clustered around shared space, cohousing cultivates a culture of sharing and caring. Residents choose their own level of engagement, and decision making is participatory and often based on consensus. "What can I give to my community?" provides the bedrock for vibrant and resilient cohousing.

Residents live in attached or single-family homes with shared spaces typically feature a common house—which may include a kitchen and dining area, laundry, and recreational spaces. Shared outdoor spaces may feature parking, walkable paths, open space, and gardens. Neighbors gather for parties, games, movies, and community activities.

At this writing, most cohousing arrangements are not set up to provide any level of assistance for specialized care—for example, dementia—and other concerns that can lead people to leave the community.

Check out the Cohousing Association of the United States (www.cohousing.org) and UK Cohousing Network (http://cohousing.org.uk). Cohousing developments are not new to most areas, but communities for adults who identify as LGBTQ may have to look a little harder. Type, "LGBTQ cohousing" into your Internet search engine.

Group Home

Fifty years ago, most people with even moderate special needs were institutionalized throughout their adult lives. Now, thanks in part to societal changes and decades of litigation, most people living with special needs, including those with very severe special needs, can live in some variation of a community setting, commonly referred to as a group home (also known as congregate care or board and care). In fact, the US Supreme Court has specifically ruled that people with special needs who receive government benefits must be housed in the least restrictive possible setting.[1]

Residents choose to live in supportive group homes with several other people. Group homes come in many varieties—with and without assistance—and can be paid for in many ways, including private payment and state programs designated for people with disabilities. A monthly fee buys three meals a day, housekeeping, and medication reminders, among other services. Resident capacity is limited, and depends on the number of bedrooms or apartments with common areas for dining, socializing, and programs.

Group Homes Online (www.grouphomesonline.com) provides listings with full details of group homes nationwide. Shared Lives (http://sharedlivesplus.org.uk) offers UK residents home care and care homes for adults living with disabilities.

Adult Foster Home

A family shares its home life and takes care of residents as it would a family member. This arrangement can be especially attractive to people who do not need constant supervision and would like to feel like part of a family rather than an independent resident.

Some homes cater to people who are relatively mobile and self-sufficient but who need basic help with groceries, bathing, dressing, and medication management. Other home settings are ideal for people who live with Alzheimer's or dementia.

In some foster homes, residents have their own rooms and share common space, such as a laundry room and bathrooms. Others offer completely self-contained quarters with only a manager who lives on the site to assist if a resident requires aid.

Contact your local Area Agency on Aging or the Eldercare Locator (www.eldercare.gov) for adult foster home referrals.

Age-Restricted Rental Apartments

Age-restricted rental apartments tend to attract independent and healthy adults who want to socialize with like-minded renters. Common areas often include fitness centers, walkable gardens, and cafés. Housekeeping and handyman services are also attractive features. Some apartments may charge a "community" fee in addition to monthly rent.

Rental apartments are specifically designed for comfort and include important modifications in the event of a health event—wide doorways to accommodate walkers and wheelchairs, emergency buttons, and bathroom and hallway balance bars. These apartment complexes generally don't include on-site medical care. Renting versus buying means you are free to roam once the lease is up.

Visit the Senior Resource website (www.seniorresource.com) to find apartments in your state.

Naturally Occurring Retirement Communities

Many individuals are now banding together to create "retirement communities" in their existing apartment buildings. The definition of a naturally occurring retirement community (NORC) is vague, but typically a large proportion of the residents are fifty-five years plus. Some are augmented with a supportive service program.

Residents of New York City NORCs, for example, can access health and social services right in their own building or building complex. With an aim to maximize and support the aging in place of residents, each NORC identifies the major health risks among the elders they serve and develops programs to improve their health status. In addition to the focus on health promotion, supportive services provide case management services, classes and educational activities, trips, volunteer opportunities, and opportunities to be part of NORC governance.[2]

Residents who pay an annual membership fee can access discounted services, such as personal care, social activities, transportation, housekeeping, handyman services, and limited nursing, on an à la carte basis. Governments and nonprofits are willing to provide many of the same services for which retirement homes charge thousands of dollars.

If you do not currently live in an apartment complex with an age fifty-five-plus demographic, you may want to consider relocating to one. You will find additional information by visiting the Naturally Occurring Retirement Communities website (www.norc.org).

Village to Village

The village concept is a variation of the NORC idea. The village is not a place per se, but a not-for-profit membership program for adults in a neighborhood who come together to help one another as they age. Support includes everything from cooking, pet sitting, and fixing the air conditioner to making doctor appointments and getting dressed. Some villages may also offer concierge services, including travel adventures for individuals and groups.

Each village member pays a yearly fee that the village uses to provide discounted services and support. Members pay the providers, but the village staff and volunteers select and screen them and coordinate these appointments. Villages may also provide social outlets, linking people who share similar interests.

Additional information is available on the Village to Village Network website (www.vtv network.org).

Active Adult Community

Single-family homes, town homes, cluster homes, and condos provide maintenance-free living and a comprehensive array of social activities to residents who are at least fifty-five years of age. In addition to the cost of the home, homeowner-association fees are extra.

The theme for this kind of living arrangement is "This is a great place to live. Improve your lifestyle here." Houses are designed with adult-friendly features—wide doorways that accommodate wheelchairs and scooters, and hand rails in hallways and bathrooms, for example. Housing developments typically offer common areas for meetings, special events, and also may include a library, fitness center, guest rooms, and dining room with meal service. This option does not necessarily provide health-care services.

Type "active adult living" and "55+ active living communities" into your Internet search engine. Also visit 55 Places (www.55places.com) to explore communities.

Life Plan Community/Continuing Care Retirement Community

This option allows the concepts of "planning" and "living" to merge. Life plan communities promote healthy living and active lifestyles, and priority access to a continuum of advanced health-care services and unique "safety net" advantages—assisted living, memory care, and skilled nursing. A full range of amenities typically includes choices in formal and informal dining, fitness centers, spas, education, volunteer opportunities, travel, art, music, language classes, and more. As it is in any community setting, you choose your level of social activity; you have the right to do as much or as little as you want.

Traditionally, this living arrangement requires an entry fee, plus monthly maintenance fees; or you may also find a community that makes rental units available. In addition to couples and people who prefer to live alone, friends, adult children, parents, and siblings are also opting to room together in life plan communities.

Be aware that the transition from independent living to higher levels of care as needs change may be problematical. A study examined experiences of residents and staff at seven multilevel sites to identify the main social features of such transitions and interactions. The first finding was that there is often a stigma surrounding the floors or units offering more intensive levels of care. Healthier residents would label such areas "Death Valley" or "the Twilight Zone." This stigma contributed to residents being uncomfortable visiting friends in higher levels of care. The next major theme was that housing the levels of care in one building or campus posed challenges to socializing across levels of care, especially when cognitive differences existed between residents. The third finding was about the impact of different levels of care on resident identity. Residents in independent living expressed a need to clearly identify as independent, and because of this, resident behaviors included concealing signs of decline. In some cases, this can involve acting preemptively to avoid rejection, such as eating meals in one's room. The power of staff to make or influence such decisions can even lead to adversarial relationships between residents and staff, as well as residents living in fear and isolating themselves from staff.[3] Researchers concluded the need for greater recognition and understanding by developers, operators, staff, and potential residents of the personal and social challenges that are typically encountered.

There are numerous life plan communities from which to choose—each a culture unto its own. Your first course of action is to use a comprehensive checklist that will help you compare one community with another. My website, Who Will Take Care of Me When I'm Old? (www.elderindustry.com), offers a customizable form titled "Senior Housing Checklist." Click the "Download I" tab on the home page to access and customize the list.

Additional information about this housing option is available on the Life Plan Community website (www.lifeplancommunity.org), LeadingAge (www.leadingage.org), and American Seniors Housing Association (www.seniorshousing.org).

Veteran Housing

The goal of these housing programs is to end chronic homelessness among veterans in our communities. More than putting a roof over their head, housing initiatives require a holistic approach that addresses the "total veteran" and his or her unique needs.

Joblessness and substance misuse, among other situations, may limit a veteran's abilities to sustain quality of life. What is needed is a full range of support services—meals, employment, training programs, legal assistance, medical advice, case management, and mental health counseling.

The National Veterans Foundation (http://nvf.org) and the National Center of Veteran Homelessness (www.va.gov/homeless) offer an abundance of information regarding veteran housing and supportive services programs.

Paid to Live Elsewhere

Some cities will pay *you* to live there. In the face of declining or slowing population growth, cities are doing whatever it takes to survive. Some are giving away free land, while others are literally handing out cash. If you are thinking about a change of scenery, why not get paid to move? Type "places that pay you to live there" into your Internet search engine.

The Isolation of Rural Living

Ahhh . . . the calm and slow pace of country living. What's not to like? A retired friend of mine from Chicago was mesmerized by the beauty of Wyoming while on vacation. She sold her condo in the city and bought a cabin in the mountains. The photo of her sitting on her screened-in front porch, surrounded by her three German shepherds, with the mountains in the background, looked like a postcard. One year later, she put the house back on the market (at a huge loss) after waking in the middle of the night short of breath. Her nearest neighbor was 5 miles away. The closest hospital was 50 miles away.

Living in a remote location is challenging. If one thing goes wrong—such as plumbing, electricity, or being snowed in—you are vulnerable in a multitude of ways, not to mention every trip you take requires getting in your car (it better start!). LGBTQ individuals in rural areas have reported refusals to be treated by local medical providers. A friend of mine who has lived on a farm in Nebraska all his life told me that he travels over 300 miles to receive routine medical care.

People who have lived their entire lives in rural areas are used to being physically isolated from other people, and consequently learn the ropes early on for getting by under these conditions.

If you were not raised with the know-how of what country living entails, and are not fully prepared for a major cultural shift, retirement-living experts agree that this is probably not the time to try it out. Type "rural health" into your Internet search engine before you make a move, and visit the following websites:

Action with Communities in Rural England: www.acre.org.uk

Administration for Community Living: www.acl.gov (type "rural" into the website's search field)

Federal Office of Rural Health Policy: www.hrsa.gov/ruralhealth

National Rural Health Association: www.ruralhealthweb.org

Rural Health Information Hub: www.ruralhealthinfo.org

US Department of Agriculture Rural Housing Service: www.rd.usda.gov

Other Housing Options

The Mobile Home

Motor homes, converted school buses, vans, and RVs—lots of folks are living with no permanent address, and the dream of unplugging full-time is a reality for many.

Some nomads work part of the year, just long enough to make money to sustain them for a few months. For engineers, project managers, and construction workers, living on the highway, and traveling from job to job is an economical low-cost housing option. Other mobile dwellers are retired and seek volunteer opportunities, as well as sunshine and relaxation.

Mobile home owners can stay in developed campgrounds or "boondock," which is the term for camping in undeveloped areas but that are federally regulated by a "14-day law."

Full-timer insurance policies, group health insurance, and towing insurance is available through the Escapees Club's RV-Alliance America (www.escapees.com), American Automobile Association (AAA) (www.aaa.com), TravelSure (www.travelsure.co.uk), Good Sam Club (www.goodsamclub.com), and Camping World (www.campingworld.com).

Escapees CARE (www.escapeescare.org), answers the question "What happens to full-time RVers whose travels are impacted because they can no longer drive or are temporarily interrupted because of health problems?" This organization provides meals, schedules medical appointments, transportation to and from the appointments, an adult day center, and more.

The Cruise Ship

Living and retiring on the high seas is another mobile, but pricey, housing option. Sometimes called "the endless cruise," residents travel as a passenger for as many days as they like, and enjoy restaurants, movies, casinos, driving ranges, spas, swimming pools, entertainment, dancing, yoga, language classes, libraries, weight loss programs, and spiritual retreats, among other fun activities. It is possible to book cruises back to back to create a floating retirement experience—port visits offer sightseeing, new people continuously come on board, and the staff starts to feel like "family."

Life on a cruise ship is similar to hotel living in that room service, daily housekeeping, and fresh linens are standard. Meals are included in the cost. Ships have doctors and nurses on call 24/7, but although medical care and emergency care is available, serious illnesses that require intensive care cannot be accommodated.

Type "cruise ship retirement" into your Internet search engine for more information and resources.

Live Outside the United States

Looking to lower your cost of living? Seeking a more laid-back lifestyle? Wanting to join friends who are already enjoying the "good life"? Before taking the expat plunge, know what you are getting into. Experts suggest that you spend several weeks in the country to which you wish to retire and immerse yourself in the local culture. Other considerations include learning how to speak the language of the natives, knowing how to hire locals for home maintenance repairs, accessing health-care needs, and arranging to have your Social Security retirement checks directly deposited into a foreign financial banking institution.

There are many countries where you can live without first obtaining citizenship, but there may be challenges if you plan to continue working. Each country has different laws. Start your research by visiting these expat-related websites: Transitions Abroad (www.transitions abroad.com) and Just Landed (www.justlanded.com). These sites offer a wealth of information about working, volunteering, teaching, studying, traveling, and retiring abroad.

EcoVillage

Get away from it all and move to a community whose inhabitants seek to live according to ecological principles, causing as little impact on the environment as possible. Awareness of caring for the world we live in and our responsibility to this planet are common threads among the ecovillagers.

Intentional living is the primary philosophy. Commonalities among ecovillages include: community gardens, shared agriculture, off-the-grid energy, and recycling and bartering systems. They also develop on-site businesses as part of their own economy that offer permaculture plant nurseries, natural building home construction, solar system installation, and herbal medicine, among others.

Further research on this type of shared housing led to discovering that many of these villages are seeking emotionally mature, cooperative people of all kinds to join them. You can find out more by visiting these websites: the Fellowship for Intentional Community (www.ic.org/directory), the Global Ecovillage Network (http://gen.ecovillage.org), and the Sustainable Ecovillages Forum (www.sustainableecovillages.net).

Niche Housing

Do you live to golf? Are you a "foodie" or an artist at heart?" Would you like to reside among other scholars in a historic district? Imagine living in a neighborhood or retirement community where you are literally surrounded by everything you love to do, including people who have the same interests as you. Alumni, artists, educators, LGBTQ, sports fanatics, fitness enthusiasts, musicians, and other like-minded people living under one roof is what niche communities are about. If you can't find what you are looking for, start your own. You only need about two hundred other Beatles fans to fill a retirement community.

As people age in these communities, they may also qualify to receive government-reimbursed services. The days where your only choices are assisted living and nursing homes are gone.

To learn more, type into your Internet search engine "best retirement community for . . . ," followed by your specific interest; for example, "best retirement community for artists." Also, type "niche retirement communities" into your Internet search engine for more information and resources.

Housing-Provided Jobs

Jobs that offer housing might be an interesting alternative to consider: Become a tour guide, work on a cruise ship or at a resort, work as a property manager or handyman, be a full-time gardener, house sit, pet sit, be a caregiver, or a nanny.

Many hotels, motels, bed-and-breakfasts, and inns require staff members to live on-site. If you have experience working as a chef, a bartender, or a general manager, you could land yourself a live-in job.

Type "housing provided jobs" and "volunteering overseas" into your Internet search engine for more information and resources.

Living out of a Suitcase

Hotel living might sound romantic and intriguing, but do your homework. People have the misconception that hotel living is a single room with little space to walk around in. There are alternatives—full kitchens and kitchenettes with dishwashers, suites with laundry and multiple bedrooms.

What also may be included in the price is parking, a room telephone number with voice-mail, cable TV, housekeeping, fresh linens, dishes/cups/flatware, free coffee/tea, free newspaper, free happy hour, complimentary breakfast, fitness center, microwave, refrigerator, high-speed Internet access, and 24-hour front desk reception. Some hotels are pet-friendly.

This housing option tends to attract freelancers and consultants whose work projects are six months or less (apartments typically require a year lease). When the work project is complete, you pack up and relocate, and you are on to the next job. In some cases, the company that hired you will pay for food and car rental. Accumulate hotel reward points to lessen the cost of your next hotel stay.

There tends to be many apartment-hotel options across North America, but not so many in Europe. In the United States they are plentiful. Type "apartment hotels" and "living in hotels" into your Internet search engine followed by the city and state for more information and resources.

Emergency Housing

Can you suddenly become homeless? When you least expect it, yes. Falling upon financial hard times or trying to keep up with the cost of chronic illness, among other challenges, could send you to the streets. Some people resort to living in their car. But there are better options. In a pinch, if you find yourself in this situation, and you cannot find an affordable apartment to move into (wait lists are long and growing), consider temporary housing. Shelters are specifically designed to assist adults who need time to get back on their feet. In the interim, case managers help shelter residents find permanent housing within a limited budget. To locate local resources, type these keywords into your Internet browser, followed by the name of your city and/or state: Area Agency on Aging, Commission on Aging and Disability, Department of Health, Community Action Committee, and Catholic Charities.

Start Dealing with Your Possessions Anyway

You own collectibles, jewelry, antiques, and designer purses, and wonder whether any of these items are worth selling. If so, you can put the money to good use now.

You anticipate relocating out of your house someday and can't fathom how you will get through the moving and downsizing process alone, particularly if not in the best of health.

You would like to give the special people in your life meaningful mementos from your past while you are alive, but are not sure how to go about this task fairly.

Your attorney asks you to prepare an inventory of your possessions to be included in your estate-planning process. You immediately feel a major headache coming on.

You decide to take everything out of your storage unit and sell anything of value but have no time to get the job done.

You are overwhelmed with mountains of papers—old tax returns, journals, magazines, junk mail, newspapers, legal documents, insurance policies, catalogs, receipts. You can never find what you are looking for and don't know what is important to keep and okay to toss.

Take control of your possessions, and reap the physical, emotional, and financial benefits:

Sell profitable items.

Make someone happy with a gift.

Donate to good causes.

Gain Peace of Mind

Where do you start? You have two choices. Do it yourself or hire experts to get the job done right, and in a timely manner. It is always in your best interest to get help with tasks that you may not be able to do on your own. Plus, sometimes you need an objective, experienced professional to help you move forward.

Besides you, who else hires moving and downsizing professionals?

Executors of someone's will

Bank and trust officers

Life care managers

Attorneys

Financial planners

Retirement community managers

Realtors

Some of the following professional services overlap, but they all have one thing in common—an extensive network of resources at their fingertips that the average person does not have. They know of closet companies, specialty movers, appraisers, storage companies, painters, brokers, auction houses, organizers, junk haulers, donation sources, shredding companies, consignment stores, insurance providers, interior designers, photo and paper scanning companies, contractors, and much more. They know who is reliable and appropriate for each budget. They have partnerships with many companies that can extend discounts to clients.

Professional Organizers

Organizers are trained to bring order and efficiency to people's lives. Their work is focused on the person, and not so much on their stuff. They can establish systems so that their clients won't fall back on bad habits, can ultimately make long-term improvements, and keep disorder and clutter at bay.

Organizers know where to sell, ship, trade, donate, buy, store, or recycle anything. They also offer storage options. For example, you have plenty of wall space, but no idea where to find good shelving to make the best use of it.

To find an organizer in the United States, contact the National Association of Professional Organizers (www.napo.net). In Canada, check out the Professional Organizers in Canada (www.organizersincanada.com). In Australia and Southeast Asia, contact the Australasian Association of Professional Organizers (www.aapo.org.au). Germany has BOOND (www.boond.de/home). The Netherlands has NBPO (www.nbpo.nl). The United Kingdom has the Association of Professional Declutterers and Organizers (www.apdo.co.uk). Japan has the Japan Association of Life Organizers (http://jalo.jp). Countries in Africa have Professional Organiser Association Africa (http://podirectory.com).

Estate Inventory Managers

Cataloging inventory; obtaining valuations; estate and business liquidation; auctions; appraisals; sales and consignment; in-home and off-site estate sales; and indexing, packing, and managing the storage and moving process—all can be arranged by estate inventory service providers.

You will need these services for estate planning; income tax returns; orderly distribution of family possessions; business liquidation; proof of inventory for insurance claims (video and/or photography) in cases of loss and theft; warranty settlements; tracking what's in storage; dividing assets and possessions in the event of a divorce; profiting from the sale of valuables and collectibles; and cleaning, cataloging, organizing, and removing inventory of a residence or business upon death of the owner.

Like organizers, estate inventory managers know where to sell, ship, trade, donate, buy, store, or recycle anything. To learn more, visit Estate Inventory Services (www.estateinventoryservices.com), or contact the National Association of Home Inventory Professionals (http://nahip.com).

Senior Move Managers

Although specific services vary per provider, these experts are typically associated with a pending move, executing a seamless action plan customized to the client's wishes. Services may include: custom floor plans and space planning; sorting and downsizing possessions; interviewing, scheduling, and overseeing movers; supervising professional packing and unpacking; and setting up the new home.

Senior move managers know where to sell, ship, donate, store, and dispose of unwanted items. They can also assist individuals who choose to stay in their own home but simply require expert organizational skills and solid knowledge of aging-in-place concepts to help them achieve their goal of staying put.

The National Association of Senior Move Managers (www.nasmm.org) is the leading membership organization for senior move managers in the United States, Canada, and abroad.

Do It Yourself

Not everyone needs the help of a professional. If organizing come naturally to you, and you have the time and energy to manage downsizing projects yourself, you are probably in good shape—physically and mentally.

Take a deep breath, and start anywhere: clothes, books, DVDs, musical instruments, mementos, sports equipment, photo albums, kitchen gadgets, furniture, cleaning supplies, keepsakes, tools—are you getting the picture? Everything and anything can probably go without being missed.

As you approach each room, categorize the household goods accordingly:
Keep
Give away
Sell
Donate
Toss

Don't Fall into the Trap of Creating a "Maybe" Pile

To refresh your memory on outlets for selling items (and making extra money), review the chapter in this book titled "The Fierce Urgency of Money," starting on page 57.

The organization and/or disposal of paperwork requires special attention. Here are a few suggestions:

Some paperwork requires long-term storage (legal and tax papers), whereas other types need varying degrees of attention (warranties, instruction manuals). Grouping papers per usage eases the stress of knowing what to keep and what to toss.

Outdated documents that contain sensitive information are best shredded (Social Security numbers, access codes, etc.). Unfortunately, identity theft is here to stay, so destroying confidential information is a must. Before making any decision on what to keep or discard, check with your accountant and attorney. Buy a shredder or engage a professional shredding service.

After you die, someone sifts through *every single piece of paper* looking for clues of unfinished business before they close your estate for good. They do the same with your computer files. If you own personal journals, or any other papers and files that you have created for your eyes only, decide what you want to do with them immediately. Many people go the route of shredding papers and deleting files for this reason. Remember to clear out your personal files and passwords from any computers, smartphones, and other such devices before giving them away or otherwise disposing of them.

Insights and Inspiration

Recommended Reading: *Big Magic: Creative Living Beyond Fear* (2016) by Elizabeth Gilbert

Recommended YouTube: *Somewhere over the Rainbow*, Judy Garland (1939)

Recommended Movie: *Life as a House* (2001)

Recommended Song: "Right Place, Wrong Time" by Dr. John

Recommended TED Talk: "Where is Home?" presented by Pico Iyer, global author, filmed January 2010

Part Three

Ties That Bind and Unwind

The Broken Hearts Club

Accepting relationships as moving targets

As years pass, family members and longtime friends will die off. The older we get, the more we are left behind. Time is not a healer, and grief is a constant companion. There may be moments when you unexpectedly cry like a baby, not because you are unhappy but simply because you miss people who have died. The heart aches as a testament to loving people deeply.

Age and death continue to transform our worlds. Whereas time used to be spent on baby showers and baptisms, retirement parties and funerals now occupy more of our days. So intensely aware of death, our attitude about living is altogether different—a combination of an underlying emotional pain paired with wondrous feelings of coming into one's own.

As life becomes emptied each time another loved one dies, we do not die *with* him or her. In fact, just the opposite may occur. We can become an even more intense version of who we already are. Death is the ultimate prioritizer that allows us to move forward and live full out, claiming what time is left for *us*.

When someone you love dearly has died, or leaves you in another way—such as divorce or estrangement—you become a member of the Broken Hearts Club. Loss, of one kind or another, is the key that opens the door. Initiation comes suddenly or slowly. The process matters not. Every loss hands you an experience you can get nowhere else. What becomes important are the choices you make and the stories you tell yourself as you journey on the path to aloneness.

Objectives

After completing the chapter "The Broken Hearts Club," you will be able to:

- Capture valuable life lessons during the caregiving years
- Be aware of the sensitivities of widowhood
- Access LGBTQ caregiver and widowhood resources
- Obtain later-life divorce resources and counsel
- Create strategies if estranged or alienated

Providing Care to Others

You are sitting at your desk at work, when the phone rings. It's your mother's neighbor. She says, "Come quick. I found your mom wandering outside the house in her bathrobe. Something is terribly wrong."

Or you and your longtime friend make a date to enjoy an afternoon lunch together the next day. When you arrive at her home to drive her to the restaurant, she becomes extremely agitated and anxious because she does not remember making a date with you. You also notice that she has not showered in days, and the house is in complete disarray. It's clear to you that she can no longer manage safely on her own.

And just like that, your world is turned upside down.

You don't choose eldercare. *Eldercare chooses you.* Caregiving goes hand in hand with growing older. You are aging, and so are the people you care about. They now need your help. Your responsibilities may be hands-on, 24/7, or simply a matter of picking up the phone and checking in every so often.

You do many things in the caregiving role. You rush to the hospital in the middle of the night, spend countless hours making telephone calls, cook and clean up, make sure they take their medications correctly, listen to them complain, take them shopping for shoes, watch television with them for hours, and sit quietly as they doze. You do what you must with the understanding that you have no way of knowing how you will deal with what happens next.

The people on the other end of your care are now on another journey. You can be present with them for a while longer, but they will ultimately leave you. *And that is exactly the point of it all.* David Horgan, coauthor of *When Your Parent Moves In: Every Adult Child's Guide to Living with an Aging Parent* (2009) writes, "It is far too easy to get caught up in your 'young' life and gloss over the sensitivities of caring for parents and loved ones as they age. Give them their dignity and empathy with the understanding that one day you will be in their place."

In the process of caregiving, you are three persons at once—carer, observer, and mourner. As you go about your daily caregiving routines, open your heart and mind so as to become the beneficiary of unique gifts. To reap your rewards, ask yourself the following questions:

What is this person I am caring for trying to teach me?
What am I learning about myself that I never knew before?
How is caregiving making me wiser?

As caregiver, you witness a variety of end-of-life events—good, bad, and ugly—and consequently become a student of what happens when someone is close to death. Perhaps you also participate in tender moments of togetherness with your loved one, and consequently say to yourself, "I hope that I am loved this much when I am at the end of my life."

If ever there were a perfect time to keep a journal of life and death experiences, it is now—when thoughts and feelings about your caregiving experiences are fresh in your mind, and lead you to express how you would like your end of life to be.

This is also a prime time to ask yourself these important questions:

Knowing what I know now, what will I do differently in my own dying process?
What plans must I put in place now to ensure a quality end of life for myself?

To further your exploration of end-of-life options, review the "'Just Shoot Me' Is Not a Plan" chapter of the book, beginning on page 227.

Caregiving in the LGBTQ Community

Most of the needs of LGBTQ caregivers are the same faced by all caregivers, but inevitably there are unique considerations. Even as attitudes have evolved, and the LGBTQ community is more visible and accepted, you will continue to hear of instances where rights are unjustly denied.

As a caregiver, if you meet resistance from one person in the health-care setting, ask to speak to someone who has training or experience working with the LGBTQ community. If hospital visitation rights are being denied, type "hospital visitation rights" into the search engine of the Human Rights Campaign website (www.hrc.org).

Be sure to assemble and complete the necessary legal documents that establish the right for you to make care decisions and treatment preferences. Seek referrals for legal advice from local LGBTQ organizations, the National Center for Lesbian Rights (which is available to all LGBTQ individuals at www.nclrights.org), and Lambda Legal (www.lambdalegal.org).

What you observe and experience in the process of caring for loved ones will not only lead you to ponder and plan for what lies ahead for you at your end of life, but special concerns will also cause you to be vigilant on protecting your rights, especially in health-care settings. Make plans for the following:

Dealing with situations where you must legalize decision-making powers and durable power of attorney for finances as a "family of choice"
Protecting your decision regarding who has visitation rights
Finding supportive health-care and service providers (e.g., in-home care, hospitals, hospice, assisted living, nursing homes)
Taking steps after experiencing mistreatment and/or discrimination

You will find additional support and LGBTQ advocacy resources when you visit the following organizations online. Type "LGBT caregiving" into the search engine of these websites:

Family Caregiver Alliance: www.caregiver.org
National Family Caregiver Support Program: www.aoa.acl.gov
National LGBT Aging Resource Center: www.lgbtagingcenter.org
SAGE: www.sageusa.org

Widowhood: Before

Can we ever prepare for the death of a spouse or partner? Perhaps not. It has been said that widowed grievers use a very simple calendar: before and after the death of their loved one.

If you are like me (in the "before" stage), there is work to do in anticipation of aging solo; when you are numb and vulnerable with grief is not the time to plan for any of this. Additionally, the poverty rate for elder widows is about three to four times higher than that for elder married women.[1] If that statistic isn't incentive enough to get planning, financially and otherwise, I don't know what is.

Act Now

When responsibilities and daily activities cause the two of you to be apart—even for a few hours—say, "I love you," before you walk out the door. It may be your last good-bye. My girlfriend's husband was killed in a car accident on his way to pick up the pizza they had just ordered. Also, take the trip. Do not put off that couple's dream vacation.

Make sure you know how to survive without your partner. For example, if you do not currently drive, learn how to get around town without your spouse's chauffeuring services that you may have come to rely on as passenger. Brush up on grocery shopping, cooking nutritious meals, and staying social. Nurture current friendships.

In the aftermath of losing a spouse or partner, the last thing you will want to think about is money, but you will have little choice. Because financial planning in the "after" stage involves your emotional state, you run the risk of being pushed to make unwise decisions—from friends, family, and even professional advisers. That said, get to know your spouse's professional advisers (attorney, accountant, banker, financial planner, and insurance provider). If you decide that you trust them implicitly, hire them later to assist you with post-death details. Or start now to find your own expert professionals.

Learn how to handle everything in your portfolio, especially when and how to pay monthly bills. If you have not done so already, create 24/7 access to paperwork, bank and credit card statements, legal documents, and online accounts that back up your financial life: insurance policies, mortgages, debts, car payments, retirement plans, account numbers, passwords, lock codes, copies of deeds, registrations, titles, wills, trusts, living wills, powers of attorney (health and finances), birth and marriage certificates, passports, military discharge papers, proof of citizenship, and safe-deposit box access.

Put check-writing in both of your names and open your own checking account.

Research spousal death benefits. Investigate what you can expect from Social Security, retirement plans, pensions, veteran programs, and employer survivor initiatives.

Decide and plan for future living arrangements. Can you afford to stay in the house where you are now? Is your current home environment age-friendly? Might you want to move and start over? Review the "Where You Live Matters" part in this book, starting on page 85.

If the death of your spouse will require you to work, start researching job and income-earning opportunities. Review "The Fierce Urgency of Money" chapter of this book starting on page 57.

Complete your estate-planning documentation, including ensuring proper titling of assets, minimizing taxes, what is subject to probate, plans for heirs, and distribution of property and assets. Now is a good time to conduct an estate inventory and appraisal of possessions. Review the "Start Dealing with Your Possessions Anyway" section in this book, beginning on page 131.

Business-ownership questions will surface if one or both of you are engaged in private business. How will you handle the transfer, sale, or closure of the business? How will you manage the existing client/customer relationship?

Know how to reach your partner's personal and professional contacts—names, phone numbers, and e-mail. Gain access to your spouse's online address book.

Expect the need to update insurance coverage, especially health insurance, disability, long-term care, rental, property, and life insurance. Learn how to obtain copies of your spouse's insurance-related documents.

Talk about end of life. Consider making arrangements with a provider of funeral or burial services through a funeral trust. Once plans are in place, make sure advance directives reflect your wishes, and those of your spouse. Also discuss related costs and how invoices are paid.

To gain specific insights on the emotional experiences of widowhood, think about offering comfort directly to the recently widowed. You will learn firsthand about their regrets, joys, and everything in-between. Widows Hope (www.widowshope.org) is an organization that is dedicated to men and women who have lost a spouse or significant other. Strengthen your relationship with your spouse's family.

Take care of your health: mind, body and soul. Aging solo means guarding your well-being with a vengeance. Work out regularly. Develop a hobby. The goal is to do what it takes to prevent the need to be taken care of in old age.

Be Aware of Widowhood Sensitivities

What I know now about the experiences of people who live within the widowhood reality has changed me forever—I had no idea of how insensitive I have been in the past. For instance, I learned recently that the use of the terms *football widow* and *baseball widow* might be offensive to the newly widowed.

I am apologetic to widowed friends when I may have remarked about the benefits of their spouse's no longer being in pain. *What was I thinking?* Here I am aiming comments at their head instead of where they hurt the most—their broken heart. I realized that I was not helping the newly widowed feel any better in the moment. Instead, here is what I have been saying and doing differently:

"I don't know what to say, but I will be here if you ever want to talk."
"I can't imagine how you feel."
"I don't know what to say, but please know that I'm sorry."

When I can't come up with the right words, tears shared and a long hug say it all.

Widowhood: After

In the "after" stage of widowhood, take these specific actions:

Funeral arrangements may consume your immediate attention. If plans were not spelled out ahead of time, look to the "Places to Go and Things to Do" chapter of this book, starting on page 241, to assist in the process of carrying out death's details.

Get organized. Hopefully, you already put the pieces of your financial puzzle together ahead of time. If not, you can and will get through this difficult period. Gather the following paperwork:

Spouse's will
Multiple original copies of spouse's death certificates
Spouse's birth certificate
Marriage certificate
Durable power for attorney for finances

Naturalization papers

Social Security numbers of spouse and dependents

Monthly bills

Insurance policies

Property deeds and titles

Rental agreements

Bank statements

Loan documents

Checking accounts

Investment statements

Stock certificates

Business-related ownership documents

Joint tax returns from the past five years

Vehicle titles, registrations, loan and/or lease agreements

Inventory of possessions

Appraisals

Employee-benefits documents

You may want to consider getting professional counseling since there is no preparation for this emotional journey. Over time, you and your therapist will discuss a variety of needs—what to do with your spouse's clothes in the closet, managing relatives who are looking for a handout, and more. Search online for supportive blogs and forums. Hospice is an excellent resource for compassionate social workers and support groups.

Contact your attorney, financial planner, executor of the will, accountant, banker, and insurance provider. Inform them of your spouse's death. Ask the following questions of these advisers:

Which financial decisions must be made immediately?

Which financial decisions can, and should, wait?

What is the process to ensure that I have money to meet my monthly expenses?

How do I revise my portfolio to fit my lifestyle needs?

What am I entitled to regarding survivor benefits?

What financial and insurance-coverage considerations must be discussed with my spouse's employer?

How do I put accounts into my name?

What is required regarding settling an estate and filing a final income tax return?

If applicable, contact Social Security (www.socialsecurity.gov) and the Department of Veterans Affairs (www.veterans.gov). Inform them of your spouse's death and inquire about survivor's benefits.

Widowhood in the LGBTQ Community

My widowed LGBTQ friends tell me stories that are incredibly sad and unjust. One friend attended a grief support group and found that no one was sympathetic or compassionate, including an intolerant facilitator. Another friend told me that she found it necessary to communicate untruthfully at times, refraining from using the word *wife*. The stories go on and on.

In addition to the many books and blogs that are available online regarding LGBTQ widowhood, visit Legacy Connect (http://connect.legacy.com). This website offers grief support groups, condolence advice, funeral etiquette, and much more. Type "LGBT" into the website's search field.

Late-Life Divorce

Divorce at any age is a major loss event. Later-life situations include spouses divorcing mates who are recently diagnosed with a chronic illness; others running off with younger, healthier lovers; some coming "out" and finding true love in same-sex relationships; some looking forward to a quiet and uncomplicated solo lifestyle.

The divorce rate among people aged fifty and older has doubled in the past twenty years, per research by Bowling Green State University.[2] What makes these divorces different can be summed up in two words: finite resources. "You have a limited amount of time, money, and energy. When you get divorced in your senior years, or even middle age, you no longer have a lifetime to rebuild your finances. Your income is unlikely to go up in any serious way. Your assets are fairly fixed and your employment opportunities are limited."[3]

Life expectancy is also playing a role in the rise in divorce rates. In the past, "people died earlier," says Pepper Schwartz, PhD, a professor of sociology at the University of Washington in Seattle, and the love, sex, and relationship ambassador for AARP. "Now, let's say you're 50 or 60. You could go 30 more years. A lot of marriages are not horrible, but they're no longer satisfying or loving. They may not be ugly, but you say, 'Do I really want 30 more years of this?"[4]

No matter who does the initiating, a legal separation or divorce is difficult for everyone involved. To protect yourself emotionally, you may want to hire a divorce coach to help you negotiate the rough spots. Type "divorce coach" into your Internet search engine to find the right coach for you. To protect yourself legally, discuss the following with a family-law or divorce attorney:

Economic risks
Division of retirement benefits and other assets
Legal separation versus divorce
Social Security
Medicare
Maintenance (formerly known as alimony)
Real estate strategies
Divvying up assets and possessions (including family pets)
Financial and legal effects of the divorce on adult children and grandchildren
Financial support of dependent children and aging parents
Legal fees and who pays

Here are a few helpful resources:

The Lilac Tree: www.thelilactree.org. Provides education, support, and access to resources for women at any stage of the divorce process—contemplating, divorcing, or divorced.

Splitsville: www.splitsville.com. Offers a social utility where you can connect with others who are divorcing or divorced, swap stories, and get ideas and solutions. It's free, and you can remain anonymous.

Estranged and Alienated

To *estrange* means to make indifferent.[5] To *alienate* means to make separate.[6]

Are you currently living with losses associated with family estrangement or alienation? Or is it you who decided to act or withdraw? One or several of the following scenarios is typically the cause behind a formerly close relationship separation:

Someone said something he or she shouldn't have.
Someone did something he or she shouldn't have.
Someone did not say something that he or she should have.

Someone did not do something that he or she should have.

Not sure what happened.

A blog post on Disinherited (www.disinherited.com) reports that family estrangement is found everywhere in society, from the wealthiest to the poorest. "Although there is a shocking lack of statistics available on family estrangement, contemporaries in other fields, such as family counsellors, report a tremendous increase in the number of family members who no longer communicate with each other."[7]

Unmet expectations, entitlement attitudes, divorce, intolerance, disapprovals, addictions, abuses, and incarcerations are among the many reasons why sons and daughters rarely see or talk to Mom and Dad, if at all; parents disengage with offspring; young children are alienated from grandparents; and siblings simply stop speaking to each other. Once upon a time there was a family connection and now there is not.

Psychotherapists readily admit that not all separations between parents and their adult children can or should be reconciled.[8] In heinous situations, where a family member is abusive, cruel, irresponsible, and/or neglectful—or even homicidal—removing oneself from the situation is understandable. Every person has the right to make decisions that keep them feeling safe.

In years past, we rarely heard about physical separations within the family unit—we literally needed each other to survive—and family members honored the natural bond between them. Today, it is a different world. The definition of "family" has evolved [9] and the traditional notion of "blood is thicker than water" appears to have gone by the wayside.

Whether you are on the receiving end of a relationship breakup or are the one who chose to leave, you may be wondering whether it's worth trying to patch up the relationship or if it is even a possibility. Seek the advice of professionals to guide you during these extremely emotional times.

The website of Dr. Joshua Coleman (www.drjoshuacoleman.com) is a perfect place to gain insights. Dr. Coleman is cochair of the Council on Contemporary Families and a psychologist with a private practice in the San Francisco Bay Area. His comprehensive website offers books, webinars, online forums, and other resources.

Search the Internet to locate a variety of support groups, some of which are designed to specifically support estranged and alienated parents and grandparents, and others to support estranged and alienated adult children and grandchildren.

Specialty Facebook groups (www.facebook.com) connect you with others who are experiencing similar situations. Groups may be posted as "closed" due to privacy needs, but ask to join anyway. Requests to join are typically recognized quickly. Once you join the group, members agree to keep all information confidential. To locate these online support groups, type "estranged and alienated" into the Facebook search engine.

The following resources also offer estrangement and alienation guidance and support:

Empowering Parents: www.empoweringparents.com
Estranged Parents Speak Up: http://peacefulparents/proboards.com
Estranged Stories: www.estrangedstories.com
Estrangements: www.estrangements.com
Parents, Families, Friends, and Allies United with LGBTQ (PFLAG): http://home.pflag.org
Rejected Parents: www.rejectedparents.net
Stand Alone: www. standalone.org.uk

Score One for Grandma and Grandpa

Personal conflicts between parents and children have a detrimental impact on the relationship between grandparents and their children's offspring. The good news is every state has provided a way for grandparents to petition for contact with their grandchildren, although there are wide-ranging differences among the individual state statutes.

"The network of state-specific laws probably worked fairly well for years, when families tended to inhabit small geographical areas. It doesn't work so well now, when families can be scattered across the nation," writes Susan Adcox, grandparent expert at Grandparents-About (http://grandparents.about.com). "This means that grandparents in search of information must conduct state-specific searches, after determining which state has jurisdiction. (It's usually the state in which the grandchildren reside.)" Type "visitation rights by state" into the Grandparents-About website search engine to locate specific states. The website also offers invaluable insights on what is meant by "grandparent rights" and steps to take to avoid court proceedings.

Also, check out Alienated Grandparents Anonymous Incorporated (http://www.aga-fl.org). This organization provides support and information, and helps validate the feelings of those suffering some degree of estrangement, alienation, or isolation.

Stop the Whispers

It is time to take family estrangement and alienation out of the closet and into the light of day. There is no place for shame or victimhood. There is no room in your life for people who behave badly or manipulate you to get whatever it is they want.

In the meantime, should someone ask about your estrangement or alienation situation, why not simply say, "Unfortunately, at this moment we are not in touch." You also have the choice of bringing up the situation in a conversation, since chances are anybody you speak with these days most likely has a similar story to share about estrangement and alienation.

You have no idea how the story will end, yet your goal of fostering close relationships to carry you through to old age remains. Family members—including "black sheep"—do not define us. We define ourselves. Continue to stay focused on your long-term care objectives and plans, and the rest will fall into place.

Insights and Inspiration

Recommended Reading: *Conscious Living, Conscious Aging: Embrace & Savor Your Next Chapter* (2014) by Ron Pevny

Recommended YouTube: *Somebody That I Used to Know*, performed by Gotye, written by Walter Andre De Backer

Recommended Movie: *Griefwalker* (2008)

Recommended Song: "This Is It," performed by Kenny Loggins, written by Kenneth Clark Loggins and Michael McDonald

Recommended TED Talk: "On Being Wrong," presented by Kathryn Schulz, wrongologist, filmed March 2011

Zero Isolation

Foraging for family

10

Parents, children, spouses, partners, grandparents, grandchildren, siblings, relatives, friends, neighbors, and strangers—these are the people we used to know, people we know well, and people we don't know yet.

Cultivate friends of all ages, advises my favorite *Chicago Tribune* columnist, Mary Schmich (@MarySchmich on Twitter). "Your friends are people in the same phase of anxiety and hope and striving, peers who know the same slang, can sing the same songs, have similar ideas of what to wear to a party. But through the decades, as my idea of old has changed, I've learned how friendship can span the age gap and how being friends with someone much older or much younger can widen your world."

You get the picture. It's only natural that people in your life of all ages will continue to come and go through a revolving door, yet you do not have to end up old and alone unless you choose to do nothing to prevent that from happening. An ongoing stream of people is available to all of us.

Home Alone

Some people choose aloneness as a means of savoring solitude and serenity. This is a common experience, not an exception, and the appeal of living alone is not at all surprising—live as neatly or as messy as you like, talk to yourself a lot, stay in your pajamas all day, be

Objectives

After completing the chapter "Zero Isolation," you will be able to:

- Create ways to enjoy mealtime
- Thrive during the holidays
- Be better prepared to age without children
- Nurture existing relationships
- Access pools of new people
- Move on when friendships end

151

extremely productive with no disruptions, choose a home decor that fits your taste, and best of all, when you get home things are exactly where you left them.

Living alone can be the farthest thing from lonely, but the bottom line is that it ultimately depends on the individual. Society nudges us to get married or at least "couple" with someone; then, somehow we are magically healthier and live longer. While there is some truth in the benefits of togetherness over loneliness, living with someone else is *not* the deciding factor. I know plenty of people (and so do you) who are miserable in their committed relationships.

Where do you stand on the concept of living alone? You may be outgoing and social, or quiet and content. Either way, you have decided that you recharge best when living alone. You may even prefer to be alone in dying and death. As long as you are governed by your beliefs and values, your choice to live solo must be respected. *You* choose how to convey this important message to others.

If, on the other hand, you find that living alone is difficult, Lauren Mackler (http://laurenmackler.com), coach, psychotherapist, and author of *Solemate: Master the Art of Aloneness and Transform Your Life* (2009), suggests, "Reframe aloneness as an opportunity to become the person you were meant to be—to treat yourself well, and shed old patterns that limit your ability to live a healthy, happy, secure, and satisfying life."

But don't expect the process to be easy. I, for one, experience great difficulty living by myself. Living alone is equally emotionally challenging when I work out of town (several weeks at a time over the course of many months). The moment I walk into my hotel room, my heart sinks. I feel sorry for myself like a kid at summer camp—homesick and sad that I am far away from everyone and everything I love. My temporary remedy is to get lost in a good book.

The Campaign to End Loneliness project (www.campaigntoendloneliness.org) believes that nobody who wants company should be without it. Perhaps you will find comfort when you visit this website and learn more about what others are doing to address this cause.

Mealtime, Loneliness, and Thoughts to Chew On

There is a poignant yet funny scene in the movie *The Lonely Guy*, where the main character, played by Steve Martin, walks into a restaurant and asks for a table for one. From that moment, he feels totally self-conscious, that all eyes are upon him. Does picturing yourself sitting at a restaurant table alone, surrounded by diners who are engaged with one another and their meals, instantly dredge up deep feelings of loneliness and thoughts of being forgotten?

For years, eating my main meal alone was a depressing experience. I struggled nightly; then, the lightbulb went on. Instead of fighting the emotional demons of loss at dinnertime,

I decided to make cooking and eating meals with other people the antidote to my anxieties about living alone. It was the perfect answer—for me.

For many, mealtime is a social experience. To this day, my tradition of dining with others as often as possible has kept feelings of loneliness at bay. Millions of solo agers eat their main meal alone. Are you one of them? If eating alone bothers you, here are some strategies that might vastly improve your outlook on living alone:

Shifting gears: You may feel like Steve Martin's character, that you're the only solo diner. Yet everywhere you look, people are dining alone. This fact may reassure you that you are not being stared at or putting your solitude on display. Because more and more people are living solo by way of widowhood and divorce, the incidence of solo dining is going to escalate for a long time.

Solo-friendly eateries: Dine in places that make it easy to strike up a conversation with a stranger (if that is what you desire) or allow you to eat alone without occupying a table for two. Benchlike seating and eating at the bar are a few ways to accomplish this goal. You can also frequent restaurants that cater to solo diners. No-interaction dining establishments are becoming hugely popular in the United States and in cities around the world where a lot of people travel alone for business. "The idea is that focus enhances food enjoyment. Diners speak to no one, not even upon arrival or to order."[1]

Guess who's coming to dinner? Take the initiative to share home-cooked meals with friends and co-workers. You are literally surrounded by others who are in the same situation as you. Invite them to your house for dinner.

In your own backyard: How many people right in your neighborhood or apartment building live alone and are housebound? Bring meals to the homes of people who typically have no one to dine with—and enjoy mealtime together.

Potluck: Start a tradition one night a week where everyone rotates having dinner at someone's house. Share responsibilities—one prepares the entrée, the other dessert.

Eat as you learn: Consider taking a cooking class one night a week. Invite fellow students and friends to your house to show off your new skills as a chef. If you are recently widowed or grieving the loss of a relationship, ask your local hospice organization about culinary grief therapy programs. Classes teach grievers how to cook for one. Mealtime is one of the most overlooked parts of grief.

Carry-out: Who says you must eat meals at home? Go on a picnic—the beach, park bench, outdoor concerts. Eat while sitting in front of your favorite outdoor landmark or at some other esthetically pleasing site.

Mix play with dining: From food courts at the shopping mall to zoos, museums, soccer fields, and baseball stadiums—you can enjoy a meal surrounded by a variety of fun and entertaining activities.

Switch it up: Eating your main meal at midday frees you up to be occupied with an activity other than eating alone when dinnertime rolls around.

Volunteer: When you volunteer to serve meals at the local homeless shelter, you are often invited to share the meal with fellow volunteers.

Group meals: Enjoy dining with others at the local senior center. The nearby life plan retirement community may also have a program that allows you to purchase low-cost meal tickets where you can dine with residents.

Rewrite Your Holiday Story

Thanksgiving. Christmas. Hanukkah. New Year's Eve. Valentine's Day. What's your story? If you dread being alone when people typically gather together to celebrate special occasions with loved ones, one of the secrets to contented solitude is to have a plan:

Stay real. The hyped "magical" expectations of the holiday are set by retailers and marketers that reap substantial economic benefits by portraying "fantasy" views of the day's expectations. In truth, real life doesn't even come close to feeling magical. One-sided media messages neglect the needs of people who are alone around the holidays.

Date yourself. Enjoy your own company and spend the day with the world's most important person: yourself. And no feeling guilty about putting you first. Indulge liberally.

Respect time as a finite resource. When you tell people that you don't have plans, they may feel obligated to invite you along because you "can't be alone" during the holiday. And not wanting to appear ungrateful, you may feel obligated to accept their kind invitation. But over the years you realize that making small talk with fifteen people you don't know, trying hard to remember names and faces, and feeling like a stranger isn't fulfilling. Think twice before filling the day with irrelevant social superficialities. A simple white lie, "I have plans," gets you off the hook.

Take on a home project. Paint a room or a wall. Rearrange your living room furniture. Clean out your closets. Work up a sweat and put your energy to good use.

Share the love. Use your day to write letters in your own handwriting to people you know would love to hear from you.

Keep a healthy perspective by serving others. Volunteer opportunities are endless. Soup kitchens and homeless shelters can always use an extra hand. Deliver meals. Cook a turkey and give it to someone in need of a meal. Visit a nursing home. Volunteer at an animal shelter or offer to dog sit so the owner can take the day off.

Heal your heart. Give yourself time if you are healing from loss, such as a breakup of a long-term relationship, divorce, or death of a spouse or partner. How much time? Everyone's needs are different. If you feel the need to be alone during the holidays, be alone.

Aging Without Children Requires Extra Work

Preferring to live alone comes with stigmas. So does aging without children. "I never wanted to have children," says a longtime friend. "While my mom told me she loved being a mother more than anything else in life, she never judged me or even suggested I do anything but follow my heart, my head and my feelings about child rearing. I think that is why I never doubted my decision. My mother's friends, however, continuously questioned me in my younger days and thought I was missing out on something special."

Other acquaintances tell of similar experiences about being judged unfavorably. People who are aging without children should not have to explain or justify why they are not parents. Add this topic to the pile of people others may discriminate against—the elderly, poor and working class, people of color, people with disabilities, and LGBTQ, among others.

Childfree (never wanted children) and childless (wanted children and not able to achieve the goal) voices must be heard. Health-care organizations, social services providers, and policy makers, among others, need to recognize and respond to people who are aging without children. There lies the opportunity for nonparents to step up and educate the professionals. The concerns specific to aging without children include:

Dealing with judgments, criticisms, and lack of empathy

Feeling ostracized in a parent-child and family-focused society

Being ignored in discussions about parenting, grandparenting, and family caregiving

Invisibility in data and local/national government policies

Paying taxes to support an infrastructure that benefits families (e.g., education)

Hospital discharging plans that assume the presence of adult children family caregivers

Educating and training staff who work directly with people living without children

Filling the void in media coverage, advertising, and sales efforts

Needing to rely heavily on extended family, friends, and strangers

Paying for expensive long-term institutionalized care

Legalities preventing LGBTQ parenthood

Assistance connecting stories, traditions, and legacy with future generations, especially when dementia is present

For additional information and support, check out Childfree (www.childfree.net) and the Ageing Without Children website: (https://awoc.org). There are also a variety of blogs, articles, and websites created by people who are in the same boat; start the process by searching for the terms "aging without children" and "childfree" online.

Committed Couples Need Outside Friendships

I only needed to learn this critically important lesson once to fully understand the value of friendships outside of marriage or committed relationship. I was twenty-one years old, and the expectation in my marriage at the time was that the partnership was supposed to *give* me something and that my husband *owed* me something—for example, I will never feel lonely again; I will never be disconnected; and I will never feel unimportant. Implicit in the union was that he was my whole world. And that is where I went wrong. The pressure of sustaining that impossible expectation crushed our marriage to pieces. What I did not realize is that I needed more "best friends" to bring a healthy balance to the relationship.

Stephanie Coontz (www.stephaniecoontz.com), author of *Marriage, a History: How Love Conquered Marriage* (2005) and director of research and public education for the Council on Contemporary Families (https://contemporaryfamilies.org), proposes that we raise our expectations of other relationships. "Emotional obligations to people outside the family can enrich, not diminish, our marital commitments. Society needs to respect and encourage social ties that extend beyond the couple, including those of unmarried individuals, as well as ties between the married and the unmarried." She further explains that taking the emotional pressure off marriage is a win-win situation. The happiest couples are those who have interests, confidants and support networks extending beyond the twosome. And such networks also make single and divorced people better off.[2]

Marrying again later in life meant that my husband and I each brought long-term same-sex and opposite-sex relationships into the marriage. This time around, nonstop communication has been the key to managing our friendship expectations.

Sustain healthy friendships outside of your committed relationship with the following guidelines:

All friendships between the two of you are open and known to the other.
You would not behave differently around your friends if your partner was present.
You do not expect your partner to enjoy the company of your friends, and vice versa.
You manage your time to be highly protective of the marriage relationship.
You communicate what is happening within your friendships.
You have established clear-cut boundaries around what you discuss within the confines of your marriage, and what is talked about with others.

Today, my husband and I have peace of mind knowing that when something bad happens to the other—illness or death—we have nurturing relationships to help get us through the rough spots.

Siblings—a Love Story?

Now is the time to assess the quality of your sibling relationships. The individuals you grew up with under the same roof may well be one of your most trusting bonds in old age. (If you have a history of an abusive or toxic relationship with a sibling, and you cannot or will not patch things up, feel free to skip this section and go on to the next; or perhaps this section contains insights you could share with a friend or apply to another relationship.)

The love and trust between siblings is like no other. You know what you went through together to survive childhood. You shaped each other's life, with each having a completely different take living within the family unit. You shared a variety of good and bad experiences. Siblings may have come to your rescue at the lowest points in your life, or vice versa. That history can never be erased. It is easy to dismiss the value of siblings because they have always been there. Nurture your sibling relationships the same as any other. Get over any residual feelings of "Mom always liked you best." If relationships can be mended, make the effort to fix them.

Staying close to siblings has other advantages. There may come a day that nieces and nephews end up taking care of you in your old age. (To this day, I am ready and poised to be the front-line family caregiver for one of my favorite aunts.) National Siblings Day (also referred to as Sibling Day) is observed on April 10. It is a day created to honor our brothers and our sisters.

Stay Connected

Stay close as best you can to people you already know, or suffer the consequences of having them drop out of your life. There is not only a need to stay connected, but to respect the value of protecting what you and the other person have already created together.

If you are divorced, your extended family also includes ex-husbands and wives, and perhaps your ex's new spouse, and their children. You loved your ex once upon a time. Is it possible to be separate without the hate? Check out Cards 4X (www.cards4x.com), a line of greeting cards that helps get certain sensitive messages across, especially when saying, "I'm sorry."

Your connections may extend beyond siblings and in-laws:

Cousins share your childhood. They share your family history—the good and the bad times. They "get" your family dynamics. They share your grandparents. They may be so close in age that they may even be considered your first friends. Reminiscing with cousins about shared experiences may become a source of comfort; retightening those bonds now can devolve into long-lasting benefits for all.

Your close friends have family, too. Stay connected to your friends' children and grandchildren. Encourage the same on your end. One day, those individuals may come to your rescue.

Reunite. Don't pass on attending your high school reunion. Former flames have been known to rekindle relationships, sometimes even leading to late-in-life marriages. Track down people you once knew via social media sites and reconnect in person. Attend alumni gatherings.

Assist a family caregiver. Do you know someone who is caring for an aging parent, parenting a grandchild, or parenting a special-needs adult child? That person can probably use a friend right now. Show up at his or her doorstep with dinner at least once a week, and you have most likely made a friend for life. You might also volunteer in other ways: do laundry, grocery shop, mow the lawn and rake leaves, do dishes, put up holiday decorations, clean the bathroom (or hire someone), organize a closet, offer to fill in while the caregiver goes to the movies or relaxes at a spa. You may also find this organization to be an invaluable resource: Share the Care (www.sharethecare.org). Learning how to organize a group to care for someone who is seriously ill may keep you connected to people who will be by *your side* when the time comes.

Does your former employer offer a "retiree club?" If you worked for a large corporation, chances are there are social and educational activities offered to former employees, and their spouses. Annual dues may get you access to picnics, sporting events, golf outings, theater productions, and more. Check the organization's website or call the human resources director.

Ancestry-type websites allow you access to family you never knew you had. Networking with long-lost relatives may pay off in terms of more permanent connections. Type "genealogy" into your Internet search engine to get started.

Are you adopted? Would you like to be? A heartwarming story describing the reunion of a mother and daughter after eighty years offers hope to people who wish to reconnect with birth parents.[3] More good news: adoption is not only for kids. Adult adoption laws focus on facilitating new family relationships. When parents adopt a child, it creates a legal relationship, just as if the child was their biological offspring. The same outcome applies when one adult adopts another adult, to formalize relationships that have endured for extended periods of time. Imagine a childless aunt who adopts her favorite niece. Or an older cousin adopts a younger cousin. Benefits to adult adoption include inheritance rights, permission to make important medical decisions, and increasing the potential for family caregiving. Guidelines and requirements for adult adoptions vary between states. If you're considering an adult adoption, obtain specific state information from your secretary of state. Also contact an experienced adoption attorney who will be able to advise you of the process and evaluate your situation.

Make New Friends

How do you feel about bringing strangers into your life? Feel queasy at the mere thought of approaching and conversing with people you do not know? Susan RoAne (www.susanroane .com), expert networker and author of *How to Work a Room, 25th Anniversary Edition: The Ultimate Guide to Making Lasting Connections—In Person and Online* (2014), says you're normal. She explains that 90 percent of us self-identify as "shy." "Maybe you find out through small talk that you went to the same school, or like the same restaurants, or even more importantly, know the same people. Entering and working a room, and overcoming being uncomfortable, can be taught."

Here are a few ways to meet new people:

Consider getting a job. Working is often a simple answer to interacting with more people on a daily basis. If getting out is difficult, and you can work from home, that will enable you to at least interact with co-workers, clients, and customers by using the phone or a computer. You may be able to find a job you can do from home, if getting a job to stay socially connected appeals to you. Also read "The Fierce Urgency of Money" chapter of this book, starting on page 57, for more ideas about reentering the workplace.

Go from volunteer to one of the "family." Certain volunteer assignments tend to lend themselves to cultivating long-term relationships—for example, Big Brothers Big Sisters of America (www.bbbs.org) and Contact the Elderly (www.contact-the-elderly.org.uk). Also, get in touch with Experience Corps (www.experiencecorps.org), RSVP (www.nationalservice .gov), Senior Corps (www.seniorcorps.gov), Circle of Care (www.circleofcareproject.org), and Royal Voluntary Service (www.royalvoluntaryservice.org.uk).

Surrogate grandparent. The idea is to become a grandparent for families who need one. Celebrate birthdays and holidays. Get together for special occasions. Even if you live far away, you can text one another and video chat as often as you like. Many faith-based groups run family programs. Your local senior center may offer similar programs. Find a Grandparent (www.findagrandparent.org.au) is a not-for-profit company that operates Australia-wide.

Also, consider joining a regional surrogate grandparent group on Facebook. Type "surrogate grandparents" into the website's search field.

Foster grandparent. Volunteers aged fifty-five and over serve children and youth in their communities. From troubled teens to premature infants, volunteers serve in schools, hospitals, juvenile correctional institutions, and daycare facilities, among others. Type "foster grandparent" into the National and Community Service (www.nationalservice.gov) website search field. In some cases, volunteers live on campus. San Pasqual Academy (www.san pasqualacademy.org), for example, is a boarding school for foster teens where "grandparents" pay below-market rent in return for devoting themselves to the kids.

Visit your senior centers. By some accounts, there may be as many as fifteen thousand senior centers in neighborhoods across America. To find one near you, visit the Senior Center Directory (www.seniorcenterdirectory.com), or type "senior center," followed by the name of your city, into your Internet search engine. If you haven't been inside your local senior center lately, you have no idea what you are missing. Meet many new people who are just as eager to know you.

Go to school. Research adult education programs at your local college, university, or public library. Studying together may cultivate friendships. Tuition is sometimes waived when the student has no intention of taking tests and being graded.

Talk to strangers. From putting a smile on your face to looking "approachable," introducing yourself to a stranger can lead to a longtime and trusting friendship. This approach is also your opportunity to not only connect with people who are aging alone but also couples and younger people; limiting yourself to wanting to associate with others who are in the same boat sabotages your goal to expand your horizons.

Make the laughter connection. If you are ready to shake things up and stretch yourself, take an improv course at the local comedy club. You'll meet people from every kind of background imaginable—from accountants to yoga instructors. Muster up the courage to belt out a few tunes at the local karaoke bar. Get ready to laugh and make new friends.

Take language courses. The process of learning a new language lends itself to after-class study groups. Students benefit by practicing and conversing with other students. Who knows? You may even end up traveling together to the country where the language you are studying is spoken.

Housing matters. Moving to age-restricted housing (starting at age 55 and over) where there is an activity director takes the pressure off you to come up with things to do. Cohousing, urban condos, naturally occurring retirement communities (NORCs), and village-to-village networks tend to attract like-minded people who want to stay active and connected. College towns tend to reconnect alumni. Type "best college towns for retirees" into your Internet search engine. Review the "Moving On" chapter of this book, starting on page 119, to read up on additional housing options that are specifically designed to enhance the community lifestyle.

Teach a course. Are you an expert knitter? Can you instruct others how to ski, play mahjongg, or paint watercolors? A friend of mine turned her garage into a beautiful art studio. Today she offers classes to children as well as adults—and has accumulated many new people in her life as a result.

Attend an adult coloring party. These are popping up in libraries, community centers, cafés, and private homes all over the country. To find a coloring event in your state, or to host a party of your own, visit National Coloring Book day (www.coloringbookday.com).

Meet locally. Build in regularity. Do something that is always on your schedule, such as participating in a book club or singing in a chorale group. Join a daily mall-walking group. Participate in a serial jam session with other musicians. Pray weekly with fellow church members or become a helper at your church or synagogue. Engage in sports that include a partner—such as golf, tennis, and bowling—or even find a team sport to play—such as volleyball or softball. Swim with performing aquatic groups. Learn how to play bridge or canasta—you will find many card-playing groups to join. The social networking site Nextdoor (www.nextdoor.com) connects you with people in your neighborhood where you can discuss community needs, ask for local recommendations, or even organize events with the people you see every day.

Be a mentor. Don't you wish somebody had shown you the ropes when you were growing up? Be an important person in a young person's life and a whole new world of relating will open up to both of you. Check out Mentor: The National Mentoring Partnership (www.mentoring.org), My Mentor Advisor (www.mymentoradvisor.com), and The Mentoring Project (www.thementoringproject.org).

Work among other people. If you work from home, and you feel as though the walls are starting to cave in, and you think that being around other people will do you good, check out Work Hard Anywhere (http://workhardanywhere.com.) Working remotely doesn't have to mean working alone. Meet fellow creatives. Share a desk, see who's getting work done around you, and network.

In addition, the following resources could bring you in touch with like-minded people:

Contact your local Area Agency on Aging for a variety of ongoing fun and affordable activities.

Visit Wikipedia (https://en.wikipedia.org) and type "social networking websites" into the website's search field.

The Transition Network (www.thetransitionnetwork.org) and the Freebird Club (www.thefreebirdclub.com) may be of interest if you are a woman, aged fifty and upward, and seeking new connections, resources, and purposeful opportunities.

Meetup (www.meetup.com) is a website that hosts groups in towns and cities around the world and connects you with people who match your interests—from the arts, politics, adventure travel, crafting, to reading, writing, movies, sports, and beyond. Meetup's strength is its intergenerational mix. Groups meet weekly, monthly or on a sporadic basis, all in person—in coffee shops and restaurants, members' apartments, and other local spots. If you can't join one, start one.

The goal of AARP Foundation's Connect2Affect initiative (http://connect2affect.org) is to create a deeper understanding of loneliness and isolation, and help put an end to social isolation among older adults. Visit the website to start building your social connections.

Ask friends to introduce you to their network of friends and family. Perhaps they know of others who share your interests and will also enjoy your company.

Making new friends takes conscious choice and effort. The most important question to ask in the process is not "What am I getting?" It is to ask, "Who am I becoming?" There will be days that you will be tempted to pity yourself or give in to your excuses as to why you can't make the date with others: "It's too hot or too cold outside," "It's raining!" Do the best you can to stave off isolation and loneliness.

Are Your "Friends" Really Friends?

"Why do many of my so-called friends keep leaving me when I get sick?" asked an attendee at one of my keynotes for a college alumni group. She further explained, "All I want is for someone to call and just be there for me. They don't need to solve anything, just listen. I've always been a good listener; is it really too much to ask someone to do that for me?"

Sadly, this is a common story. It rarely matters what the illness is. The unspoken trauma is that people we believed would be there for us simply desert us.

Achieving the goal of growing old with others at your side is made possible through a balance of giving and receiving, listening and speaking, cooperating and forgiving. While your network of surviving is made up of people, places, and things, thriving when the going gets rough ultimately depends on committed and trusting relationships that have been developed (and tested) over time.

Your Social Network May Be Wide, but Is It Deep?

Creating a dependable circle of support requires time and hard work. It also includes contemplating the following:

Knowing when to stop being a "friend collector," including social media "friends"
Cutting ties with toxic people and constant complainers
Getting good at recognizing when a relationship has run its course
Knowing the difference between a friend and an acquaintance

Certain indicators can tell you whether a new person is worth your time and effort to cultivate a dependable friendship. For example, reliability and trustworthiness are not the same in my book. I have a friend that I can always rely on to have dinner with me every once in a while, but this same person gossips about everyone. She has proven to me that she betrays confidences. Our values and moral standards of trust are not aligned. I enjoy her company, but I do not share information beyond "small talk."

Another way you can size up people has to do with the way they enter a room. Some look around and say, "Here I am." The people I am attracted to say, "There you are." These individuals are the givers of the world. Are you more a taker than a giver?

When I hold a relationship to a higher standard, and decide to fold you into my inner circle, you know it, and feel it deeply in your heart. You get preferential treatment—the kind of caring that money can't buy. I do many important things for my close friends and they do the same, and even more, in return. Here is how true friends demonstrate a committed friendship:

Friends ask how you are doing and listen for problems.
Friends do not lie to you and are brutally honest.
Friends answer their phone at all hours of the night.

Friends drop everything and help you.

Friends sit with you when you are sick.

Friends tell you they love you.

Friends express gratitude that you are in their life.

Friends trust you and ask you for advice.

Friends always make time for you.

Friends stick up for you.

Friends keep promises.

Friends make you feel safe.

How Do Your Friendships Stack Up?

If you already know that it is time to part ways with certain people in your life, and you have not made a move in that direction, what are you waiting for? Seek professional counseling if you would need additional emotional support. The part in this book titled "Ties That Bind and Unwind," beginning on page 139, offers additional tips and resources when dealing with troubled relationships.

At the core of friendship decisions is self-respect. You deserve quality friends who stay by your side no matter what because of what *you* bring to the table. It is your responsibility to think strategically about who they may be. Kind, caring, ethical, and warm-hearted people are truly rare. I personally work hard at finding (and keeping) them. I cherish them beyond measure. In the end, I only need a handful of real friends to get me through this life.

When and if people choose to part ways with you, you may never really know the reason for their departure since their explanation may not be the whole truth. People outgrow each other or grow apart. If you have done something wrong, and the other person does not accept your apology, accept that the decision is final; then, move on.

If you are abandoned by so-called friends when you are sick, you have other options for temporary support. When you are at your most vulnerable, ask for help. Join a support group. That's what they are there for. You will instantly be surrounded by people who are experiencing what you are going through.

Make Relationships "Stick"

You go to the gym so your body stays strong and healthy. Maybe you regularly go to the dentist. You spend time sleeping so your brain can refresh. What are you doing to take good care of your existing relationships?

Family and friends require ongoing love and attention. If you love them and they love you, stick together through thick and thin by integrating some of the following suggestions:

Throw parties for no reason. Keep celebrating life.
Make a habit of scheduling daily (morning or evening) walks.
Take a fitness or yoga class together.
Agree to meet one another's friends. Validate each other outside the relationship.
Binge watch favorite TV shows together.
Initiate a group activity—playing cards, bowling, golf, gardening, book club, movie club
Become tourists in your own community. Meet monthly to attend lectures and free tours.

Insights and Inspiration

Recommended Reading: *How to Be an Adult in Relationships: The Five Keys to Mindful Loving* (2002) by David Richo

Recommended Pinterest: Visit Joy Loverde's "Aging Solo" board: www.pinterest.com /joyloverde

Recommended YouTube: *You've Got a Friend in Me*, Randy Newman (*Toy Story* Edition), published March 25, 2015

Recommended Movie: *The Lonely Guy* (1984)

Recommended Television: *The Golden Girls*

Recommended Song: "While You See a Chance" by Steve Winwood

Recommended TED Talk: "Why You Should Talk to Strangers," presented by Kio Stark, stranger enthusiast, filmed February 2016

Love Is Love:
Pets Are Family, Too

11

Adopting a pet for two-way love and caring

Objectives

After completing the chapter "Love Is Love: Pets Are Family, Too," you will be able to:

- Self-assess whether you feel mentally up to the responsibility of being a pet owner
- Determine whether you are able to physically handle a pet
- Create a backup pet-care plan if you become unavailable
- Prepare for the possibility of rehoming your pet
- Obtain grief support when your pet is near death and dies

What does it feel like to be greeted by a friendly, adoring companion day after day? If you really want to know, ask a pet owner. In additional to being the center of a pet's love and attention, research offers additional benefits of pet ownership.

Among older adults, pet ownership might also be an important source of social support that enhances well-being. In one study, older individuals who had a dog or cat were better able to perform certain physical activities deemed "activities of daily living," such as the ability to climb stairs; bend, kneel, or stoop; take medication; prepare meals; and bathe and dress oneself. There were not significant differences between dog and cat owners in their abilities to perform these activities. Neither the length of time of having a dog or cat nor the level of attachment to the animal influenced performance abilities. Companion animals did not seem to have an impact on psychological health but researchers suggested that a care-taking role may give older individuals a sense of responsibility and purpose that contributes to their overall well-being.[1]

The benefits of owning a pet don't end there. A 2013 study from the American Heart Association (www.heart.org) indicates that pets can help lower blood pressure through sitting together and stroking.[2] These and other findings about pet ownership are important to know as you journey toward old age. Think about it. What if the missing link in your overall well-being is something as simple as giving your love and attention to a pet?

Can you see yourself welcoming a pet into your life for companionship? (After all, pets are never unavailable or off duty.) Are you open to establishing a routine like getting out of bed at a certain hour to walk the dog? Does taking care of something appeal to you? Sure you need your pet, but your pet needs *you*. Would you find making a commitment to be involved in another life rewarding?

Is Pet Ownership Realistic Now?

Not everything is as grand as portrayed in advertisements. Cats and dogs, among other pets, can suffer physically and emotionally every bit as much as humans—allergies, memory problems, hip dysplasia, you name it. Plus, if you tend to be impatient or are easily frustrated, acquiring a pet can result in disappointment for you, and the animal, adding to your stress, rather than easing it.

Most people begin the process of adopting a pet by asking, "What kind of pet should I get?" The better question to ask is "What are the needs of this particular kind of pet, and can I realistically provide them?" And how do you really feel about having to get dressed and go outside to walk the dog, regardless of the weather, the lateness of the hour, or how tired you are at the moment? I live in a high-rise and am witness to pet owners walking their dog at all hours of the night—especially puppies or mature dogs that have become incontinent.

Pets require different levels and amounts of personal interaction. Are you home enough hours of the day and night? Are you up to the nonstop give and take of this social bond? A cat, for example, may be perfectly content curled up on a sunny windowsill and left alone for hours at a stretch. A dog, on the other hand, may whine, beg, and bark incessantly until you toss it a ball or give it a treat. As you grow older, are you willing and able to give a pet the care and attention it needs? And what are the odds of sustaining your energy level? If you are not in shape now—physically and mentally—how will you be able to keep up with the demands of a pet down the road?

Keeping a pet under control is another consideration that cannot be overlooked. Cats dashing out the front door never to be seen again and dogs running into the street, narrowly missing getting hit by a car, are all-too-common occurrences. Are you physically able to handle a pet that wants to run for its freedom? Training the animal to be better behaved is certainly an option, but that, too, requires time, energy, patience, and money.

If you are seriously thinking about bringing a pet into your life, or even if you already have a pet, assess if you are in a position to sustain the cost of pet ownership as well as being able to fulfill the pet's needs.

Money

Do you have the money to cover all the expenses associated with a pet? Are there other places your money should go first?

ID tags/microchipping	Water bowl
Certifications	Pet food
License	Special diets
Pet insurance	Treats
Grooming	Chew toys
Dental care	Pet-proofing the house
Meds/vaccinations	Training
Emergency vet bills	Safety monitoring
Disease prevention	Pet-sitting
Neutering/spaying	Boarding
Bedding	Pet-friendly hotel fees
Collar	Travel tote
Leash	Crate or cage
Clothes	Pet therapy
Food bowl	Hospice

If money is tight, many national, state, and local organizations provide assistance with pet food and other essentials, behavioral advice and training, and low-cost or free spaying/neutering and other veterinary care. Local animal shelters and rescue groups are also invaluable resources for free or low-cost pet assistance. For more information visit the Humane Society (www.humanesociety.org) and the Shelter Pet Project (www.theshelterpetproject.org).

Housing

Are pets allowed where you live?
Are you going to be moving to a place where pets are allowed?
Is the animal in a safe environment—for example, no steep stairs, poisonous plants?
Will it be easy to make your house "pet-proof"?
Do you have sufficient living and sleeping space for the pet?
How will the animal be walked and/or exercised on a daily basis?
How will "poop patrol" be managed?

Is a security system needed to prevent the animal from running away or going missing?

How easy will it be to create boundaries where the animal can and cannot roam within the house?

Does your insurance cover if the animal damages property, harms another person's pet, or causes injury to another human being?

Are there other animals living in the house that need to be "consulted"?

Foster a Pet

Let's say you are not quite ready to take full responsibility as a pet owner, or have no desire to own a pet, yet crave the interaction of and affection of a furry or feathery friend. Shelters and rescue groups rely heavily on volunteers to temporarily take pets into their home or onto their property. Cats, dogs, pigs, birds, rabbits, horses, rodents, reptiles, and many other homeless pets need nurturing and valuable human interaction until they are adopted to a permanent home.

If taking in a foster pet full-time is impossible, you can make arrangements for shorter stayover visits. Shelters and rescue groups typically cover medical costs for fosters, and they may foot the bill for food and other day-to-day expenses.

Fostering is a crucial part of socialization—foster pets learn that they are lovable, and doing something that makes the world a better place makes you feel great. Everybody wins. Most shelters and rescue groups offer information on their websites about how to get started as a foster.

Pet-Care Backup Plan

If you live alone, who will be there to take care of your pet if you become incapacitated or are unable to return home for any reason? Have you made arrangements for someone you trust to access the inside of your house in the event that you become unavailable?

Someone needs to be informed that you are a pet owner. A sudden hospitalization, for example, puts your pet at serious risk. If you choose to do nothing, and your pet ends up home alone, hospital social workers have no choice but to call the local animal shelter to have your pet picked up.

A lot of people mean well and may promise to take care of your pet when you need a backup, but they may change their mind and leave you hanging at the last minute—your pet is too much trouble and now you are stuck. To avert this scenario, you are wise to make a more formal arrangement for emergency pet care.

Research professional pet sitters ahead of time—people who can come to your pet's rescue for any reason. Add their names and contact information to your emergency contact list.

Make sure that your doctor has the pet sitter information as well as the phone number of your veterinarian.

Check out Care.com (www.care.com) and CareGuide (www.careguide.com) to hire people who are looking for pet care jobs. Look for pet sitters who have gone through specialized training. Learn more about certified pet sitters by exploring the following resources:

International Boarding and Pet Services Association: www.ibpsa.com
National Association of Professional Pet Sitters: www.petsitters.org
Pet Sitters International: www.petsit.com
Volunteers of America: www.voa.org

Formal and legal arrangements in the event of your death are another matter. Include pet care in your estate planning. A document called a pet trust spells out what happens to beloved animals following the death of their owner. The trust specifies a "guardian" who carries out the owner's wishes for care including food the animal should eat and how the pet should live. Funds or property, or both, must be set aside to pay for the care. Not every state permits pet trusts, according to the American Society for the Prevention of Cruelty to Animals (www.aspca.org). If you go this route, obtain agreement from the designated guardian ahead of time, and give him or her a copy of the trust, because your will may not be read immediately. If you have adopted a pet from an animal shelter, check whether you are under contract to return the animal to the shelter if you can no longer care for it, to ensure it goes to another good home, and that your guardian is aware of this arrangement.

Another option, which is much less expensive and does not require a lawyer, is a "pet protection agreement." This document is available online. Type "pet protection agreement" into your Internet search engine.

Pets as Care Partners

If you are hospitalized, would you like your pet to visit you? According to an article posted on Vetstreet (www.vetstreet.com), more hospitals are letting pets visit their sick owner. "When a family pet visits, it's a real morale booster for the patient. It's comforting for them to be able to bring a piece of their normal life to the hospital."[3] Most pet owners would jump at the chance to have their pet at their side—to soothe their shaky nerves especially during the rough patches. It's a magic moment when patients and pets are reunited.

Now, the question is how to go about making this happen, especially if you live alone. If you have not done so already, plan with someone you trust to care for your pet when you are unable to do so. Candidates include neighbors (and neighbor's children), friends, a pet sitter, and a friendly landlord.

Most hospitals and rehab centers have a no-dog/cat-from-home-allowed policy, but those rulings are changing by the minute. Hospice is almost always the exception to the rule. In the meantime, try and bring a pet into the building, and the volunteers at the front desk will stop you dead in your tracks. Perhaps a call to your doctor will be enough to arrange for a one-time visit.

Inpatient roommates must be considered, especially if they have a genuine fear of dogs or suffer from animal-hair allergies. It is hard enough sharing a hospital room with a stranger and their human visitors. Ask roommates first whether they have any objections.

For health-care institutions that have a "pets can visit" policy, a doctor's order is usually required, along with proof from the veterinarian that the animal is healthy and up to date on vaccines. Carriers for smaller animals and leashes are a must. So is grooming several days before the visit. Pets must be accompanied by an adult who takes responsibility for the pet. Pets must be housebroken. Disruptive and aggressive pets will be escorted out of the building immediately.

If the medical institution is adamant about pets not entering the building and refuses to give permission for a visit, you might ask (beg) about a pet visit in a room off the main-floor lobby or in an outdoor courtyard. A short-and sweet encounter can make all the difference in the world during difficult times—for you and your pet.

Many hospitals have pet-therapy programs. Animals are assigned to work in both outpatient and inpatient departments. If you are craving the company of an animal, ask how you might participate.

On the other hand, if you are planning to move to an assisted living community or nursing home, find out about their pet policy ahead of time. Many are open to the idea of you bringing your pet with you. And thanks to the Eden Alternative philosophy (www.edenalt .org), many house community pets as well.

Emotional Support Animals

Emotional support animals, usually a dog or other common domestic animal, help individuals with emotional problems—for example, anxiety, depression, bipolar/mood disorders, panic attacks, and other conditions—by providing therapeutic support through companionship and affection. This certification is different from service animal certifications that assist people who live with disabilities.

Why You Should Consider Adopting an Older Pet

Don't rule out adopting an animal because it is not young. Mature animals teach owners to be compassionate and more present in the moment. A relationship of this nature is truly about quality, and not quantity of time.

These adoptable dogs and cats come to shelters in a variety of ways—their owners die or they cannot care for them any longer.

Generally, the pets are housebroken and have been trained by at least one person. They are less likely to chew on the furniture, and tend to be more settled and calm.

If you are considering an older pet, ask what medical care is included in the adoption. If adoption is not an option for you at this time, you can always ask about being a foster carer until an owner chooses to take over full-time.

Some shelters also have programs for terminally ill cats and dogs, which also includes palliative care and hospice until the animal passes away. You will also find a wealth of information about terminally ill dogs when you visit The Grey Muzzle's website (www.greymuzzle .org). The Grey Muzzle gives grant money to programs that help senior dogs all over the United States.

Three excellent resources to learn more about animal certification programs are: Pet Partners (https://petpartners.org), Service Dog Central (www.servicedogcentral.org), and Service Dogs, Inc. (www.servicedogs.org).

Re-home Your Pet

Things change, and now there is no way you can keep your pet—for instance, you may be moving and pet-friendly housing is not available to you, you can no longer afford pet care, or you may be diagnosed with an illness that makes it impossible to properly care for the pet. What must be considered is re-homing the animal responsibly:

Get the word out. Post color photos on social media. Include the pet's name and advertise its best traits, endearing qualities, and guidelines—such as no small children, no other pets, or does not like to be left alone. Ask friends and followers to share it on their social streams.

Solicit friends and family. Either they want the animal, or know someone who can give your pet a good home.

Let your vet know. Maybe he or she knows someone who is looking to adopt.

Seek a "no-kill" rescue shelter. Look for those that are dedicated to fostering animals while finding your pet a good home. Be sure to confirm the "no kill" status with the organization. The term "no-kill" means that a shelter does not end the life of healthy animals due to the lack of cage space after a specific time period (typically 10 days or 2 weeks). However, there are conditions when a shelter may end the life of an animal; find out those criteria.

A comprehensive resource for more information is Best Friends (http://bestfriends.org).

Parting Ways Through Death

Grief, confusion, anger, guilt, and depression are all typical responses to the death of a loved one. Researchers have come to realize that the death of a beloved pet evokes equally intense emotions.

The veterinarian is the best-qualified person to guide owners through the pet's various stages of life and death, including discussing the possibility that the animal is suffering and experiencing a greatly diminished quality of life.

When a person you love dies, you can speak openly, and consequently people surround you with sympathy and support: cards, flowers, food, attending the funeral service, and visits. Everybody understands why you might cancel important meetings, why you get teary-eyed at the drop of a hat, why you may feel like taking time off work. Everybody understands—until the one who died is a pet.

Love for pets is real and deep, and the experience of losing a pet to death is intense. And you often mourn alone. The point is not whether a pet's death should be treated with equal social weight as that of a human being. Pet owners deserve to be consoled openly after losing a much-loved pet and companion.

Feeling alone in your grief is not an illusion. You may even wonder whether you are crazy and if something is wrong with you. Expect insensitivities from other people right away—from the animal hospital that wants to put your pet in a heavy-duty plastic garbage bag and bury it in a mass grave at a pet cemetery to people saying, "Well, you can always get another one." You may also experience being accused of taking the death of your pet far too seriously.

If the opportunity presents itself, take time off. By allowing yourself to grieve honestly and openly, you can, in time celebrate and honor the pet who so enriched your life with his or her unwavering companionship. Surround yourself with others who do understand what you are going through. Realize that your other pets may be grieving the loss as well, and it may comfort you to comfort them. Numerous books have been written on pet loss–related topics. You might also want to consider the assistance of a therapist.

For additional support and guidance type "pet hospice" and "pet death café" into your Internet search engine. Also visit the International Association of Animal Hospice and Palliative Care (www.iaahpc.org). Hospice care for pets isn't free; home visits from the vet usually cost more than office visits.

One final note: Pet cemeteries are now beginning to accept the human ashes of pet owners for burial alongside their pets.

Pet-Owning Alternatives

So, you have determined that now (or maybe never) is not the ideal time to acquire a pet, but the desire to put your emotions and attention to something remains. There are plenty of alternatives. Here are a few suggestions:

Meet the animals on their turf. Visit petting zoos and pet shops. Hang out at doggy beaches and doggy parks. Visit an aquarium. Go on safari. Snorkel in the ocean.

Offer your help at an animal shelter. Shelters are always in need of volunteers—to play with and comfort animals, walk dogs, and assist with administrative or other aspects of the organization. You might also volunteer to assist at the next shelter pet-adoption event.

Also check out these two programs for veterans:

Pets for Vets (www.petsforvets.com), dedicated to supporting veterans and providing a second chance for shelter pets
Serenity Park Parrot Sanctuary (http://parrotcare.org/serenity-park), a special place where parrots and veterans heal one another

Adopt a stuffed animal. Petting and stroking a stuffed animal can be calming, and the animals go almost everywhere you go—tuck them next to you in a wheelchair, in bed, and in your bicycle basket. Battery-operated "breathing" stuffed animals look and feel alive (the stomach area actually moves up and down). The weight, the size, the fur, the paws, everything about the stuffed animal is unbelievably realistic. Type "breathing stuffed animals" into your

Internet browser. New technologies are also making it possible to hire specialty companies that make uncanny stuffed animal replicas of your beloved pet.

Befriend pet owners. Babysit the neighbor's pet occasionally. Offer to walk someone's dog.

Engage from afar. Hang a bird feeder outside the window. Watch animal shows on television. Stare at a fish tank. Subscribe to Internet cams that visit with animals virtually. Type "animal cams" into your Internet browser.

Love a robot. Through sophisticated artificial intelligence systems, pet robots tell owners when they are hungry, "speak" their own unique language and also learn yours, develop personalities, chase balls, bark for attention, respond to voice commands, exhibit facial expressions and what seem like real emotions, pick themselves up when they fall down, spring to life when you say their name, and purr and coo when they are "content." Some models also take photographs and videos and relay the images back to concerned family members. Type "robotic pets for adults" into your Internet browser.

Insights and Inspiration

Recommended Reading: *What Pet Should I Get?* (2015) by Dr. Seuss

Recommended YouTube: *Ultimate Dog Tease*, published May 1, 2011; *Ultimate Cat Tease*, published April 12, 2012

Recommended Movie: *The Secret Life of Pets* (2016)

Recommended Song: "No One" performed by Alicia Keys

Recommended TED Talk: "Four Legged Citizens," presented by Francis Battista, one of the founders of Best Friends Animal Society, September 10, 2014

Part Four
Safety Nets

Doctor Me

Reframing sickness and health

12

After completing the chapter "Doctor Me," you will be able to:

- Establish a healthy partnership between you and your doctor
- Check the credentials and ratings of your health-care providers
- Opt in for telemedicine
- Avert the possibility of medical identity theft
- Create a personalized formula for aging
- Obtain resources for medical tourism
- Learn the ropes of hiring a transition coach

Did you know anyone who died in his or her sleep? Are you aware of family or friends who were diagnosed with a terminal disease, then died within a month or so of the diagnosis? Have you ever been surprised to learn of the sudden death of people who appeared to be healthy and vital the last time you saw them? No nursing homes or assisted-living stays. No in and out of hospitals or rehab centers. Sick one day and gone soon after.

What is interesting about the people I know personally who "died short" is that they were nothing at all alike. They came from all walks of life and a variety of cultures. They also had a unique approach to going about their business of daily living. While some settled into a nightly cocktail routine, others never drank a drop of alcohol. Some abstained from eating red meat. Others enjoyed a steak accompanied by a baked potato smothered in real butter and sour cream. Some were early risers and others were night owls.

The fact that these people were so different from one another begs a variety of questions: How did they manage to lessen the need for care in their later years? What did they do to help keep suffering to a minimum at the end of their life? Did they follow a formula that anyone can latch on to? It turns out that the answer is yes.

According to David Gobble, PhD, director and professor emeritus, Fisher Institute for Wellness and Gerontology at Ball State

University (http://cms.bsu.edu/academics/centersandinstitutes/wellness), how to live well and long is simple to describe, but hard to do. Dr. Gobble says,

> To age successfully, you need to manage your life to maximize your physical, mental, spiritual, and social-life choices. You need to be physically active almost every day, pushing yourself to do enough to feel challenged. You need to challenge your mind with novel, complex, and stimulating activities every day. You need to engage in spiritual activities that give you purpose and energy to meet daily challenges. You need to partake in social activities that have meaning, and stimulate you to want more time with others. What makes this all hard is that you usually do almost half of your activities of daily living on auto pilot, never considering the consequences. So, become more conscious about these critical dimensions of aging, and you radically increase your odds for a long, meaningful life.

The common thread shared by each of my friends who did not have a lengthy dying process was a daily conscious decision-making process that touched upon the four elements of wellness as Dr. Gobble describes: physical, intellectual, social, and spiritual.

Looking back, one of my friends who had a short dying process *never* turned down a party invitation. She got herself dressed and out of the house, no matter how "lousy" she felt. A popular partner on the dance floor, she used to joke about being the world's oldest social butterfly. She stayed socially active until two weeks before her death. Another friend produced lavish Broadway plays after she moved into a life plan community. She was the casting director, set and costume designer, and acting coach. Her productions were first class all the way. She, too, was active until a few weeks before her death.

What these women had in common was a conscious aging process. They were diligent about growth and development throughout their life and into their old age. They were also purpose-driven. Coincidently, they both died in their mid-nineties after a short illness.

According to the experts, aging consciously is a process that is available to us all—sick and well—and it is never too late to get started.

Update Your Health-Care Paradigm

If you could, how would you change the current health-care system? Yes, that's a tall order, but surely you have had some unpleasant experiences—as a patient or a caregiver—that you wish had never happened. Did you sit in doctors' waiting rooms for hours? Did you leave a physical exam confused about treatment options? Were you treated like a statistic instead of a human being? Was your medical treatment denied by your insurance company?

You go to the doctor when you are sick. What if the opposite were true? What if you sought medical attention to improve and sustain health? Imagine a process that begins in the waiting room when you sign in and are asked to complete the intake forms. The questions on the form are indicative of a deeper level of involvement on the part of the medical staff. How would you answer the following questions:

What gets you out of bed in the morning?
What is going on in your life right now—good and bad?
Are you lonely most of the time?
Are you particularly religious or spiritual?
Is your cup typically half empty or half full?
What kinds of situations frighten you?
What makes you angry?
Who are the influencers in your life?

After the intake process is completed, you are called to the examination room. The doctor looks you over, discusses your intake form, takes a few notes, then prescribes a customized health-care regime that includes specific foods to enhance brain fitness, antistress yoga exercises, monthly volunteering, weekly dinner with friends, routine playdates at a playground for adults, and power-walking five days a week. Plus, your health insurance policy pays you a yearly dividend to stay healthy. *So much for fantasy.*

You are in charge of your health and well-being up to a point: you choose to eat and drink certain foods and beverages, whether to exercise or not, try to get a good night's sleep, and carefully choose your health-care team. On days when something minor goes wrong with your body, you do what it takes to heal yourself. When you run out of the necessary skills to fix what ails you, your doctor enters the picture.

You are the CEO of your body. The doctor *works for you* and is the manager of your care team. You and your doctor are engaged in an equal partnership, but you have final say on all matters, including how you die. You hire your health-care professionals, and can fire and switch providers if necessary.

Finding Dr. Right

Life does not travel in a straight line, and neither does the process of sustaining health and well-being. Sometimes there is a cure, and sometimes not. You are responsible for conducting your own research and keeping expectations in check. Doctors do not have the power to perform miracles, nor do they have a crystal ball to see into the future.

Your research can yield a lot of valuable information, including the name of your condition, how you got it, and treatment options. The more you learn on your own, the better your questions will be when you meet with the doctor. You'll also gain insights on whether you are seeing the right doctor for what ails you.

At the same time, the process of researching your particular medical needs can be overwhelming. It is important to realize that the Internet is filled with inaccurate information. Unless you have a background in medicine, discriminating between different sites is next to impossible. For this reason, the Physician's Practice website (www.physicianspractice.com) offers guidance regarding online health resources to recommend to patients, including:

Drugs.com: www.drugs.com
Hopkins Medicine: www.hopkinsmedicine.org
Mayo Clinic: www.mayoclinic.org
Medivizor: www.medivizor.com
Medline Plus: https://medlineplus.gov
National Institutes of Health (NIH): www.nih.gov/health-information
Pharmacy Checker: www.pharmacychecker.com
Women's Health: www.womenshealth.gov

The patient-doctor relationship is a two-way street. Both parties have specific roles to fulfill. Both decide on treatment options based on knowledge, experience, and preferences. Take a look at the following lists. Are you keeping up with your end of the deal? Is your doctor?

Patient Responsibilities

I carry notification of allergies and emergency contacts at all times.

I conduct doctor and health-care provider background checks.

I track and update my medical and medication history as needed.

I am committed to following the doctor's instructions.

I track what does and does not work.

I choose to get educated about my illness and conduct my own research.

I come to every doctor appointment with questions.

I keep asking questions until answers are fully understood.

I invite advocates to accompany me to important health-care appointments.

I have completed the durable power of attorney for health-care directives (also known as a health-care proxy).

I fully understand the do not resuscitate (DNR) guidelines.

I fully understand the do not intubate (DNI) guidelines.

I fully understand the do not hospitalize (DNH) guidelines.

My DNR order is known to my doctor and posted for first responders.

If I am unsatisfied with my doctor, I do not hesitate to search for a new doctor.

Doctor Responsibilities

Creates a comforting wait-room environment

Keeps patient wait times under thirty minutes

Treats a patient as a person, not as a statistic

Offers ample time in the examination room

Answers all questions with a patient-first focus

Engages the office staff and the care team in a patient-first mentality

Accepts patient fear-driven behaviors, and treats them respectfully

Educates and empowers patients to practice well-being

Distributes printed materials and brochures

Offers several treatment options

Is accessible by phone and/or e-mail

Knows patients beyond illness (e.g., solo ager, LGBTQ, triathlete)

Agrees to implement patient advance directives orders

Equal patient-physician partnerships are founded on mutual respect. To gain a better perspective of what is possible including how this philosophy of care plays itself out, research the following organizations:

Planetree: www.planetree.org. A mission-based not-for-profit organization that partners with health-care organizations around the world and across the care continuum to transform how care is delivered. Powered by over fifty thousand focus groups with patients, families, and staff, and over thirty-five years of experience working with health-care organizations.

The SCAN Foundation: www.thescanfoundation.org/learn-more-about-person-centered--care. An independent public charity devoted to transforming care for older adults in ways that preserve dignity and encourage independence. SCAN envisions a future when high-quality, affordable health care and supports for daily living are delivered on each person's own terms, according to that individual's needs, values, and preferences.

In addition to doctors, nurses, physician assistants, nurse practitioners, pharmacists, and dentists, consider adding the following wellness resources to your health-care team:

Academy of Nutrition and Dietetics: www.eatright.org. Offers dietary guidelines, food allergies information, recipes, fitness workout ideas, and a Find a Registered Dietitian Nutritionist online referral service.

American Academy of Pain Medicine: www.painmed.org. The goal of the website's Patient Center is to help you find general information about pain and offer assistance in finding a dedicated pain specialist in your area.

American Association of Acupuncture and Oriental Medicine (AOM): www.aaaomonline .org). Serves to advance the practice of AOM and educate patients by providing a variety of resources, including an online newsletter subscription, interesting research results, learning more about the pricing of acupuncture treatment, and what to expect at your first acupuncture visit.

American Association of Naturopathic Physicians: www.naturopathic.org. Aims to increase awareness of naturopathic physicians, help its members build thriving medical practices, and expand the body of naturopathic medicine research. The site also includes a bookstore as well as a search engine to find a doctor.

American Massage Therapy Association: www.amtamassage.org. Learn more about the benefits of massage, investigate current massage research, and find a therapist.

Health in Aging: www.healthinaging.org. Offers information on common diseases and disorders that affect older adults, with resources tailored to specific topics, tip sheets, and instructions on how to find a geriatric professional.

Mouth Healthy: www.mouthhealthy.org/en/adults-over-60. Get the facts about dental life stages, terminology, and nutrition. The site also offers a symptom checker.

National Association for Continence: www.nafc.org. While it might be uncomfortable to learn that you are dealing with incontinence and not some insignificant complaint, over

25 million people in the USA are in the same situation. The good news is, most cases of incontinence are treatable or at the very least manageable. The first step is getting informed.

National Center for Complementary and Integrative Health: https://nccih.nih.gov. Serves as the federal government's leading agency for scientific research on the diverse medical and health-care systems, practices, and products that are not generally considered part of conventional medicine. NIH research helps answer important scientific and public-health questions about complementary health approaches—what is promising, what helps and why, what doesn't work, and what is safe.

National Center for Homeopathy: www.homeopathycenter.org. This site answers such questions as: What is homeopathy? How does homeopathy differ from conventional medicine? When do I need to go to a professional homeopath? What are the costs? Will my health insurance cover it? Where can I find a practitioner?

Medical Marijuana

The WebMD website (www.webmd.com) answers a variety of questions, including: How does marijuana affect you? What are the physical effects? How does marijuana affect your brain? What are the risks of marijuana use? Additionally, the Cannabis Infoline has a medical marijuana toll-free national call center: 844-446-3665. Upside Edibles (www.upsideedibles .com) offers education and testimonials of persons enjoying the health benefits and relief of many conditions, the upside to ingesting edibles vs. smoking cannabis, and insights on the variety of medical marijuana products that are available to patients seeking information.

Reviews and Ratings Count

Fancy diplomas, licenses, and board certifications hanging on the walls of health-care providers may offer some level of comfort, but how do you know for sure whom you are dealing with? With the Internet at your fingertips, it has never been easier to research and compare health-care professionals, including the provider's experience, patient satisfaction, and the quality of the health-care setting. To obtain ratings and reviews, follow these tips:

> Conduct an online search by typing the person's name into your Internet search engine.
> Confirm graduation and said degrees with medical and trade schools.
> Type the person's name, followed by the keyword "ratings," into your search engine.

Type the person's name and "malpractice" into your search engine, which will bring up any past or present lawsuits concerning that individual.

You can also find a wealth of background information on your health-care providers by visiting the following websites:

AIM Doc Finder: www.docboard.org
American Board of Medical Specialties: www.abms.org
American Medical Association: www.ama-assn.org
Best Doctors: www.bestdoctors.com
Federation of State Medical Boards: www.docinfo.org
Health Grades: www.healthgrades.com
Surgeon Scorecard: https://projects.propublica.org/surgeons
To review hospitals, visit Centers for Medicare and Medicaid Services: www.cms.gov

The Doctor Is All In

No one ever feels like getting dressed and heading to the doctor's office when feeling sick. Besides, who has time to sit for hours in a waiting room, not to mention catching everybody else's germs? Living in rural settings where having to travel long distance to obtain medical care can make it even more mentally and physically challenging.

Initial doctor-patient conversations are always in person; after that, your care may not require face-to-face interaction or physical touch. Technology eases access between providers and patients. If there is an Internet connection, "telemedicine" is a possibility. What is needed in terms of equipment may include a computer or Tablet equipped with a microphone, speakers, and webcam; and a smart phone.

If you are game, ask your health-care providers what they offer remotely, and how to sign up. One app in particular to ask your doctor about is TapCloud (www.tapcloud .com), especially if surgery has been recommended. In addition to capturing how you are feeling day to day, TapCloud watches for symptoms that are clinically important for your personal health situation. A brief, one-minute check-in each day creates an unprecedented, real-time stream of data. This data helps your doctor and staff actively manage risks, identify onset of new complications, assess medication effectiveness, and help manage your quality-of-life needs.

Also, find out whether your employer offers "telehealth" as part of your employee benefits package. Applications may include:

Video-chats for routine checkups

E-mail surveys

Educational videos and handouts

"Smart" wearables, clothing, toothbrushes, smartphones

E-therapy with mental health professionals

Wireless monitors to track existing health conditions

Electronic medical records

GPS trackers

Price transparency

Patient support groups

Reminders and alerts

Not everyone is a fan of cyber-based home doctoring. While the convenience factor is a huge plus, a significant part of medicine is the touch and comfort of traditional healing when a doctor sits down beside you, especially when you are feeling anxious or in pain.

Electronic Medical Records

Medical records, personal health records, and medical charts—call them what you will, health-care providers who take care of you over time use these to keep track of your health affairs: They record observations as well as phoned-in reports of pain or other symptoms you may have; make note of prescribed drugs, exams, and therapies; list your allergies; chronicle past and current illnesses, conditions, surgeries, and hospitalizations; and document immunization reports and the results of tests, X-rays, and treatments. The records also contain personal information—age, race, where you live, your health insurance provider, payment methods, and occupation and place of employment.

Traditionally, written medical records were compiled and maintained in folders stored in filing areas in the doctor's office, with handwritten new information added per office visit, but advances in online data-storage systems have made it possible for providers and patients to maintain records simultaneously. The idea is to encourage "participatory medicine" in the hopes of improving health-care outcomes, reducing medical errors, and increasing patient satisfaction.

As a patient, consumer, or caregiver, an important goal of electronic medical records is to enhance patient relationships with their health-care providers, and the providers' relationships with one another. The following resources offer foundational information on topics related to quality medical care and technology:

Center for Technology and Aging: www.techandaging.org. Focuses on projects aimed at improving the well-being and independence of older adults, self-management of chronic disease, and patient engagement through technology solutions. Additional technology initiatives include increasing work force efficiency; reducing disparities and costs in health care by developing and integrating advances in telehealth, sensors, services, and gaming; improving communication and coordination of care; and improving health-care delivery nationally.

Health IT: www.healthit.gov. Click on the "For Patients and Families" website tab for a wealth of insights on important topics, such as protecting your privacy and security, better health care, greater convenience, more patient involvement, and tools and resources.

Ownership and the safekeeping of medical records vary from country to country. In the United States, the data contained in the charts belongs to the patient. Health Insurance Portability and Accountability Act (www.hhs.gov/hipaa) places the responsibility of the security of the data on the organization that is maintaining the records.

If you have not yet made arrangements with your doctor about accessing your medical records, you may want to do so immediately. Catching mistakes and oversights are good reasons to access your charts. Have they correctly recorded your blood type and allergies? Do they have the most recent emergency contact information? Did they accurately describe your family medical history?

If you are refused access to your medical records by your health-care provider, file a health-privacy complaint with the US Department of Health and Human Services (www.hhs.gov) or call toll-free 800-368-1019.

Lack of Transparency

If you have ever foregone seeking medical attention, skipped a visit to the dentist, never signed up for health insurance, or decided not to fill a prescription because of the cost involved, then join the millions of others who realize that the health-care reimbursement system for products and services is broken and out of control.

Emergency room doctor turned journalist Elisabeth Rosenthal writes about the dilemma in her book *An American Sickness: How Healthcare Became Big Business and How You Can Take It Back.* She suggests that health-care consumers "start a very loud conversation" that will be "difficult politically to ignore." We have all created this mess by remaining silent, and it will take a village to get out from under it. Her book offers readers specific action steps including the following:

Questions to ask during your hospital stay
Questions to ask before every doctor's appointment
How to deal with bills
Templates for protest letters

Stop, Thief!

The health-care provider is responsible for the information in your medical records. What is recorded is highly sensitive and personal, and you probably have the expectation that what is being noted is private. And you may be dead wrong.

Medical identity theft is a vicious crime that has emerged because of easy access to your personal and medical information, as well as your health-insurance policy number and Social Security number—creating the potential for a variety of criminal acts, including filing false claims against your health insurance company, making a profit on the black market, and obtaining prescription drugs to sell or satisfy addictions.

Thieves heist the information in a variety of ways—from photocopying what is written in your charts to hacking into online medical databases. Who does this? Bad apples include cybercriminals who know the ropes of taking advantage of online systems that do not have checks and balances. Other suspects fall into the category of doctors, pharmacists, nurses, and employees at nursing homes; providers of medical equipment, such as wheelchairs; and other medical personnel who know how the insurance billing system works.

The damage that medical identity theft can cause is long-lasting—ruined credit, loss of health coverage privileges, and higher insurance premiums, to name a few. To complicate matters, a health-care provider or health plan may unknowingly send copies of your altered and inaccurate records—with your permission—to another provider when additional treatment is needed. Your personal medical history is now not your own.

Be vigilant about safeguarding hard-copies of medical and insurance statements as well as any online documentation (including e-mails). Thieves are looking for information about appointment dates, names and addresses of healthcare service providers, lab results, prescribed medications, and medical procedures. Review your health-related documents for billing and insurance errors especially the possibility of being billed for another patient's care. Question all procedures that you believe should be fully covered by your insurance provider. The sooner you catch documentation errors, the better. The process of filing billing complaints is time sensitive.

To file a medical-identify theft complaint, visit the Federal Trade Commission website (www.ftc.gov) or call the toll-free hotline 877-438-4338.

Medical Tourism

A patient who dreamt of an attractive smile had her teeth capped in Hungary; weight-loss surgery was an affordable option in Mexico; while on vacation in Seoul, a couple decided to get a comprehensive health screening; hip surgery in India brought new life to an uninsured middle-aged American.

The world population is aging and becoming more affluent at rates that surpass the availability of quality health-care resources, reports Patients Beyond Borders (www.patients beyondborders.com). "In addition, out-of-pocket medical costs of critical and elective procedures continue to rise, while nations offering universal care are faced with ever-increasing resource burdens. These drivers are forcing patients to pursue cross-border health-care options either to save money or to avoid long waits for treatment."[1] Individuals are also taking advantage of airfare specials and quality low-cost treatments combined with sightseeing and tourist activities—thus the term *medical tourism*.

Considerations for obtaining medical care abroad require specific steps in finding the right provider, researching patient safety, transparency in quality health care and pricing, quality of services provided by the doctor and staff, accreditation from an internationally recognized institution, possible health insurance coverage, and aftercare follow-up when returning to the home country.

It goes without saying that there are numerous risks associated with medical tourism, and with the medical procedure itself. If you are considering this health-care alternative, you will want to know the answers to the following questions before booking your flights:

How do hospital and physician business practices and ethics standards vary from policies back home?

What are the country's physician and facility licensing and certification protocols?

How are the risks of infections managed, especially needle usage and practices?

What are the documented medical risks regarding the specific procedures?

What public health risks are patients exposed to abroad?

What is the screening process for blood supplies?

What are the risks of traveling long-distance after the procedure?

How long is the recovery process?

What are the aftercare and rehab protocols for this procedure?

How is patient autonomy protected?

Which laws apply if patients find it necessary to seek damages for malpractice?

Will your insurance or Medicare/Medicaid cover such procedures, aftercare, or possible effects on your health once you return home?

As you begin to research your options, check out these invaluable resources for more information about medical tourism:

Centers for Disease Control and Prevention: http://www.cdc.gov. Type "medical tourism" into the website's search field.

HealthCare Trip: www.healthcaretrip.org

International Medical Travel Journal: www.imtj.com/medical-tourism-associations

Medical Tourism Association: www.medicaltourismassociation.com

US Travel Insurance Association: www.ustia.org

WebMD: www.webmd.com. Type "medical tourism" into the website's search field.

Be Well and Purposeful Longer

None of us is bound to the aging process that befell our ancestors; the journey to old age is not an inevitable decline from vitality to frailty. We are wired to grow and learn from birth throughout our entire life—we just have to be smarter about *how* we age. Surround yourself with experts who understand the full spectrum of wellness—physically, intellectually, socially, and spiritually.

The wellness industry unites a broad range of organizations and professionals. You may have an interest in learning more about brain fitness. Perhaps longevity and "slow medicine" practices are of interest to you. Spiritual health and playgrounds for adults also fit into this category. The flow of research in this field continuously paves the way for breakthroughs of all kind—especially for people who are living with a chronic illness.

Wherever you are in your aging journey, a visit to the International Council on Active Aging website (www.icaa.cc) is sure to inspire you. This organization offers a variety of resources, including a wellness facility locator, preventive foot health, a walking center, fitness guides, and lifestyle tips. "All of us have the potential to create a seismic change within our life course. Science has told us we have the potential to not just live longer but better. Active-aging offers us the opportunity to fulfill our potential, regardless of age, socioeconomic status or health," says Colin Milner, founder and CEO of the International Council on Active Aging.

Here are a few additional resources to explore:

Age Brilliantly: www.agebrilliantly.org. This site offers a community platform for adults determined to live a longer, healthier, and happier life. Through engaging with peers, experts, and service providers, community members are empowered to take charge of their life and live better!

Association of Nature and Forest Therapy Guides and Programs: www.natureand foresttherapy.org. Also known as *shinrin-yoku* and forest bathing. Take a slow walk in the woods. Inhale the surroundings through your senses. No need to think or analyze; simply relax and let your natural sense of enjoyment guide you. Your body, mind, and spirit will thank you.

Changing Aging: www.changingaging.org. Founded by William Thomas, MD, this organization teaches that aging is a strength, rich in developmental potential and growth. Dr. Thomas says, "Aging is quite insistent and determined to have its way with you. The culture of aging, however is phenomenally flexible and adaptable."[2]

Genome: www.genomemag.com. This organization explores the world of personalized medicine, empowering you to use customized treatments to help you live better, longer.

Montessori for Dementia: http://montessorifordementia.com.au. You may be familiar with the term "Montessori" as it applies to education. This is a new way to deliver care that requires us to change all we thought we knew about dementia. The focus is supporting both the person and the environment, which is adapted to support memory loss and independence.

Philips Breathless Choir: http://philips.to/breathless-choir. Can people who experience severe breathing problems lead a fulfilling life? Philips believes they can. Learn how the singers have coped in their daily lives with such conditions as cystic fibrosis, reduced lung capacity, asthma, and COPD.

Rock Steady Boxing for Parkinson's: www.rocksteadyboxing.org. Gives people who are living with Parkinson's disease hope by improving their quality of life through a noncontact boxing-based fitness curriculum. Boxers condition for optimal agility, speed, muscular endurance, accuracy, hand-eye coordination, footwork, and overall strength to defend against and overcome opponents.

SingFit: www.singfit.com. This interactive music-making program is a cognitive and physical stimulation activity that fully engages the body and mind. People who are living with dementia and vision impairments enjoy singing and recording their favorite songs.

Music Man

Participating in the arts—singing, poetry writing, playing an instrument, dancing, painting, quilting, and more—can pump new life into your body, mind, and spirit. If you get the acting bug, check out your local theater group and audition for the next play. Dance studios also offer classes that may be of interest to you.

Maestro David Dworkin "sparkles with high-spirited virtuosity," reports the *New York Times.* He served as conductor and artistic consultant for three PBS television documentaries in the series *Grow Old with Me.* Upon his "retirement," the energetic and inspiring Dworkin launched his exhilarating new "fitness fusion," Conductorcise (www.conductorcise.com), a sound workout for mind, body, and soul, as a natural outgrowth of his lifelong passion for conducting, performing, educating, and physical fitness.

This conductor is a perfect example of how music can enhance well-being on many levels. Whether you are hitting the gym, commuting to work, or humming a favorite tune, music touches your soul. Music has also proven to be so powerful that doctors are now prescribing music for a variety of ailments.

According to the American Music Therapy Association (www.musictherapy.org), "Music therapy has been shown to be an efficacious and valid treatment option for medical patients with a variety of diagnoses. Music therapy can be used to address patient needs related to respiration, chronic pain, physical rehabilitation, diabetes, headaches, cardiac conditions, surgery, and obstetrics, among others. Research results and clinical experiences attest to the viability of music therapy even in those patients resistant to other treatment approaches. Music is a form of sensory stimulation, which provokes responses due to the familiarity, predictability, and feelings of security associated with it."[3]

Check out these websites for a variety of additional creative-aging insights:

Alive Inside Foundation: www.aliveinside.org. This nonprofit organization is dedicated to inspiring an "empathy revolution" through education, intergenerational practices, music, and film. An important goal is to reduce elder loneliness, boredom, and overuse of antipsychotic drugs, with a special focus on the 4 million elders living with dementia at home.

National Center for Creative Aging: www.creativeaging.org. This organization is dedicated to fostering an understanding of the vital relationship between creative expression and healthy aging, and to developing programs that build upon this understanding. Their vision is a world where all individuals flourish across their lifespan through creative expression.

Just Kidding

Whoever said that laughter is the best medicine was on to something. In his research, Michael Miller, MD, director of the Center for Preventive Cardiology at the University of Maryland School of Medicine, and author of the book *Heal Your Heart: The Positive Emotions Prescription to Prevent and Reverse Heart Disease*, reports that fifteen minutes a day of laughter is as important as thirty minutes of exercise three times a week. Dr. Miller also "prescribes" laughter as a stress buster and friend maker.

Choosing to laugh when times are tough creates distance between you and a painful situation. For a moment, you are *beside* your pain, not *in* it. Joke books, funny movies, and your favorite comedians make it easier for you to find reason to laugh. Here are few other ways to find laughter insights:

Connect with a professional laugher. Type "laughter network" into your Internet search engine.

Laugh café. Type "laugh café" and "online laughter session" into your Internet search engine.

Laughter yoga: www.laughteryoga.org. This concept is based on a scientific fact that the body cannot differentiate between fake and real laughter. One gets the same physiological and psychological benefits.

Insights and Inspiration

Recommended Reading: *The Four Things That Matter Most—10th Anniversary Edition: A Book About Living* (2014) by Ira Byock, MD

Recommended YouTube: Subscribe to *Attitude Is Altitude*. Type "attitude is altitude" into the YouTube search engine.

Recommended Movie: *Awakenings* (1990)

Recommended Song: "Stayin' Alive" by the Bee Gees

Recommended TED Talk: "What Makes a Good Life? Lessons from the Longest Study on Happiness," presented by Robert Waldinger, psychiatrist, psychoanalyst, and Zen priest, filmed November 2015

Chronic Illness: The Game Changer

13

Repairing holes in your safety net

Objectives

After completing the chapter "Chronic Illness: The Game Changer," you will be able to:

- Address the costs associated with chronic illness
- Create a work-transition plan
- Compare effective advocates
- Anticipate decision-making powers in the event of incapacity
- Consider housing alternatives when care is needed
- Become more aware of staffing challenges
- Take advantage of technology to enhance well-being

Arthritis, cancer, dementia, heart disease, diabetes—no one plans to be sick. When sickness is here to stay, it takes its toll on the body, mind, and bank account.

Few people escape an illness and/or have an accident-free old age. Every one of my old friends is managing the physical and emotional challenges of a chronic condition. I would never think of my friends as "broken" just because they are sick; after all, *they* certainly don't.

I marvel at their courage and grit. They fight resenting others who are healthy and pain-free. They fight the urge to pull inward and isolate themselves. They fight with egos that would prefer they hide signs of weakness. They fight hating medical treatments and procedures. They fight feeling victimized and marginalized by disease. They fight the anger of knowing that life goes on with or without them. They tell me that while they greatly appreciate the companionship of others who make their best attempts to understand what they go through daily, they fight feeling isolated and overwhelmed with worry. They fight fear every day.

With no cure in sight, the diagnosis of a chronic illness comes as a blow. What lies ahead is a veritable minefield of uncertainties—your safety net now has a hole in it.

Jill Morris, president of ChoiceWorks (www.choiceworks.com), a firm that specializes in helping people achieve personal power and high performance, has personally fought a lifelong battle with a chronic medical condition. She writes, "Though dealing with a chronic disease seems all consuming, it is only one part of who we are. We can make wise choices every day. By learning to accept and become more educated about the illness, we can connect with what remains strong—many of our bodily functions, plus our mental, emotional, and spiritual wellbeing. We are much more than the condition."

Manage Costs

A long-term chronic illness is an expensive proposition. Upon diagnoses of a chronic condition, there is an immediate need to seek financial advice from a variety of professionals—the doctor, financial planner, elder law attorney, your employer, and people who are managing similar medical experiences. Another invaluable resource for financial information is the website of the national organization for that illness. For example, if you are diagnosed with diabetes and you want to create an estimated budget for care, contact the American Diabetes Association (www.diabetes.org).

Meet with financial advisers as soon as possible. If you are employed, review your company's employee handbook and research insurance and benefits options. Look for guidance from financial advisers regarding the following: sick leave, disability benefits, veteran benefits, health insurance, flexible spending accounts, individual retirement accounts (IRAs), and annuities. Also, review the chapter in this book titled "The Fierce Urgency of Money," starting on page 57.

When you are in the presence of professionals who can give you answers to financial questions, here are a few additional basic questions to ask:

What will I be spending my money on in the short-term?
What will I be spending my money on down the road?
What resources are available to me to help cover the costs of my chronic condition?

Transition Your Work Responsibilities

If you are working full-time when you receive a diagnosis of a chronic illness, your career may be altered one way or another. In the meantime, you might be wondering about the following: Do I hide my illness for a while? When do I tell my employer, and what exactly does he or she need to know? Who are my allies at work? Should I quit my job or stick it out for as long as possible?

As you process your situation, keep in mind that business owners are breaking new ground as they integrate employee chronic disease and disability solutions into the workplace. For example: if travel is a substantial part of your job, you may be transferred to a position that allows you to work in the office; if working the cash register has resulted in a wrist injury, you may be asked to work in the customer-service department.

Upon diagnosis of a chronic condition, what you need is a work-transition plan.

Step One: Before *Disclosing Your Illness at Work*

1. **Evaluate your finances.** Meet with financial advisers as soon as possible to make plans for a time that you are no longer employed.

2. **Become familiar with federal workplace policies.** Visit the Job Accommodation Network (http://askjan.org) or call toll-free at 800-526-7234 and learn about the Americans with Disabilities Act (www.ada.gov).

3. **Evaluate work impact.** You may have to decide whether quitting your job now or being asked to leave later is the better approach. Safety comes first. For example, if you are a nurse, surgeon, medical technician, airline pilot, or taxi driver, errors can cost lives. Ask your doctor how your current set of symptoms will immediately impact your ability to work and how your symptoms will change over time. Also ask for estimated timelines regarding symptom changes. Discuss your ability to realistically operate an automobile if you depend on your car to get to work.

4. **Seek workplace counsel.** If your company has an employee assistance program (EAP) or an employee health department, you may want to schedule an appointment with one of the counselors to work through personal needs, and examine how your health and emotional well-being may impact your job performance. Sessions are confidential.

5. **Seek advocacy.** You may want to bring an advocate to the workplace meeting for emotional support and to be an extra set of eyes and ears. Make arrangements with someone you trust to accompany you.

Step Two: *Inform Your Employer*

Your immediate supervisor, the human resources department, and fellow co-workers will have their fair share of questions, and you want to anticipate how they will react to your news. You will be asked many times over to define your illness and the severity of your symptoms.

1. **Schedule a meeting with your employer.** Come prepared to share disease-related brochures and recommended websites that help explain your condition.

2. **If the plan is to continue working,** create a transition plan such as reducing hours or taking on a less demanding role within the company.

3. **Let your employer know your specific needs.** For example, you may require more frequent breaks or additional time off for medical treatments.

4. **Ask for your employer's assistance** when applying for benefits and other company programs.

5. **Agree to a confidentiality and/or communication strategy** with your boss regarding co-workers and customers.

Obtain Additional Support

When the need arises, you go to the doctor: You ask questions, conduct your own research, manage your medications, follow treatment instructions, buy health-related products and services, and hopefully, eventually you get well. The cycle of getting sick and getting well continues until one day you become too sick to manage most illness-related tasks on your own. Therefore a chronic illness is a game changer—you are now entering the world of care-givers and advocates.

Caregivers come on the scene by way of a variety of informal arrangements with friends, neighbors, and family. They care about our well-being and agree to perform a variety of home-based tasks on some level that helps us get by—cooking, housecleaning, laundry, providing transportation, managing medications and finances, companionship and emotional support, and even tucking us in at night.

The reality is that none of that care is a sure thing. Friends, neighbors, and family who are caregivers are aging alongside you. There is a good chance that they will be less able and un-available to you in the long run. Sooner or later, when your network of support can no longer manage your care, and you have the money to pay for services, you may consider hiring pro-fessionals to take over the tasks.

If you know now that you will not have the money to hire people to help you, and you are aging alone with no friend and family caregivers, start planning by researching the kinds of organizations that may be available to come to your rescue. Contact the following resources:

Eldercare Locator: www.eldercare.gov
Medicaid: www.medicaid.gov
National Care Planning Council: www.longtermcarelink.net
US Department of Health and Human Services: www.hhs.gov

To research local caregiver resources, type the name of your city and state into your Internet search engine to access your city's main website; then, type the following key words into the website's search field: "health department," "department on aging," "social services," "public guardian," "professional fiduciary," "elder care," "respite care," "senior hot line," and "senior care."

Even more options are available if you type the name of your chronic condition, followed by the keyword "organization" in your Internet search engine—for example, "Parkinson's organization" will lead you to the National Parkinson Foundation (www.parkinson.org).

Plan on Advocacy

As it is with caregivers, advocates are equally important members of your care team. Oftentimes, the caregiver and advocate are one and the same person, but not necessarily.

An advocate is the individual who shows up (usually in person) when you are most vulnerable; he or she rights wrongs, helps to prevent dangerous medical errors, sticks up for you when you cannot speak, and takes over when you run out of energy to fight your own battles. When you are sick, the presence of an advocate makes all the difference in the quality of care that you receive from service providers, health-care professionals, advisers, and anyone else who is involved in your daily activities.

Advocates know how to build relationships and get messages across effectively. With a specific agenda in mind, they think nothing of questioning health-care professionals about procedures and precautions. They are also perfectly comfortable confronting individuals when services are not up to par.

When troubles are upon you, and you are not getting your way, sometimes gender is the problem. Would a male or female advocate make a difference?

While being compassionate and fiercely committed to you, advocates are bulldogs when they have to be—and all in the name of making things better for *you*. Here are a few examples of what I am talking about:

Situation: You are transferred to a rehabilitation facility from the hospital to recover from a fall at home. While in the rehab center, you push the call button to request assistance to use the bathroom. The nurse arrives thirty minutes later, and by then it is too late.

Solution: The next day, your advocate appears at the nurse's station, with a large pizza in hand. He invites everyone to enjoy the meal, then calmly brings up the subject of last night's bathroom incident, and kindly asks for better service.

Situation: For years, you have enjoyed a scoop of vanilla ice cream around two a.m.—one of the little pleasures in life that you look forward to. You recently move into a nursing home. They refuse to honor your request to continue your evening ice-cream ritual, due to lack of staff on the night shift.

Solution: Your advocate makes a call to the owner of the establishment, and you get your wish.

Situation: You are being discharged from the hospital and you think that your Medicare-covered hospital services are ending too soon.

Solution: Your advocate helps you file a claim with the Beneficiary and Family Centered Care Quality Improvement Organization (www.medicare.gov/claims-and-appeals).

Situation: The fitness professional hired to train you in your home is consistently late. No matter how many times you complain, nothing changes.

Solution: Your advocate greets the trainer at the door when he arrives late for the next session, and questions him about his scheduling practices. The trainer arrives on time thereafter.

Consider Professional Advocates

There may also come a time when it is appropriate to call upon people with specific credentials and expertise to act as your advocate representative. Do you know a public official who would benefit from knowing what is happening in this situation? Would the local newspaper, television, or radio station consider your story newsworthy?

When all else fails and you have exhausted your free resources, you may find that paying for advocacy is well worth the cost. For example, would a letter from an attorney get better results?

As a health-care consumer, you have rights. In a health-care setting, request a written copy of the patient's bill of rights that guarantees access to patient information, fair treatment, and autonomy over medical decisions, among other rights.

Review the following descriptions of professionals who can work directly with you in a variety of settings including hospitals, community health centers, and long-term-care communities. Also, ask your insurance company if they offer patient advocate or care manager services.

Patient representatives: Also known as patient care representatives, these professionals serve as a liaison between patients, families, and hospital and medical staff. They advocate for patients' rights; promote patient safety; are a point of contact for organization-wide complaints, grievances, and concerns; and provide patient feedback to the organization to continually improve the patient experience. Start your research with these resources: AdvoConnection (http://advoconnection.com), National Association of Healthcare Advocacy Consultants (http://nahac.memberlodge.com), and My Elder Advocate (www. http://myelderadvocate.com.

Medical social workers: Also known as health-care social workers, these professionals are adept at helping patients meet their emotional, financial, and social needs. They may serve as case managers, patient navigators, and therapists. The largest percentage of health-care social workers work in hospital settings. Some work in outpatient health centers. In hospital settings, social workers may handle discharges and also review new admissions for needs that require addressing. They may help patients locate various resources within their communities. A medical social worker may also handle crises as they arise. This may involve offering counseling or therapy.

Ombudsman: This public advocate, usually appointed by the government, but with a significant degree of independence, represents the interests of the public by investigating, addressing, reporting, and helping to settle complaints and/or a violation of rights in hospitals, assisted living, nursing homes, among other locations. Complaints about practices at hospitals, long-term care facilities, and residential care facilities should be directed to your local state department of social services, department of health services, and county licensing offices. Licensing and certification reports are public information.

Life care managers: Formerly known as geriatric case managers, the expertise of these professionals includes attending doctor appointments and facilitating conversations between medical staff and patients, determining types of health services needed, monitoring services, overseeing bill paying, consulting, assistance with insurance claims, selecting appropriate housing, family mediation, advocacy, referrals for legal counsel, and crisis intervention in the medical setting. Start your research at Aging Life Care Association (www.aginglifecare.org).

Patient navigators: These professionals offer a full range of clinical advocacy and care-management services, including medical research and insurance resolution. Research more by visiting Patient Navigator (http://patientnavigator.com).

Patient advocates: Also known as health advocates and health advisers. When you have questions or are unsure of treatment options, when you are looking for resources, or are in need of health insurance counseling, or simply want to better understand your illness, professional advocate organizations offer patient-centered navigation, education, and decision-making support. For more information about accessing advocates, visit the following websites:

Aging Life Care Association: www.aginglifecare.org
Alliance of Professional Health Advocates: www.aphadvocates.org
Center for Patient Partnerships: www.patientpartnerships.org
Governed Advocacy Information Network: www.gain.org.uk
Kind Ethics: http://kindethics.com
Patient Advocate Foundation: www.patientadvocate.org
Veterans Health Administration Patient Advocate: www.va.gov/health/patientadvocate

Anticipate Incapacity

How is it possible for people to represent you if they do not know what you want? Do not delay. Execute a durable power of attorney for health care. This important document gives another person (agent) legal authority to make medical decisions in the event of incapacity. The form specifies how life-support decisions are to be made, and under what conditions. It is not necessary to hire an attorney to complete this document; the forms are available free of charge at hospitals, doctors' offices, senior centers, nursing homes, and online. Each state has its own form.

The Health Insurance Portability and Accountability Act (HIPAA) protects your privacy, and limits who has access to your medical information. If you want others to be briefed about your condition, you must make formal arrangements with your health-care providers ahead of time.

Also, ask your doctor or hospice agency for do not resuscitate (DNR), do not intubate (DNI), and do not hospitalize (DNH) forms, if any or all of these are to be your desire. Type "do not resuscitate," followed by your state, into your Internet search engine to obtain the form where you reside. At this writing, health-care professionals are debating a new name for the DNR, namely "allow natural death" (AND). Subsequent action on the part of the health-care team would be exactly the same. The definition of "do not resuscitate" remains unclear among professionals as well as patients and their caregivers. Be informed before signing.

If you do not have anyone in your life that you can call upon to act as your caregiver, advocate, or durable power of attorney, you lose control over what happens next. Chances are, you will find yourself in court, with a judge appointing someone to manage your medical and financial decisions for you. This person is variably called a conservator or guardian. To say the least, this is not an ideal situation.

Putting your paperwork in order and making caregiver and advocate arrangements ahead of time will make all the difference in your quality of life—in sickness and in health.

Decide Where to Get Care

If a debilitating illness strikes, and you think that you want to remain in your own home, review the chapter in this book titled "Aging in Place Alone—What You Need to Know," beginning on page 85.

Staying home may be ideal in the beginning, but face up to the possibility that over time your abilities to manage your care, among other challenges, can change. Even if you have the financial wherewithal for 24/7 home care, finding reliable and competent in-home workers, and managing them every day, is more difficult than you can ever imagine. Even after hiring the "perfect" care worker, you must have a backup plan in place for the inevitable no-show or sudden resignation. Also, be aware that some in-home care agencies only allow their staff to provide assistance up to a point. For example, if you stop walking and are bound to a wheelchair, the care agency may no longer be licensed to provide caregivers because of the heavy lifting required to transfer the person from the bed to the wheelchair.

The in-home care process can easily drag you down physically and emotionally. If you go this route, it is wise to use the services of a professional home-care agency who can substitute caregivers at a moment's notice as well as manage any other in-home care problems you may encounter.

Depending on your needs, and assuming you can afford it, assisted living (also referred to as catered living, board and care, supported care, and personal care homes) is an alternate housing option. Assisted living is not synonymous with nursing homes. An assessment from your doctor, as well as the facility's health-care provider, determines where you will live within the assisted-living facility, as well as the level of care provided. Expect to encounter long wait lists to get into the "good" ones.

At first, the idea of assisted living may seem like a logical choice, especially if you currently live alone. *But not so fast.* If you visit a facility and have the know-how to assess for yourself what it truly means to live in an assisted-living environment, you might immediately do an about-face, and walk back out—unless of course you agree to surrendering your autonomy and personal dignity, you agree to letting your illness define you, and you agree to give up on thriving, growing, and contributing to society. If that's the case, welcome home.

Assisted-living staff are the kindest, most caring people you will ever meet. The first few weeks of moving in, you may relish the personal attention you receive. Soon after you settle in, when your basic care and safety needs are met, and the nurses, personal care attendants, and activity directors go home for the night, and your private room with the flat-screen TV starts to close in on you, and you are jarred out of your sleep by loud echoing clinking sounds emanating from medication carts rolling down institutional hallways, and the constant screech of walkie-talkies penetrates your eardrums, and you are surrounded by other residents who are in the later-stages of dementia and you have no one to talk to, and the person in the next room starts screaming at the top of her lungs at two a.m.—*then what?*

Over time, a disempowered environment will wear you down and send you into an emotional spiral of despair, boredom, and helplessness. Keep in mind that the grossly underpaid staff is also trapped in the same system that is mostly defined by medically related tasks.

Abraham Maslow uses the terms "physiological," "safety," "love," "belongingness," "esteem," "self-actualization," and "self-transcendence" to describe patterns that generally motivate humans in their pursuit of happiness. When it comes to residing in an assisted-living community, this natural process that we all depend on is typically nowhere to be found.

And what's with the housekeeper who accidently invades the privacy of two mentally competent consenting adults who are in the middle of having sex? How prepared is the staff when it comes to resident sexual relations, bed-sharing, hand-holding, and knowledge about sexually transmitted diseases? Do you think that living in an assisted-living community should end's one's sex life?

A wonderful organization in the United Kingdom, the King's Fund (www.kingsfund.org .uk) has studied healing environments in all aspects. It envisions that the best possible health care is available to all. It accomplishes this through research and analysis that will shape policy and practice; by developing individuals and teams that build on the capability to improve care; promoting understanding of the health- and social care system; and bringing people together through events and networks to learn, share knowledge, and debate. This website is worth a visit.

The Green House concept (www.thegreenhouseproject.org) and the Eden Alternative (www.edenalt.org) are also worthy attempts to right the shortcomings of long-term care settings, but pets, plants, and small, homelike settings are not enough. And while there are numerous articles written to instruct prospective residents on questions to ask before moving into assisted living, the information as it stands today is not as extensive or up to date as it needs to be, and certainly does not reflect the needs of a resident who has no intention of "hanging it up" anytime soon.

Desirable assisted-living and skilled nursing communities do exist—to find them, you need to ask the right questions. Inquiring about sexual rights and dating policies, resident-led programming, purposeful-living initiatives, LGBTQ training, end-of-life education, bereavement support groups, and other resident-centered needs are a must.

Shopping for a long-term care facility begins by preparing a list of questions to ask and things to look for when visiting on-site. A list of standard questions is offered in the "Housing" chapter of *The Complete Eldercare Planner* (www.elderindustry.com), or you can find articles online by typing "tips on choosing an assisted-living community/nursing home" into your Internet search engine. In the event that you are a potential resident for a nursing home, there are grading sites, such as the Medicare Nursing Home Guide, found at www.medicare.gov.

Short-term assisted-living stays are also available. Seniorly (www.seniorly.com) makes booking a short-term stay in an assisted-living community as easy as booking a hotel room. Use its platform to support your temporary care needs.

As you begin your research, keep in mind that using the services of a placement company to assist in your selection of a facility is not a quick fix; you must continue to be diligent in your own selection process, or hire an advocate to assist with your choices. Referring agencies are no guarantee of quality care—they may give out the names of the communities with the highest rankings because finder's fees and commissions will be higher. Worse yet, if there is a problem, the placement agency may not be there to advocate for you. You are wise to conduct background checks on the ombudsman website (www.ltcombudsman.org).

Competition in the long-term care industry is fierce. As a prospective resident of assisted living, you are at an advantage since you have many housing alternatives—including the option of remaining at home. Here are a few more consumer-oriented websites when researching quality care:

Argentum: www.argentum.org/alfa
Center for Excellence in Assisted Living: www.theceal.org
National Center for Assisted Living: www.ahcancal.org/ncal
National Consumer Voice for Quality Long-Term Care: http://theconsumervoice.org
Senior Housing Forum: www.seniorhousingforum.net

By the way, you are not home free when you are accepted into an assisted-living community. Among other reasons, if you exceed the level of care that the facility can provide (for example, in cases of obesity or the onset of dementia), or you pose a danger to yourself or others, and the facility feels it is in your best interest, you can be involuntarily discharged or asked that you consider skilled nursing care. (Now you know why residents may hide an illness or a fall. They fear moving to a nursing home.)

Staff Problems Are Your Problems, Too

You may be ready to move into an assisted-living community, but it may not be ready for you. In fact, you can expect to be turned away if the community cannot get qualified people to work there.

Owners and sponsors of assisted-living communities have long banked on employees finding it emotionally rewarding to provide for the needs of residents. This is no longer the case. Employee turnover is high and job satisfaction is low. What keeps potential workers away from the care industry are minimum wages, unpredictable work schedules, language barriers, risk of injury from heavy lifting, emotional demands, and in many cases, no health-care benefits. The situation being what it is, how can developers continue to build more assisted-living communities when they find it extremely difficult to properly service the ones they currently have?

Some organizations are known to fill vacancies with workers from temp agencies. In a regulatory work environment such as assisted living, this option can be dangerous. Proper staff integration takes time. In the event of a fire or weather-related emergency, newly hired untrained staff may not know what to do; consequently, people are going to get hurt, and even die.

Care workers deserve to be paid a living wage with benefits and better job training—and an open pathway to citizenship. Many live on public assistance. To get more involved, contact the following organizations: the Marguerite Casey Foundation (www.caseygrants.org) and National Domestic Workers Alliance (www.domesticworkers.org).

The staffing crisis may not be fixed anytime soon. In the meantime, if you are thinking about moving to an assisted-living community, the staffing problems will affect you on several levels. For starters, you will no doubt come to care deeply for certain care workers, and when you least expect it, they will quit their job and move on. People living with dementia will find staff turnover especially confusing and upsetting. Staff response time within the community will also be affected since their numbers may be dwindling. Language barriers between foreign-born caregivers and English-speaking residents as well as cultural differences will also negatively impact the quality of care. Expect the situation to get worse before it gets better. All the while you can expect to pay more for care services. Go figure.

Now that you are more aware of why people say, "Promise that you will never put me in a home," the revolution to change the concept of assisted living starts now, and starts with all of us. The right place for you to thrive when you are managing a chronic condition is one that can fulfill all of your basic human needs regardless of abilities and disabilities. Before you commit to moving into a long-term care facility, consider all of your living arrangement options by reviewing the chapter in this book titled "Moving On," which begins on page 119.

Get Me out of Here

Your doctor will soon prescribe virtual reality (VR), 180-degree videos, and other experiential technologies for what ails you. It matters not whether you are frail, housebound, in pain, or immobile: put on a VR headset, and you are immediately and totally immersed, and in the middle of the action—physically and emotionally. And for a moment in time, your chronic condition does not hold you back.

VR experiences—real, fictional, and story-telling—reach far beyond entertainment and gaming. In "passive" VR, sit back and enjoy the ride. The "interactive" VR pulls you in and wakes up your senses. Go where you have never gone before—climb Mount Everest, swim in a fish tank, paint the Sistine Chapel, drive the Indy 500, ride wild horses in Montana, live among people in a foreign country, play football with the New York Giants. Learn more about virtual reality by typing "virtual reality for adults" into your Internet search engine.

I am also content using my smartphone as a tool to stay connected with my housebound chronically ill friends. For example, when I am out and about, and feel the urge to share an experience I know others will enjoy, I turn on the video chat feature of my phone, and off we go—to the park and walkways along the beach, Chicago's Navy Pier, to cheer for the Chicago Cubs at Wrigley Field, and laugh like there's no tomorrow as we ride roller coasters at amusement parks. These and other real-time tours are an inexpensive way to make a friend's day if they can't get outside themselves. My homebound friends tell me they feel alive and vital once more, and they are forever grateful that they can forget about their physical and emotional pain for a few moments. Share the gift of your freedom with your friends and perhaps one day someone will do the same for you.

Insights and Inspiration

Recommended Reading: *29 Gifts: How a Month of Giving Can Change Your Life* (2010) by Cami Walker

Recommended YouTube: *What Is Social Justice?* published by PragerU, March 24, 2014

Recommended Movie: *The Sessions* (2012)

Recommended Song: "We Gotta Get Out of This Place," written by Barry Mann and Cynthia Weil, recorded by the Animals

Recommended TED Talk: "How Frustration Can Make Us More Creative," presented by Tim Harford, economist, journalist, and broadcaster, filmed September 2015

Early-Onset Alzheimer's: The Value of Knowing

14

Preparing for the day you hope will never come

Objectives

After completing the chapter "Early-Onset Alzheimer's: The Value of Knowing," you will be able to:

- Weigh the advantages and disadvantages of getting tested early
- Create plans to finance long-term care
- Get your legal affairs in order
- Track the disease per well-defined stages
- Make a workplace plan
- Effectively share the diagnosis with grandchildren
- Help change the face of Alzheimer's disease

Forgetting the name of a best friend or adult child. Getting disoriented in one's neighborhood.

Losing things and being unable to retrace steps to find them.

Regularly failing to complete tasks at home and at work.

When you notice that people you care about become increasingly forgetful or confused, you might encourage them to seek the advice of a doctor, right? When you exhibit the same symptoms, would you follow your own advice?

While the notion of being diagnosed with Alzheimer's disease is frightening, there are benefits to knowing early on, as you can:

Stay in control of making important decisions

Minimize risk of accidents, self-injury, and injuring others

Create a team of people to oversee your care

Avert financial scams and abuse

Strategize to finance long-term care

Be a voice to change the culture of dementia

However, some experts advise that you should not proceed with being tested for Alzheimer's under certain circumstances. "Checking people who have no symptoms of dementia using questionnaires, blood tests, or brain scans has long been controversial. One key sticking point is that tests available today can't paint an accurate picture of future dementia risk."[1] Doctors report that poor sleep, depression, and stress can also affect memory.

If, on the other hand, you are regularly displaying symptoms that are causing you to worry, be prepared for the far-reaching and profound effect a positive diagnosis of dementia will have on every aspect of your life—work, relationships, money, insurance, care, and end of life. Making plans now to avert avoidable personal, professional, and financial crises will pay off.

Money, Memory, and More

Something is not quite right. People who know you well are regularly remarking that you are repeating your questions and commenting on your extreme mood swings. You are also beginning to mistrust longtime friends and work associates. If you suspect that you are a likely candidate for Alzheimer's, and have yet to be tested, making decisions now about finances and estate planning keeps you in the driver's seat. You may be comfortable financially at this time, but as the disease progresses it can rapidly devour your resources.

Financing the rest of your life will no doubt weigh heavily on your mind. Now is a good time to review the chapter of this book titled "The Fierce Urgency of Money," starting on page 57.

Sources for paying for certain kinds of care may include private funds, health insurance, Medicare, Medicare supplement (sold by private insurance companies, not the federal government), Medicaid, Supplemental Security Income (SSI), Social Security Disability Income, and long-term care insurance. Keep in mind that once you are diagnosed with Alzheimer's disease, an application for long-term care insurance will surely be declined.

If you are employed at the time of the diagnosis, you will also need to calculate and compensate for any lost wages. Work with a certified financial planner to create a budget that will cover the costs of the following dementia-related expenses:

Insurance
Medical treatment
Nutrition and special diets
Prescription drugs
Professional care workers
Safety measures and technology

Home modifications and medical equipment
Personal care, grooming, and bathing
Incontinence products
Physical and brain fitness activities
Socializing and entertainment
Transportation and travel

Housing, Including Possibility of Full-Time Residential Care

Work with an elder law attorney to draft legal and important documents. To accomplish this goal, you must be an adult with the mental capacity to understand the extent of risks and benefits, since instructions will create binding provisions giving away your rights to make certain decisions. Ask your attorney when you will be cut off from signing legal documents. Also, make a plan with the attorney regarding the process of storing your documents, and how they will be distributed when you are unable to handle this yourself. The documents to draft are as follows:

Durable power of attorney (specific duties)
Durable power of attorney for finances
Durable power of attorney for health care
Advance directives/living will
Guardianship (for yourself as well as dependents)
Will
Living trust

Work with your attorney to add an "Alzheimer's provision" to your living will. Highlights of this provision include:

Where you want to live
How you will finance your care
The process of suspending driving privileges
Preferences and instructions about care and treatment
Provisions for pets
Participation in dementia drug trials (or not)
Who makes decisions on your behalf and the extent of their decision-making powers

Court-appointed guardian provisions
When the document goes into effect and for how long
When and how to revoke the document even if you are incapacitated

End-of-life preferences are also a component of the Alzheimer's provision in your living will. To enable others to respect and carry out your final wishes as you would want them to be fulfilled, put your plans in writing. Read the chapter of this book titled, "'Just Shoot Me' Is Not a Plan," starting on page 227. Also read "Places to Go and Things to Do," starting on page 241. As you begin to formulate your plans, consider the following:

Care and treatment at end of life
Physician orders for life-sustaining treatment (POLST)
Where you want to die
Do not resuscitate (DNR) orders
Do not intubate (DNI) orders
Do not hospitalize (DNH) orders
Spiritual and religious support
Hospice
Brain autopsy and donation
Funeral arrangements

At some point, you will find it necessary to delegate routine financial responsibilities. Seek guidance from your financial planner and your attorney regarding options on how financial affairs will be handled. Money-related tasks include:

Paying bills
Arranging for benefit claims
Making investment decisions
Managing bank accounts
Incoming and outgoing mail management
Preparing tax returns

On a Scale from One to Seven

Depending on training, physicians and other professionals are known to use terminology that refers to dementia stages, descriptions, or both. There are seven stages of dementia:

Stage One: "Normal aging"—no cognitive decline or problems in daily living.

Stage Two: "Very mild cognitive decline"—trouble finding words, forgets names, forgets the location of objects.

Stage Three: "Mild cognitive decline"—difficulty handling responsibilities and solving problems at work, finding traveling to new locations challenging.

Stage Four: "Moderate cognitive decline"—finding ordinary tasks difficult; for example, managing finances and shopping, planning, and cooking dinner.

Stage Five: "Moderately severe cognitive decline"—beginning of the "late stage." Can no longer live without assistance. Needs help choosing clothes and tending to personal hygiene concerns.

Stage Six: "Severe cognitive decline"—loss of awareness of experiences and events, may fear bathing, decreased capability in toilet functions or incontinence.

Stage Seven: "Very severe cognitive decline"—limited vocabulary, ambulatory needs, requires help with eating.

Two excellent education resources to consider:

Alzheimer's Association Green-Field Library: www.alz.org/library. Located at the national office of the Alzheimer's Association in Chicago, Illinois, the library catalog is searchable, and includes borrowable resources, such as DVDs, books, websites, and videos, among others.

Alzheimer's Reading Room: www.alzheimersreadingroom.com. This is a searchable website that contains more than five thousand articles written to answer and address the most difficult problems and issues faced in Alzheimer's and dementia care. The goal of the site is to educate and empower Alzheimer's caregivers, their families, and the entire Alzheimer's community.

The Day You Hoped Would Never Come

Unpaid bills. Getting lost. Missing assignment deadlines at work. You fear the worst. You muster up the courage to get your brain checked out with a gerontologist or neurologist who specializes in dementia—and the test comes back positive for dementia. Coming to terms with an early-onset Alzheimer's diagnosis is extremely difficult, but it is the only way to move forward. Follow these strategies to get a better handle on what is to come:

Update professional advisers. Get in touch with your attorney, financial planner, and insurance provider. Meet with your advisers *before* you disclose any information to your employer. Ask for assistance in creating a "hand-off plan" in anticipation of when you are no longer mentally able to handle your own financial and legal affairs. Also, ask for advice on creating financial and legal protection systems to avert scams, fraud, and financial abuse.

Get back in touch with the doctor. Schedule a follow-up appointment. There is a good chance you absorbed little else that was said after you heard the diagnosis the first time. Hearing partial information may mean you missed out on treatment options and participation in clinical trials. During the meeting also discuss driving concerns if you depend on your car to get around town. If possible, arrange to have someone accompany you to this important appointment—to take notes, ask more questions, and calm your nerves.

Choose support wisely. You decide who to tell what, and when. It can feel liberating not having to mask shortcomings and hiding your medical condition any longer. The Alzheimer's Associations helpline is available 24/7. Call 800-272-3900 (TDD: 866-403-3073).

Participate in a support group. In-person or online support and message boards may prove to be an invaluable resource. Facebook (www.Facebook.com) offers closed groups for the purpose of venting and sharing resources. Social workers, grief counselors, clergy, and end-of-life professionals are also extremely helpful during this difficult transition.

Stay the course. You are experiencing a personal crisis, yet the intensity of your initial feelings won't last forever. Experts suggest establishing routines and resuming most activities, as long as it is safe to do so. Posting reminder notes, using day planners, and writing down your thoughts in a journal are also advised.

Seek Specialized Dementia Care

Surrounding yourself with health-care professionals who have been trained and certified to nurture your emotional, social, physical, and spiritual well-being is hugely important. What to look for is a philosophy of care that sees those who are living with dementia as people, rather than focusing on their illness or on abilities they may have lost. Instead of treating the person as a collection of symptoms and behaviors to be controlled, person-centered care specifically delivers customized care that considers everyone's qualities, abilities, interests, and preferences. Person-centered care treats every person as an individual. Consequently, the care plan reflects the person's unique needs.

Well-trained staff get to know you and can support you in ways that are personally meaningful. You might like to sit in the lobby and greet people as they walk by. You prefer to play the piano rather than participate in an art project. Publications, books, and educational sessions are worth exploring to gain a better perspective of the kind of care you deserve. To better understand the person-centered approach to dementia care, visit the Best Friends Approach to Alzheimer's Care (http://bestfriendsapproach.com).

The goal of the National Council of Certified Dementia Practitioners (www.nccdp.org) is to develop and encourage comprehensive standards of excellence in the health-care profession and delivery of dementia care. There is a profound difference in how you are cared for based upon staff sensitivity and training. Look to this website to gain additional insights on person-centered quality care.

Many people who live with the symptoms of dementia move into a care home once their disease progresses to a certain stage. Choosing the right care home can be difficult. The Alzheimer's Society (www.alzheimers.org.uk) offers a factsheet that explains how to find a care home and what high-quality dementia care should include, including tips on things to consider when visiting different home-care options.

Receiving a Diagnosis While Employed

If I tell my boss, will I lose my job? Good question.

While many people who are diagnosed with early-onset Alzheimer's disease remain at work in the early stages of the diagnosis, your employer might not agree to that kind of arrangement. Consequently, you may be tempted to conceal difficulties at work from co-workers and managers for fear of a negative response or, worse yet, being let go.

The Americans with Disabilities Act provides limited protection to people living with Alzheimer's disease in the workplace. It requires that companies with at least fifteen or more employees make "reasonable" accommodations for employees with physical or mental disabilities.

What is needed if you are diagnosed with Alzheimer's disease is a work-transition plan. See the section "Transition Your Work Responsibilities" featured in the chapter of this book titled "Chronic Illness: The Game Changer," starting on page 197.

Employees and employers are breaking new ground as they put dementia-related workplace needs into context. Type "dementia-friendly workplace" into your Internet search engine to access a variety of innovative workplace initiatives, guidelines, and resources.

Sharing the Diagnosis with Grandchildren

As you begin to confront the realities of the disease, people around you are experiencing struggles of their own, especially grandchildren who may not completely understand how your illness will eventually take its toll *on them*. It's natural to want to protect them, but if you are assuming that they do not notice that something is wrong, you are probably mistaken.

Initially, they may be wondering why you no longer ask them to do fun activities together or feel hurt that you don't laugh with them as much as before. They may think that it is strange that you don't remember their names. The reality is that children are observant and worry when someone they love changes their behavior toward them and, worse yet, seems to have disappeared from their life.

Grandchildren will have questions that deserve straight answers. If you are newly diagnosed and are able to do so, the best person for that job is *you*. Take charge of the relationships you have with the children in your life and talk with them about your Alzheimer's diagnosis. To begin, experts advise the following:

Treat each child individually.

Disclose the type of information that child is capable of understanding.

Decide how much information that child can handle in one sitting.

Allow children as much time as they need to discuss their feelings.

Share your own feelings of sadness or worry, but balance the conversation with how being a family and helping one another is important.

Make good use of communication tools, such as books written especially for children and teens.

The National Institute on Aging (www.nia.nih.gov) website offers tips on talking with children about the disease. Type "resources for children and teens about Alzheimer's disease" into the website's search field.

Teepa Snow's website offers communication tips as well as a comprehensive list for suggested books to read to children. Visit http://teepasnow.com/resources/for-kids-teens.

Type "kids and teens" in the Alzheimer's Association website search engine (www.alz.org).

Alzheimer's: Not a Prescription to Stop Living

What people say and do after you disclose to them the fact that you have been diagnosed with Alzheimer's disease is not a reflection of *you*; rather, it is indicative of their lack of exposure to the disease and education. Be prepared for others to behave badly:

Family members are quick to feel stressed and prepare for the worst.

So-called friends are quick to disengage or disappear altogether.

The medical community is quick to prescribe pharma-centric treatments.

Employers are quick to disempower and dismiss.

The general public is quick to stigmatize and discriminate.

Blogger, radio host, and dementia advocate Lori La Bey, founder of Alzheimer's Speaks (www.alzheimersspeaks.com), understands all too well. She recalls many stories, especially one told by her good friend, Dr. Richard Taylor, a leading voice living with dementia. "He said that once he told family and friends about his diagnosis, he knew by the way they would hug him if he would ever see them again. Richard's insights were a profound showing of the power of non-verbal communication, which for most of us is an unconscious mode."

When it comes to how Alzheimer's disease is typically described, the media is doing more damage than good. News reports and advertisements typically employ fear-mongering rhetoric, such as *dreaded, nightmare, burden, unraveling, disappearing*, and *sufferer*, to paint a picture of total despair.

Forgetfulness and memory loss are not "normal" or expected outcomes of aging, yet biases, negative labeling, misunderstandings, and injustices prevail—this is how the world behaves toward men and women who are living with Alzheimer's disease. Stigmas are what many people who are living with dementia fear the most.

On the other side of the disease, the more enlightened clinicians are turning to people who are living with forgetfulness, and asking them for advice on how to change the culture of dementia. Here are a few examples of innovative dementia initiatives you will want to explore:

Alive Inside: www.aliveinside.us

Dementia Action Alliance: http://daanow.org

Dementia Alliance International: www.dementiaallianceinternational.org

Disrupt Dementia: https://drbillthomas.org/local/disrupt-dementia

Giving Voice Chorus: www.givingvoicechorus.org

Purple Angel Dementia Awareness Campaign: www.purpleangel-global.com
Together in This: http://togetherinthis.com
To Whom I May Concern: www.towhomimayconcern.info
Young Dementia UK: www.youngdementiauk.org

People who are living with early-onset Alzheimer's disease are pushing back on biases: writing books, giving speeches, raising funds for dementia organizations, creating blogs, engaging social media outlets, and producing videos, among other communication activities. Michael Ellenbogen (http://michaelellenbogenmovement.com) is a tireless advocate, writer, husband, and father. In 2008, at age forty-nine, he was diagnosed with Alzheimer's disease after struggling to get a diagnosis since his first symptoms at age thirty-nine. He explains that he got into advocacy because he saw firsthand how society was not treating those with dementia fairly. "There is so much negative stigma around this disease. A person with dementia loses the freedom to drive, freedom to conduct financial affairs, freedom to travel alone, freedom to choose how to die, and lack of funding towards the cure and quality of life. A person should not lose their freedom because they get Alzheimer's. That is the mission I have hoped to change."

If you are so inclined to join the cause or want to learn more about creating a dementia-friendly initiative in your neighborhood, read the chapter of the book titled "Bring Livability Home," starting on page 103. You might also want to check out my Pinterest board, "Early-onset Alzheimer's," for hundreds of innovative ideas for living with dementia (www.pinterest.com/joyloverde).

In January 2006, the Alzheimer's Association established an advisory group composed of people in the early stages of Alzheimer's disease. The group is helping the association provide the most appropriate services for people living with early-stage Alzheimer's, raise awareness about early-stage needs, and advocate with legislators to increase funding for research and support programs. The association continues to seek dynamic individuals living with early-stage Alzheimer's or related dementias to join the Early-Stage Advisory Group. This important group of advisers brings the unique perspective of persons living with the disease to key efforts of the national association, including advocacy, education and programming, and consumer awareness initiatives. For more information, visit the Alzheimer's Association website (www.alz.org/about_us_early_stage_advisory_group.asp).

You Say You Want a Revolution

When asked, most people say that discovering a cure is a top priority for dealing with Alzheimer's disease. And it's safe to say that many people who realize how daunting a prospect "cure" truly is, would also push for the development of individualized practices that slow down the onset and progression of the disability.

If a magic wand is waved today, and all cases of Alzheimer's disease are cured, the result is an increase in a population of people in their upper decades (who we are already ill equipped to properly care for), of which many will develop other age-related chronic conditions. The number one risk factor for developing Alzheimer's disease is age. The world's population has never been older, and never more vulnerable.

In the meantime, the Alzheimer's dilemma begs the question: What if progress in drug treatment and/or cure never happens in our lifetime, and we continue to increase life expectancy?

There is great focus and expenditure of funds on the "cure" and too little on the "care" for the millions of people who are currently living with dementia. Someday, hopefully, a cure for Alzheimer's disease will be discovered, and it will be a happy celebration for all. However, until that day arrives, how about applying some of the funds already accumulated as a means to support other equally critical needs? Supplementing care costs of people who are living with Alzheimer's disease as well as affordable caregiver respite programs are extremely worthy causes that could use financial backing right now. Here are a few other dementia-related causes that deserve our immediate attention:

Person-centered training
Long-term care financial assistance
Alzheimer's reimbursement policies
Dementia and sex education
Caregiver respite, loneliness, burnout, and isolation
Dementia-friendly city and workplace initiatives
Public education and awareness
Assistive technologies

Fund-raising efforts are in full force, and you can always donate money to the cause, but wait! There are a lot of scams out there. What does the organization do with the money they receive from donors? How does the organization prove that a contribution is tax deductible? Is the organization legitimate?

To conduct a background check, add the words "complaint" and "scam" after you type the name of the organization or charity into your Internet browser. To ensure the quality of a charitable organization, also look into these resources:

Better Business Bureau Wise Giving Alliance: http://give.org

Charity Navigator: www.charitynavigator.org
Charity Watch: www.charitywatch.org
Federal Trade Commission Charity Scams: www.consumer.ftc.gov
GuideStar: www.guidestar.org
Internal Revenue Service: www.irs.gov/charities
National Association of State Charity Officials: www.nasconet.org

Despite an Alzheimer's disease diagnosis, people are speaking out publicly and demonstrating that their experience of the disease is "dynamic and fluid." Will you be joining them? Figure out which skills and resources you want to devote to your cause, and how much time and effort you can realistically dedicate. Invite others to participate alongside you. Here are the many ways you can get involved in this worthy cause:

Tap into your "superpowers." Do you have the gift of gab? Are you comfortable speaking in front of an audience? Is writing a passion of yours? If public speaking is your thing, decide where you can address and educate a large number of people who may be concerned about Alzheimer's disease and open to receiving information about it.

Raise funds for a dementia nonprofit organization. If you are up to the task of asking for donations from others, roleplay with someone who will help you get your pitch right. Read articles about fund-raising. Type "how to ask for donations" into your Internet search engine.

Initiate discussions. Type "dementia online forum" into your Internet search engine to access a variety of forum websites. You will also find discussion groups that are already engaged in conversations about the rights of people who are living with dementia.

Create a website. Secure a domain name, and research the many website templates online to get started. If you are not computer-friendly yourself, hire someone to complete web-related tasks.

Hook up with heavyweights. Is there a school, business, association, celebrity, journalist, or other entity that might want to hook up with you and support your efforts? If you know of no one, keep asking others who may have friends in high places.

Set up an information table. Get permission to set up a table in a strategic location, or rent a booth at a conference. Hand out free stuff, such as stickers and brochures. Many towns have fairs and other events that attract a lot of people.

Gain steam through social media and e-mail. Create an online presence for your cause—blog about it, create a podcast, tweet (www.twitter.com), and gather "likes" on Facebook (www.facebook.com). The more interactive you are with your online audience, the better. Social media is powerful and reaches a global audience.

Picture it. Make your cause come alive with photographs and videos to assist in telling your story. YouTube (www.youtube.com), Instagram (www.instagram.com), and Pinterest (www.pinterest.com) are among the many visual online outlets to get your online message across. "A picture is worth a thousand words."

Remember the power of art and music. Write songs and poems. Integrate your artistic talents into your online social media and websites.

Seek media coverage. Contact the media about your cause: try for local radio and television stations, especially the morning news and talk shows, as well as the local newspapers and magazines. As your cause gains momentum, so will the coverage. Do you know a public relations professional who will work with you pro bono? Check out the WikiHow guide (www.wikihow.com) on how to write a press release.

Organize letter-writing campaigns. Write to politicians, congresspersons, and city officials. Congress.gov (www.congress.gov) will help you navigate current politician activities. Research which public officials agree with your point of view, and vote for them if you think it will help your cause.

Be a billboard. Advertise your cause with wristbands, T-shirts, caps, buttons, and bumper stickers.

Crowdfund. Propose an idea and/or dementia-related project to be funded through a variety of crowdfunding websites. Type "crowdfund websites" and "fundraising websites" into your Internet search engine.

Host virtual phone meetings. Besides tracking goals and coordinating efforts toward a common project, connecting with same-minded, purpose-driven people may keep you energized.

Write about it. Send letters to newspaper and magazine editors. Write op-ed pieces. Submit articles online and in printed publications. Publish a book.

Whether or not you decide that you are a candidate for getting tested for Alzheimer's disease, planning and putting your affairs in order offer you the opportunity to stay in control of what you want and need as you journey to old age. You owe it to yourself to plan for the best possible care.

Insights and Inspiration

Recommended Reading: *Alzheimer's Early Stages: First Steps for Family, Friends, and Caregivers*, updated edition (2013) by Daniel Kuhn

Recommended YouTube: Subscribe to the Alzheimer's Society YouTube channel. Type "Alzheimer's Society" into the YouTube search engine. Also, type "I have Alzheimer's" into the YouTube search engine to access many excellent videos on the topic of early-onset dementia.

Recommended Movie: *Still Alice* (2014)

Recommended Song: "Both Sides Now" by Joni Mitchell

Recommended TED Talk: "How I'm Preparing to Get Alzheimer's," presented by Alanna Shaikh, filmed June 2012

Part Five

No Tomorrow

"Just Shoot Me" Is Not a Plan

Learning lessons from the dying

Objectives

After completing the chapter "'Just Shoot Me' Is Not a Plan," you will be able to:

- Control incoming information about medical conditions
- Speak candidly about dying and death
- Tap into religious and spiritual resources
- Create instructions in the event of incapacity
- Receive quality care at end of life

The small plane took off from a runway that was closed by fog, narrowly missing striking an automobile as it crashed to the ground and burst into flames between two houses. One of the four victims in the aircraft was Father Thomas J. Fischer, the associate pastor at Sacred Heart Catholic Church, and one of my school's all-time favorite teachers. He was younger than the other priests (twenty-seven years old) and known for his quirky sense of humor. Everyone liked him.

My siblings and I were informed of Father Fischer's death as we dressed for school on that rainy April morning in 1963. Throughout the next several weeks, the priests and nuns, and the rest of the school staff, would gather occasionally in small groups in the school hallways and classrooms, stopping to whisper to each other so that we children could not hear their conversations. The intention of these adults was honorable: do not upset the children by talking about the death.

Father Fischer was not my first encounter with death. By that time, I had already "buried" my fair share of pet goldfish and the family dog, Spike. I also regularly encountered dead rabbits and birds, among other wildlife in the creek behind our house. Citywide, we had also mourned the ninety-five victims of the 1958 Our Lady of the Angels School fire in Chicago, Illinois.

But *this* death felt far different than those other experiences. Father Fischer was someone I would be seeing that morning when I arrived for religion class with my classmates. He was going to be greeting us at the door and making jokes as he always had. I understood the "death" part, but struggled terribly with how quickly he completely vanished from my life—I interpreted being "sheltered" from adult conversations that it was wrong of me to want to talk about his death, and my feelings.

Fast-forward. By now hundreds of people in my life have since died, with each of these deaths leaving its mark in my head, and on my heart. It happens to everyone. When someone we are close to dies, the death event tends to get us thinking about our own mortality. Over the years, what have you personally experienced, witnessed, and observed related to dying and death? Were any of the deaths sudden and unexpected? Did people die slowly and painfully? Did they struggle even though they were in hospice care? Did they die alone? Do you recall some of the things the dying said and did? Was death a taboo subject to be avoided at all costs?

Slowly but surely, the more you live among the dying, the more they influence your thinking and preferences about end of life. You know this to be true if you have ever mumbled to yourself or expressed this phrase to another person, "Just shoot me if things ever get this bad."

Is Ignorance Bliss?

A nagging cough here, a recurring chest pain there—you suspect that your health is seriously in jeopardy. Or perhaps you end up in the intensive care unit after a serious accident. You are very sick, and you know it, but do you want to hear directly from the doctor if you are dying? Doctors use different communication approaches to acknowledge the reality of life's end being at hand:

"You are not going to get better."
"You have a life-limiting condition."
"I am not good at an exact prognosis, but in general terms you have six months."
"This is what you will eventually die from."
"What you have is a terminal condition."

Although some people believe that knowing they are dying is a good thing, not everyone feels that way, for fear of giving up hope or feeling powerless. I can point to one friend in particular who told me that he will never ask his doctor for that kind of information. At the time, he was in the hospital recovering from emergency brain surgery and asked me to respect his right to make that choice. He has since died, but not before returning home, immediately quitting his job, selling all his belongings, putting his legal affairs in order, and hopping on a plane to Greece to live the rest of his life (two years) in peace and reflection.

What is your take about being informed about dying? Here are a few questions to ponder:

Would you want to hear the graphic details about your medical condition?

Would you want to opt out of learning if your illness is terminal?

Would you want to know how the medical condition will ultimately cause your death?

Would you want to know how long you have to live?

Consider the story of Eric and Lyn Harvey. They say that their daughter, Vickie, twenty-four, had fought leukemia twice but went rapidly downhill after being told 'in graphic detail' how she was going to die. The Harveys felt powerless and all they could do was comfort their daughter and wait for the inevitable. Vickie died barely two weeks later. Her parents have since launched a campaign to give the dying the right not to know they are terminally ill allowing patients can "opt out" of bad news.[1]

Whether or not you want to know if you are dying, you, the patient, are the boss and in total control of the amount of information you receive from the doctor. Think about what is important to you and what you are hoping for, and make your wishes known to your health-care team. The upside of knowing what is to come allows time for you to put your affairs in order and initiate discussions with others to help relieve their fears and anxieties.

Don't assume that your doctor knows for certain if you are dying. Yes, it's important that doctors don't give up on you too soon, but are there limitations to medical treatment? A close friend of mine has been dealing with widespread disease from cancer for the past year. She was recently told by her doctor to continue radiation treatments and see how things go, rather than giving her the option to initiate hospice. She is scared and confused. Much of her time is spent managing intense chronic pain. Living a while longer may deny her of being comfortable and stopping the suffering now. Is her doctor treating a dying patient? And why hasn't palliative care been introduced as an option?

In every medical situation, doctors help patients make decisions. When asked, they will explain what can and cannot be done, what the experience of the treatment will be like, what happens if you decide to forego treatment, how certain medications might be the next option, and how long medical treatment should be administered. Opening the communication channels averts big problems down the road—emotionally and financially.

Speak Freely About Dying and Death

Whether or not you are terminally ill or perfectly healthy, what stops you from talking about your own dying and death? Perhaps it's a matter of timing. *You* may be ready to open that can of worms, but that is not necessarily the case when it comes to communicating your wishes with family and close friends. They may dodge and deflect, and even steer conversations about end of life in another direction. As far as they are concerned, you are not going anywhere anytime soon—so why talk about it?

There are many questions and concerns that deserve to be discussed candidly between people who are open and willing to talking about dying and death:

What calms a person down if he or she becomes terrified during the dying process?

Is refusing to eat and drink considered suicide?

Do people who are living with Alzheimer's disease know that they are dying?

Is it true that deceased loved ones "visit" you before you die?

What is it like to die and come back to life?

Is it possible to die of a broken heart?

After someone dies can they still hear you?

Why don't people want to die?

What really happens when you donate your body to science?

If you have curiosities about dying and death, you'll find people from every walk of life, and in all parts of the world, who gather together regularly face-to-face and online to participate in deep discussions about dying and death—writers, artists, psychics, musicians, spiritual directors, hospice volunteers, teachers, funeral directors, doctors, nurses, lawyers, you name it. But make no mistake about it. These gatherings are not for grief counseling. There is no agenda. No profit motive. The idea is to get people talking so they are less afraid of dying and death when the time comes.

If you would like to join others who openly talk about dying and death in an engaging and interactive way, check out the following resources:

Axiom Action: http://axiomaction.com

Best Endings: www.bestendings.com

Betsy Trapasso: www.betsytrapasso.com

CaringBridge: www.caringbridge.org

Death Café: http://deathcafe.com

Dying Matters: www.dyingmatters.org

End of Life University: www.eoluniversity.com

The Ground Swell Project: https://thegroundswellproject.squarespace.com

Impermanence: http://impermanenceatwork.org

Let's Have Dinner and Talk About Death: http://deathoverdinner.org

Life. Death. Whatever.: www.lifedeathwhatever.com

Slow Medicine: www.facebook.com; type "slow medicine" in the website's search field

You're Going to Die: www.yg2d.com

Quality Care at the End of Life

How is dignity introduced into the dying process? As you plan ahead, you will want to give this question serious thought. *How* you die is something you can affect. You have at your disposal tools and resources to create a strategy for quality care in your dying experience. Peruse the following list to get answers to your specific questions, and in the long run, to gain peace of mind.

Palliative care: To receive palliative care, you do not have to be dying anytime soon. *Think comfort.* Palliative care provides an extra layer of support for relief of pain, symptoms, and stress for people with serious illness. Care focuses on expert treatment for pain and other disabling symptoms (e.g., fatigue, depression, and nausea). Medical marijuana may also be introduced as part of the treatment. Care can be started at any point, and throughout the course of a serious illness. Ask about palliative care home visits.

Hospice: Hospice doctors, nurses, and social workers provide comfort and support when a life-limiting illness no longer responds to cure-oriented treatments. Physical pain, discomfort, and suffering are addressed under hospice care. Caring, rather than curing, is the focus. Hospice is a *philosophy* of care, not a bricks-and-mortar location. Hospice takes place in the person's home or wherever "home" may be. Hospice care neither prolongs life nor hastens death. Signing up does not mean giving up all medical care or hope. If you choose, you can still see your regular doctor. You can opt out at any time.

Do not resuscitate (DNR) order: The DNR is a medical order signed by a physician, instructing health-care workers not to perform cardiopulmonary resuscitation (CPR). A person executing a legal DNR has decided to decline measures in the event his or her heart or breathing stops, and instead is allowed to die naturally.

Do not intubate (DNI) order: The DNI is a medical order signed by a physician, instructing health-care workers not to intubate you or place you on an artificial ventilator if your breathing is failing.

Do not hospitalize (DNH) order: The DNH is a medical order signed by a physician, instructing health-care workers not to send you to a hospital from your home or nursing home. DNH orders often are based on what is written and expressed in a person's advance directive.

Aid in dying: Terminally ill, mentally capable adults are eligible for medical aid in dying. The dying person controls the process from beginning to the end. The Compassion and Choices website is a source for extensive information (www.compassionandchoices.org).

Physician orders for life-sustaining treatments (POLST): A serious illness, medical frailty, and a chronic progressive condition (as defined by the doctor), combined with your wishes to not have your life prolonged are indications to execute a POLST form. This approach to end-of-life planning is based on conversations between patients and health-care professionals. For more information, visit POLST (www.polst.org).

Suicide tourism: Type "suicide tourism" into your Internet search engine, if that option is of interest to you. The term describes the practice of potential suicide candidates' traveling to a jurisdiction to commit assisted suicide or suicide.

Additional resources to explore the subject of dying and death include:

Americans for Better Care of the Dying: www.abcd-caring.org
Death with Dignity: www.deathwithdignity.org
Exit International: https://exitinternational.net
Final Exit Network: www.finalexitnetwork.org
Growth House: www.growthhouse.org
Hospice Net: www.hospicenet.org
National Association for Home Care and Hospice: www.nahc.org
National Hospice and Palliative Care Organization: www.nhpco.org
National Social Worker Finder: www.helpstartshere.org
The Peaceful Pill Handbook: www.peacefulpillhandbook.com
Suicide Prevention Lifeline: https://suicidepreventionlifeline.org
World Federation of Right to Die Societies: www.worldrtd.net

The Rest of the Story

There are three important reasons why the subject of hospice and palliative care deserves more airtime right now. Be aware of the following:

1. You have a choice of hospice programs.

Hospice is likely to be the most important health-care decision you make. However, be aware of various discrepancies between hospice organizations. Even though your doctor or hospital attending physician may make a recommendation of one provider over another, you are wise to do your own homework and shop around.

The *Washington Post* tells the story of an eighty-five-year-old hospice patient who was close to death. "Ying Tai Choi lay on a hospital bed arranged in the living room of her daughter's house. A pulse oximeter pinged an intermittent warning about her oxygen levels. She heaved for breath sometimes and panted at others. Sounds of gurgling and congestion came from her throat. The skin behind her fingernails was turning dark. 'She is leaving soon,' the hospice nurse told Choi's daughter. Then the nurse left the house and drove away."[2]

Not providing "continuous care" under the hospice umbrella of services happens for many reasons. For one, the scarcity of qualified care when the patient is most in need once again rears its ugly head and may leave you wondering why a hospice organization takes on so many patients in the first place. Also, employees versus "nurses under contract" dictate the allowed level of care under certain circumstances. Economics is also to blame—providing continuous bedside nursing care to needier patients can be a financial drain for small and midsize agencies. Sadly, unattended patients in crisis have been known to forego hospice services altogether by going by ambulance to the emergency room when they are frail and dying or left to suffer in their final hours.

While most hospice organizations provide quality care, hospices are among the least inspected organizations in the US health-care system, with most operating for years before an inspector calls.[3]

Make sure that your hospice research includes the following:

Size: Ask how many patients they currently have and their capacity to serve.
Employees: Ask about staff versus "employees under contract" and their qualifications.
Accreditation: Ask about recent inspections, and accreditations by which organizations.
Years in business: Ask about operation and ownership history.
Emergency: Ask whether the hospice provides immediate, 24/7 services in a crisis (e.g., pain, struggling)

To further ensure quality hospice care, the National Hospice and Palliative Care Organization (www.nhpco.org) has developed specific questions to help identify factors that may be important to you when selecting a hospice. Type "choosing a quality hospice" into the website's search field.

2. Despite palliative medicine, many people continue to suffer at the end of life.

All individuals, suffering or not, have the right to refuse life-sustaining medical treatment, including artificial nutrition and hydration (ways of giving liquid and nutrients through a tube). But what about the people who are living with advanced stages of dementia? How do they exercise this option if they have diminished comprehension or means of expression?

Additionally, to accelerate the dying process, some people choose to cease eating and drinking (referred to as voluntarily stopping eating and drinking, or VSED) as an exit option. Nevertheless, VSED may be resisted by health-care practitioners either because they think that it is or may be illegal.

No matter the situation, limiting life-sustaining medical treatment and refusing to eat or drink must be discussed ahead of time and exercised through an advance directive or a surrogate decision maker. Do not put yourself in the position of being at the mercy of a health-care practitioner who holds opposing views to what you want at the end of life.

3. There are other options besides hospice care.

People who are terminally ill sometimes choose not to enroll in hospice because they are "not ready." Other times, they may lack the specifics, and consequently make assumptions as to what hospice is about.

People who do not choose hospice have four options: hospital care, but not in a hospice bed or unit; nursing home without hospice care; home care with support from a home-health agency; and home care with help from family or friends without support from hospice or a home-health agency.

I have been witness to patients who die without the care and compassion of hospice. Please don't be one of them.

No One Dies Alone

No one is born into this world alone, and in the best of circumstances, no one dies alone, yet there are a variety of reasons that this happens:

Outliving family and friends

Alienating themselves from family and friends, and vice versa

Distance keeping family and friends from being present at the time of death

Experiencing a catastrophic event has caused one to be face-to-face with death unexpectedly

Some people prefer to be alone when they die, but most want someone to be with them. If dying alone is something you want to avoid, be proactive and research options ahead of time. Check out the following resources and strategies:

No One Dies Alone (NODA): This is an international program that provides the reassuring presence of a volunteer companion to people who would otherwise be alone when they die. Volunteers do not provide any medical care. They sit at the bedside of the dying, holding a hand or stroking an arm. Volunteers are there to listen (every volunteer signs a confidentiality agreement). Others read aloud or play music. The shared time is calming, and not always somber. Volunteers offer the ultimate gift—a dignified death. To find a NODA program, visit the No One Dies Alone website (www.peacehealth.org), and type "no one dies alone" into the website's search field.

Death midwife: Death midwives (also known as end-of-life guides) work in concert with doctors, nurses, and other health-care professionals, but do not replace them. They can perform mundane tasks—sort medical bills, legal paperwork, manage advance directives—as well as provide spiritual and emotional support at the end of life. They can step in early in the process, helping both the healthy and the terminally ill. Services and fees vary widely. Be aware that there are currently no national regulatory groups governing standards for death midwives. To locate resources, type "death midwife" into your Internet search engine as well as the Facebook (www.Facebook.com) search engine. Type "end-of-life guide" into the National Home Funeral Alliance website's search field (www.homefuneralalliance.org). Also contact the International End of Life Doula Association (www.inelda.org).

Hospice chaplain: One of the important roles of a chaplain is to help people get to a calmer place. Sometimes that means helping dying people accept their own mortality. Sometimes that means sitting with them and listening as they express regrets and fears.

Hospice vigil volunteers: In addition to hospice doctors, nurses, and social workers, vigil volunteers pay regular visits to offer emotional and practical support to a person who has a life-limiting illness. Contact the Hospice Foundation of America (www.hospice foundation.org).

Professional caregivers: Bonded, licensed, and insured care professionals ensure the dying of receiving 24/7 quality care and attention. Services and fees vary widely. Contact private home-care agencies.

Senior companion volunteer: There are a variety of local programs that match volunteers with people who seek companionship and emotional support. The services are often free of charge. Type "senior companion volunteer" into your Internet search engine. Visit the Elder-care Locator website (www.eldercare.gov) or call 800-677-1116. Your local Area Agency on Aging also provides information on senior companion volunteer programs as well as support groups for the terminally ill. Visit the National Association of Area Agencies on Aging (www.n4a.org).

Certified music-thanatologist: Musicians work within the broader subspecialty of pallia-tive care, uniting music and medicine in end-of-life care. The music-thanatologist utilizes instrument and voice at the bedside to lovingly serve the physical, emotional, and spiritual needs of people who are on death's doorstep. Visit the Music-Thanatology Association Inter-national website (www.mtai.org) for more information.

Aging life care experts: You can hire an aging life care professional to assist you in finding volunteers and professional caregivers. Formerly known as geriatric case managers, they are also instrumental in answering practical questions in times of uncertainty and can steer you to the appropriate resources. Services and fees vary widely. For more information, contact the Aging Life Care Association (www.aginglifecare.org).

Out of Your Control

You may have heard firsthand accounts of people who struggle with their dying: "Why me?" "Will I be missed when I'm gone?" "What has my life been about?" "My world is falling apart." "What happens after I die?" "Why does God allow me to suffer this way?" Anxieties, unresolved conflicts, regrets, fears, hopes, and despair—what is a dying person to do?

Highly skilled spiritual guides are available to assist the dying. Methods to connect with spirituality and religious practices include:

Meditation

Prayer

Rituals and sacraments

Scripture readings

Relaxation techniques

Spiritual guides are also instrumental in assisting with filling out advance directives forms and making difficult health-care and end-of-life decisions.

Seek the services of a priest, rabbi, minister, chaplain, or other religious representative for guidance. Regulations regarding HIPAA (Health Insurance Portability and Accountability Act) dictate that the health-care institution may not take the initiative to inform others of your situation. In the hospital setting, ask for assistance from a representative from the pastoral-care and/or ethics department.

There are a variety of resources to assist the dying with spiritual and religious practices:

Because Hope Matters: http://becausehopematters.com

Living and Dying Consciously Project: www.livinganddyingconsciouslyproject.org

The Metta Institute: www.mettainstitute.org

Soul Care Project: http://soulcareproject.org

Spiritual MD: www.karenwyattmd.com

A Traveler's View: www.atravelersview.org

Veriditas: www.veriditas.org

Seal the Deal

Whatever it is that you would like to have happen at the end of your life, have you put your thoughts in writing? Have you told anyone about your wishes? Stay in control of your end-of-life decisions with the following suggestions.

Written instructions called advance directives allow you to specify the kind of treatment you receive when you are gravely or terminally ill. Through a living will and medical durable power of attorney, you name an agent/proxy to speak on your behalf when you are incapacitated and unable to communicate your wishes. To complete the advance directives you must be at least eighteen years of age.

The assistance of a lawyer to complete this form is not required. Advance directives can be obtained from your physician and/or the Internet. Type "health care proxy," followed by the name of your state, into your Internet search engine. Forms must be applicable to the state where you reside. Create a reminder that if you move out of state, you will need to complete a new form.

Need help deciding what you want at the end of life? The following resources will assist you in the process:

Five Wishes: www.agingwithdignity.org/five-wishes. A nonprofit organization with a mission to help people plan in advance for a health crisis. Resources are available in twenty-eight different languages. This organization serves people of diverse cultures and faith traditions. The "Five Wishes" directive allows you to put your end-of-life wishes in your own words. Educational workshops and a national toll-free hotline are also available.

The Conversation Project: www.theconversationproject.org. Offers a Conversation Starter Kit as a guide to help get your thoughts together and then have the conversation with others about what you want for end-of-life care. Please note: The document does not seek to provide legal advice.

The next step is to determine who should be contacted in an emergency and is in the position of carrying out your advance directives. The person you have in mind must be willing to be your agent. Ideally, he or she is someone who can handle conflicting opinions from family, friends, and medical personnel; who can be a strong voice if a doctor or institution is unresponsive; who you trust implicitly to carry out your wishes; and who lives nearby or can travel to be with you at a moment's notice.

Choose at least one backup person if your first choice is unavailable. If no one comes to mind to act on your behalf as your agent, ask for candidate recommendations from an attorney who specializes in elder law, or you can set up a bank trust officer as fiduciary. Also type "public guardian" and "professional fiduciary" into your Internet search engine, followed by the name of your city and state. Now is the time to research your options and establish trusting relationships when it comes to managing your end-of-life affairs.

Give your agent(s) a copy of your advance directives plus any special instructions (e.g., pet care). Make sure your agent knows where you store the original document. Reconfirm that your agent is on board with your wishes, or else find someone else to represent you. Also make sure that your agent knows your Social Security number, where you keep your insurance card, and instructions on accessing funds to pay for your care.

Give your doctor a copy of your advance directives to include in your medical records. Get your doctor's assurance that he or she will support your wishes. If your doctor has objections, either work them out or find another doctor.

Yellow Dot (www.nationalyellowdot.org) is a growing statewide program. You place a sticker on the rear windshield in the bottom left-hand corner that alerts first responders to the fact that your medical record is in the glove compartment of your car. Check out the website for more details.

If you plan to obtain care in an assisted-living community or nursing home, take a copy of your advance directives with you and ask that it be added to your medical records.

Keep the original copy of your advance directives and copies of medical durable power of attorney in a place where they can be easily found. Do not store these documents in a safe-deposit box, safe, or other inaccessible location.

Create a "just in case" envelope and attach it to your refrigerator. In the envelope keep copies of all of your important documents: advance directives, powers of attorney (financial and health care), and emergency contact information (family, friends, doctor, accountant, lawyer, clergy, and neighbors). Keep a copy of what is in the envelope in your purse and in the glove compartment of your car. Keep a list of emergency contact information in your wallet. Download important information to a flash drive and attach it to your keychain. A medical ID bracelet is equally important if you have allergies and serious medical conditions. Type "emergency response devices" into your Internet search engine for additional support.

Easy access to advance directives and other important information is also available from your smartphone. Check out the American Bar Association website (www.americanbar.org), and type "My Health Care Wishes App" into the website's search field.

Insights and Inspiration

Recommended Reading: *Too Soon Old, Too Late Smart: Thirty True Things You Need to Know Now* (2008) by Gordon Livingston

Recommended YouTube: Check out the *Ask a Mortician* video series.

Recommended Movie: *Up* (2009)

Recommended Song: "Softly As I Leave You," sung by Andy Williams, composed by Giorgio Calabrese and Tony De Vita

Recommended TED Talk: "What Really Matters at the End of Life," presented by BJ Miller, palliative care physician, filmed March 2015

Places to Go and Things to Do

Facing to be and not to be

You, too, are going to die. You've known this for quite some time. You don't know how you're going to die—it may be quick and pain-free, or prolonged and traumatic.

Knowing you are going to die *for real* changes perspective on everything. I suspect that coming to terms with the idea that life is going to be over sooner than expected must be awful, yet also, at the same time, amazing. If I were given a terminal diagnosis, I imagine that a million thoughts would start swirling around in my head— How long do I have? What is there for me to do in what little time I have left? Was I a kind person? Did I love enough? Will anybody care that I am dead? How will I be remembered?

A friend of mine had a health scare that left her waiting for one entire week before she found out whether she was terminally ill. It was good news. She was not going to die anytime soon, and she said something interesting to me after she learned her fate. She wished everybody could have had her experience on some level. Although the waiting was unbearable, she said her mind was cleared of things she was afraid of and immediately prepared to get on with the joy of living.

A reassessment of priorities is not unusual among the dying, but is it possible to achieve similar clarity without being terminally ill? I'd like to think that the answer is yes.

Objectives

After completing the chapter "Places to Go and Things to Do," you will be able to:

- Leave something of yourself behind
- Create an ethical will
- Share special belongings
- Complete unfinished personal business
- Determine the destiny of your remains
- Celebrate your life now or later
- Fulfill a final wish
- Manage death's details from the grave

Why Leave Your Mark?

What is this concept called legacy? And why the disconnect between the popularity of the topic and people actually working toward leaving one? Perhaps it's because we assume it always involves money. Perhaps it's because the word *legacy* has everything to do with being dead. We live in a culture that wants to believe we will live forever—so who needs to think about leaving anything behind if we are always going to be around?

Like many people, I am more attracted to the idea of creating something that brings value to the world while I am alive. And I prefer to live in the here and now. I wonder, what can I create that did not exist before me? What is something in the world, however small, that is a little different, and better, because I was here? What will expand me beyond myself? The more I ponder these questions, the more it makes sense to start the process with the legacy I inherited.

After reading an article about obtaining dual citizenship in *Fra Noi* (www.franoi.com), my go-to magazine for Italian Americans, I decided that becoming an Italian citizen would accomplish several goals: to extend citizenship rights to my children and grandchildren if living and working overseas appeals to them, to constitute a gift of continuity bequeathed to the family by my beloved ancestors, and to put a smile on my mother's face.

After a two-year process of creating an extensive paper trail, signature-gathering, translating, and form-completing, which included siblings, spouses, former spouses, adult children and their spouses, and grandchildren, I was able to prove, once and for all, that my grandfather had never renounced his Italian citizenship after he arrived at Ellis Island.

Never in my life did I look forward to getting fingerprinted as much as I did on the day I became an Italian citizen. Perhaps the only other experience that will forever be embedded in my memory was the look on my mother's face when I told her that the mission was accomplished, and her legacy lives on.

If my story inspires you to leave a legacy, perhaps starting with the past is a path you may also want to pursue. What did your ancestors leave for you? How did they shape who you are? What do you care about the most? Did past generations influence how you like to spend your time?

You do not have to go to great lengths, such as obtaining dual-citizenship, to create a legacy. A little something goes a long way. A friend of mine bakes his mother's family apple pie recipe every Thanksgiving, then serves it to her—as a show of thanks and a display of her legacy. He says that he will continue this tradition for as long as he lives, but not before passing the recipe along to his children and grandchildren.

Pick up a pen and send a close friend a letter about why you love him or her as much as you do. Send a handwritten thank-you note to your doctor and nursing staff. Compose a note of gratitude to a teacher or coach. On your next vacation, send a postcard to someone back home. Include a handwritten sentiment in a get-well card. Sign the guest book at funerals and weddings. And guess what? You have just left a legacy. Your handwriting is unique—a part of your self-image and an expression of your personality no less than the way you dress and speak—and is one more way that people come to know you. Devote time to the art of handwriting. For more inspiration, visit the National Handwriting Association website (www.nha-handwriting .org.uk). Keep in mind, legacy is about creating anything that changes another person for the better—anything that lasts. Perhaps some of the following ideas will jump-start your journey:

Help a young person overcome a challenge or obstacle.
Organize family photographs. Skip a generation and create albums for next of kin.
Mentor a young adult.
Give a speech to high school students.
Donate items of historical value to a museum.
Dedicate land or a building to a good cause.
Teach a child to fish, ride a bike, play a sport.
Create a cookbook of traditional family recipes.
Help launch someone's career or business idea.
Make an important family reconnection.
Donate to public television and radio programs that benefit others.
Plant a tree in honor of someone or something.
Turn your blogs into a book.

Additional legacy-related resources for you to consider at this time are Legacy (www.legacy .com), ePassing (www.epassing.org), the History Project (www.thehistoryproject.com), and StoryCorps (www.storycorps.org). Each of these websites takes a different approach to reminding you how much your life stories matter and the importance of sharing them with others.

Consider an Ethical Will

There is a lot of talk these days about ethical wills, even though the tradition began over seven hundred years ago, when elders orally conveyed their values, advice, experiences, and concerns to the next of kin. In many ways, an ethical will can be a manifestation of your legacy.

An ethical will is strictly personal, carrying no legal implications or instructions on the distribution of material wealth. From handwritten letters and do-it-yourself scrapbooks to videos and audio recordings, ethical wills can accomplish the following, and much more:

Explain what you accomplished and why it was important for you to do so
Describe how you lived your life, and why
Provide in detail the life lessons you learned
Express what you hope future generations will learn from you

There are no rules or guidelines—an ethical will is solely an individual, creative endeavor and a labor of love. It is a heartfelt expression of what truly matters most in your life. Ideally, you may want to consider sharing your ethical will with others while you are alive. For more information and resources to guide you, type "ethical will" into your Internet search engine. You will also find a wealth of information on the Celebrations of Life website (https://celebrationsoflife.net/ethicalwills) and Personal Legacy Advisors (www.personal legacyadvisors.com).

Take Five

All my life I have lived with goalposts—relentless real-life demands pull me in every direction imaginable: A co-worker wants the status report by tomorrow; I need to prepare a new keynote for a fund-raising event but I want to squeeze in a workout; my mother needs a ride to the doctor—and I wonder whether I will ever again get a full night's sleep. Running ragged slowly creeps into a life. I, for one, am guilty of cramming in one more household task immediately after declaring I am heading straight to bed.

No one is impressed with exhaustion, overscheduling, and busyness, and there is no one better to guide me on the art of respecting time than my old and trusted friends. They, of all the people I know, understand the true value of time.

Over the years, they not only taught me that every breath is a precious commodity, they also liberally dish out sage advice when I am prone to treat time with disregard.

When I overschedule, they tell me: "You are running yourself ragged for nothing. You will never get it all done."
When I fail to prioritize, they tell me: "You will regret missing what is important."
When I allow others to misuse my time, they tell me: "Chronically late people are not your friends."

When I waste other people's time, they tell me: "Soon enough you will alienate them."

When I feed my phone distraction, they tell me: "You will never get those hours back playing games and checking e-mail."

When I thrive on being busy, they tell me: "Your busyness is nothing more than an ego booster."

When I move through time mindlessly, they tell me: "Having no set plans means someone else eventually decides for you."

When I am procrastinating, they tell me: "Take it one step at a time."

When I resist delegating tasks and responsibilities, they tell me: "Your way is not always best. You do not have all the answers."

When I multitask, they tell me: "You are not doing any task well."

When I overthink and overanalyze, they tell me: "Quit stalling and make a decision."

If ever there is a need to give time the respect it deserves, it is when you are contemplating the end of life—like right now. Savoring the present moment is one way to accomplish this goal. However, it is difficult to slow down if you never learned how.

For many who move through tasks quickly, moving at a slower pace takes getting used to. When we first start the process, we might feel extremely uncomfortable just thinking about slowing down; the ever-present and ever-growing to-do list constantly demands attention. (I eventually overcame my own anxieties by telling myself over and over that taking it slower is an investment in me.)

Take the Slow Lane

In her article "Baking with Kids a Reminder That Quick Isn't Always the Best Fix," *Chicago Tribune* reporter Heidi Stevens says, "I want to demonstrate to my kids (and myself) that fast isn't everything. That fast, in fact, can be the wrong thing. I want us to recognize that some problems—whether they're algebra problems or humanity's problems—are worth our dedicated time and patience."[1] These days, Heidi looks for ways to insert slow into her family's life. One thing they do together is bake.

In our fast-paced world, switching gears from fast to slower is often easier said than done. To get used to the process, consider integrating one of the following suggested activities into your routine at least once a week. Whichever activity you decide to do, trust that the rewards of taking it slower will come.

Pick an activity. Pay close attention to what you are doing in the moment. Stay focused only on the task—no multitasking:

Wash dishes by hand—slowly and carefully.

Get in the longest line at the bank or supermarket. Breathe deeply as you wait.

Draw a picture and color it in. Doodle.

Sweep a floor or sidewalk.

Rake leaves.

Stare at a fish tank.

Savor your morning coffee.

Do nothing for 10 minutes.

Spread a blanket on a beach. Listen to the waves. Take in the smells.

Fill a glass with water. Sit down. Drink the water slowly.

Pluck weeds.

Listen to the rain.

Get a shoeshine.

Bake a pie.

Eat lunch slowly while sitting outside on a park bench.

Listen to the sound of birds or crickets.

Observe butterflies or hummingbirds.

Arrive 15-minutes early to your next appointment.

Attend a baseball game and stay for the entire nine innings.

Get a manicure and sit there quietly until your nails are completely dry.

Look up. Take a few minutes to marvel at a brilliant blue sky.

Go for a slow 15-minute walk.

Play a musical instrument (whether you know how or not).

Cook a meal from scratch. Set the table. Sit down and slowly enjoy your meal.

Lie in bed a few moments longer and express gratitude for the day.

Watch a sunset or a sunrise.

During a traffic jam, thank everyone on the road for slowing you down.

You Can't Take It with You

If my house were on fire, I know exactly what I would grab before I run out the door—a pair of scissors—but these are no ordinary scissors. They were given to me by my mother, who, in turn, got them from her mother.

My grandmother darned socks using these scissors; my mother made my wedding dress using these scissors, and she taught me how to sew using these scissors.

One day, Mom invited me into her bedroom and asked me to sit next to her on the bed;

TIE UP LOOSE ENDS WORKSHEET

This worksheet is available to download and customize at www.elderindustry.com.

The clock is ticking. Keep that in mind as you review the list below. Finish the sentences, then create an action plan to carry out your desires:

Things I want to start but haven't started

_____

Things I want to change but haven't changed

_____

Things I want to stop but haven't stopped

_____

Things I started but haven't finished

_____

Things I want to do but haven't done

_____

Things I want to say but haven't said

_____

Things I want to learn but haven't learned

_____

Things I need to return that do not belong to me

_____

Things I want to give away to someone while I am alive

_____

then, she opened the nightstand drawer—and there they were, shiny and silver, and more precious than gold. My mother proudly handed the scissors over to me and asked that I be the keeper of them now. We both cried. I will never forget that moment as long as I live.

Look around. You've got stuff. Most likely much of what you have can, and should be, tossed (sorry to be so blunt). Some of the items can be sold, donated to charity, or left on the curb. But look again, *only deeper this time.* Some of what you own is attached to invaluable memories—a belt of your grandfather's, a ring from a beloved aunt, a book from your childhood.

The value of the item is not its price tag; rather, it is the story you tell to the person you give it to. Do not underestimate the significance of this transaction. In addition to the memory of the special occasion, you pass on a piece of you. It is as simple as that, yet this is one of the most meaningful interactions you can create while you are alive. Go ahead—make someone's day.

Determine Your Ultimate Destiny

Preplanning a burial, funeral, or memorial service just makes sense. Not only do you remain in control of what you want, but planning eliminates the need for the grieving to deal with details at a time when minds are unclear and hearts are overburdened.

Begin the planning process by contemplating these basic questions:

Where do I want my body to be taken immediately after I die?
What is to become of my remains?
What is my budget?
Who will carry out my wishes?

To budget for death-related expenses, read "The Fierce Urgency of Money" chapter in this book, starting on page 57, then choose from a variety of burial-related alternatives by reviewing the following list:

Embalming: Get the entire picture of what it means to be embalmed by reading about the process online before you decide to have the mortician drain your bodily fluid and replace with embalming fluid. Enough said here—type "I want to be embalmed" into your Internet search engine for more.

Flame-based cremation: The deceased is taken to a crematorium, where a heating process reduces the remains to ashes and bone particles (also known as a direct or simple cremation).

Alkaline hydrolysis: An environmentally friendly method (also known as biocremation, aquamation, resomation, green cremation, flameless cremation, and water cremation) for the disposition of human remains, producing fewer pollutants than traditional cremation. For more information, type "alkaline hydrolysis" into your Internet search engine to find out whether the process has been legalized in your state.

Burial of ashes: Store your cremated remains in a vault, tomb, mausoleum, or crypt. You can also arrange to have ashes buried in a special place, such as someone's yard or garden. Have your ashes planted in a biodegradable urn to nourish the ground near a favorite tree. Insert ashes into a cement mix to help rebuild coral reefs; visit Eternal Reef (www.eternalreefs.com). If you are a space lover, you might entertain the concept of having some of your ashes shot into space; for more information, type "memorial space flights" into your Internet search engine.

Scattering of ashes: Investigate regulations regarding the scattering of ashes on land or into bodies of water, since jurisdictions may have ordinances in place that prohibit you such use of your site choice. Keep in mind that you can have your ashes scattered and buried in more than one location. Turn your remains into a firework display. Visit Angels Flight (www.angels -flight.net). To launch your ashes in a helium balloon, visit Eternal Ascent Society (www .eternalascent.com).

Cremation urns, jewelry, and keepsakes: Turn locks of hair into a certified diamond. Infuse ashes in a glass paperweight. Mix ashes with tattoo ink. Insert ashes into an hourglass as a beautiful mantel piece—you get the picture; the sky is the limit. For more ideas, type "cremation urns," "cremation jewelry," "cremation keepsakes," "memorial tattoo," "memorial glass artwork," and "art from ashes" into your Internet search engine.

Whole-body donation: You can make arrangements ahead of time to donate your body to a medical school for research. Donations can also occur after a funeral or memorial service. The cremation option remains available after the school has completed its use of the body.

Traditional burial: The deceased is placed in a casket and set in a grave. Burial occurs after a ceremony or service, or without any service. Burial at sea also is an option. Entombment is an option where the deceased is placed in a casket and laid to rest above ground in a tomb, mausoleum, or crypt.

Veteran burial: Burial assistance depends on the veteran's benefits status at the time of death and whether the veteran's cause of death was a service-related disability. Eligibility also extends to surviving spouses and civilians who provided military-related service. Contact the regional Department of Veterans Affairs (www.veterans.gov) for details.

Home funeral: The body is washed and anointed with essential oils. The oils have a pleasant scent and help to remove the bacteria from the body. Dry ice keeps the body cool. If you are leaning toward this death-care approach, and suspect that you will need to delay your home funeral, make arrangements ahead of time with a funeral director who agrees to store your body for up to ten days or more. Sometimes people who want to attend your funeral live far away. Type "home funeral" into your Internet search engine for more information. A death midwife will be quite helpful in the planning process. Type "death midwife" into your Internet search engine.

Green burial: Interest in green burial is growing. Usually the body is washed and prepared, but not necessarily embalmed, then wrapped in a shroud or placed in a biodegradable casket to decompose naturally (also known as a simple burial or natural burial). Natural cemeteries double as nature preserves. The Green Burial Council (https://greenburialcouncil.org) is an environmental certification organization. Visit the website to learn more and to find a provider of products and services.

Cryonics: Begins immediately after a person is declared legally dead. The process is low-temperature preservation for people who hope to be resuscitated and restored to full health, vitality, renewed youth, and an extended life span in the future. For more information, visit the Cryonics website (www.cryonics.org).

Mummification: Not just for ancient Egyptians anymore. At this time, finding a funeral director who is willing to perform this form of preservation may be difficult, if not impossible. Check with the National Funeral Directors Association website (www.nfda.org). Also, type "I want to be mummified" into your Internet search engine to access resources.

Plastination: Much like mummification, plastination involves preserving the body in a semirecognizable form. The process involves dissecting the body into bits, embalming it with a hardening fluid and reposing the body into various lifelike poses. The result is used for instruction and scientific research, or you can also choose to send your corpse on a tour of museums. Visit Body Worlds (www.bodyworlds.com) and click on the "donate body" tab.

Sky burial: The body can be flown to Tibet or India where, instead of burying bodies in the hard ground, the corpse can be left on the top of a mountain to decompose while exposed to the elements, and eaten by vultures and scavenging animals. There may be restrictions regarding offering this service to foreigners. For more information type "sky burial" into your Internet search engine.

Celebrate

If your plan is to host a celebration of your life, customized funerals and memorial services are simply a matter of preference and budget. If you want to go all out, consider consulting an event planner. Although people are not legally required to use a funeral home to plan and conduct a funeral, a funeral director can very well serve as a consultant. Confessions of a Funeral Director (www.calebwilde.com) offers sage advice. Details to consider include the following:

Death notifications
Obituary
Cultural traditions
Military honors
Master of ceremonies, celebrant, and/or clergy
Religious and/or spiritual rituals
Eulogies
Location
Photos
Videos
Audio recordings
Food and refreshments
Music and musicians
Resting-place services
Scattering of ashes ceremony
Online services (guest books and real-time attendance for long-distance mourners)
Death anniversary event

Why Wait to Celebrate?

If time is limited, and you know the end is near, you may want to host a "living funeral," also referred to as reminiscing parties, transition parties, or living tributes. An event of this nature allows you to soak it all in while you are alive—hear the eulogies in advance, take in the praises, share laughs, and express gratitude. Invite friends, family, neighbors, colleagues, advisers, clergy, and pets to celebrate a lifetime of togetherness. Include in the invitation a request for them to come prepared to share a memory or two.

Gatherings can be as formal or informal as you like. The setting could be a home, banquet hall, place of worship, park, theater, boat, restaurant—anywhere that is special to you.

You will be expected to give a speech of one kind or another. If that thought makes you uncomfortable, there are plenty of ways to get around it. Write a letter and have someone read it aloud, or prepare a video or audio recording ahead of time. Ask for assistance with this task.

There are many wonderful and creative ideas on how to go about planning for such an event. Type "living funerals" into your Internet search engine for inspiration.

Fulfill a Final Wish

If you are diagnosed with a terminal illness, might you have a final wish to fulfill? Dreams can come true with the generosity of several organizations. Contact the following resources to see whether you qualify:

Dream Foundation: www.dreamfoundation.org
Second Wind Dreams: www.secondwind.org
Twilight Wish: www.twilightwish.org

Manage Death's Details from the Grave

To ensure that your burial, funeral, and/or memorial services are carried out according to your plan, write everything down. This is also the time to compose your obituary. Distribute copies of instructions to those you designate will carry out your plans.

Also incorporate instructions as part of your will, including details on accessing funds to pay for all death-related expenses. If you pay for products or services ahead of time, include receipts in your documentation as proof of payment.

Insights and Inspiration

Recommended Reading: *Modern Death: How Medicine Changed the End of Life* (2017) by Haider Warraich

Recommended YouTube: Amy Krouse Rosenthal's *Thought Bubble: Kindness Thought Café*, uploaded April 16, 2010

Recommended Movie: *Two Weeks* (2006)

Recommended Song: "Instant Karma! (We All Shine On)" by John Lennon

Recommended TED Talk: "Before I Die I Want to . . . ," presented by Candy Chang, artist, designer, urban planner, filmed July 2012

Cross It Off Your List

Did you do it? When did you do it? Are you sure you did it? With everything else that you have on your plate, it's easy to lose track of which tasks you completed and what is still left to do. Let this chapter of the book help you pull it all together.

If organizing your important and legal documents is also on your to-do list, check out the Documents Locator offered in *The Complete Eldercare Planner*. Click on the "Downloads I" tab on the Who Will Take Care of Me When I'm Old? website homepage (www.elderindustry .com), then customize the form according to your needs.

Use the following guide to stay on top of your goals.

1. Meet Your Future Self   TO DO BY   COMPLETED

Use the concept of time travel to plan.

Prioritize and tackle planning tasks.

Create filing systems to get organized.

Connect with your future self.

2. Good-bye Change, Hello Transition   TO DO BY   COMPLETED

Understand change vs. transition.

Fill out Manage Change Worksheet.

Engage advisers.

Strengthen "fear muscle."

Fill out Risky Business Worksheets.

Apply principles of proactivity.

Access resources for better sleep.

3. **Think Like a Strategist**	TO DO BY	COMPLETED

Pay attention to your thinking process.

Challenge self-sabotaging thoughts.

Practice strategic thinking.

Create vision boards.

Research Law of Attraction.

Use thinking out loud for better outcomes.

Complete the What Should I Do? Worksheet.

4. **You Are Tougher Than You Look**	TO DO BY	COMPLETED

Strengthen "resilience muscle."

Practice living in the moment.

Focus on time-worthy endeavors.

Find ways to stay motivated to accomplish goals.

Commit to establishing trusting relationships.

Learn to steer the direction of difficult conversations.

Get a handle on guilt.

Manage grief responsibly.

Learn to laugh more.

Prepare for shifting responsibilities and roles.

5. **The Fierce Urgency of Money**	TO DO BY	COMPLETED

Review current money-spending habits.

Seek legal counsel.

Hire certified financial planner.

Make a plan to control digital footprint.

Draft durable power of attorney for finances.

Get legal affairs in order.

Establish memory loss precautions.

Create cybersecurity safeguards.

Begin the downsizing process.

Bring in additional income.

Consider your house as a financial strategy.

Obtain product and service discounts.

Access thrifty shopping outlets.

Consider PACE.

Lower grocery bills.

Find freebies.

Get healthier to lower caregiving costs.

Create budget for death-related expenses.

Review and prepare for grandparent as parent financial resources.

6. Aging in Place Alone—What You Need to Know	TO DO BY	COMPLETED

Ask for help.

Accept help.

Contact certified aging in place professionals.

Understand age-friendly community values.

Understand dementia-friendly community values.

Understand LGBTQ community values.

Fill out the Age-Friendly Home Checklist.

Size up physical obstacles to aging in place.

Size up financial obstacles to aging in place.

Size up social obstacles to aging in place.

Size up service obstacles to aging in place.

Size up location obstacles to aging in place.

Complete the Beat the Odds to Age in Place Checklist.

7. Bring Livability Home	TO DO BY	COMPLETED

Review the concepts of livability.

Explore livable-city and community options.

Access home repair and remodel programs.

Implement home-safety precautions.

Research adaptive clothing options.

Research independent-living products.

Expand circle of support.

Obtain resources to access volunteers.

Consider alternative transportation options.

Upgrade to smarter technologies.

8. Moving On	TO DO BY	COMPLETED

Think strategically about relocating.

Think strategically about staying put.

Review housing options.
Make a plan to access affordable housing.
Evaluate rural-living options.

9. **The Broken Hearts Club**	TO DO BY	COMPLETED

Identify learning experiences from the caregiving years.
Tap into widowhood resources.
Access LGBTQ caregiver resources.
Access LGBTQ widowhood resources.
Seek later-life divorce counsel.
Create strategies if estranged or alienated.

10. **Zero Isolation**	TO DO BY	COMPLETED

Take a stand about living alone.
Create mealtime with others.
Stay social.
Sustain quality of existing relationships.
Access pools of new people.
Cut ties with toxic relationships.
Create a strategy to move on when friendships end.

11. **Love Is Love: Pets Are Family, Too**	TO DO BY	COMPLETED

Compare pros/cons of pet ownership.
Review budget considerations.
Decide pet type for current lifestyle.
Secure certification for pet as emotional support.
Consider pet alternatives.
Create pet-care back-up plan.
Create re-homing alternatives.
Seek bereavement support.

12. **Doctor Me**	TO DO BY	COMPLETED

Establish doctor-patient partnerships.
Check credentials and ratings of health-care providers.
Opt in or out for telemedicine.
Make plan to protect against medical identity theft.

Research medical tourism.

Create custom strategy for aging.

Consider hiring a transition coach.

13. Chronic Illness: The Game Changer   TO DO BY   COMPLETED

Create budget for chronic illness.

Create work-transition plan.

Seek caregivers and advocates.

Compare and utilize effective advocates.

Draft decision-making legal documents.

Establish HIPAA documentation for caregivers.

Consider housing alternatives for care.

Remain aware of staffing challenges.

Take advantage of technology for caregiving and well-being.

14. Early-Onset Alzheimer's: The Value of Knowing   TO DO BY   COMPLETED

Decide to get tested or not.

Put financial house in order.

Put legal affairs in order.

Track Alzheimer's disease according to stages.

Create workplace exit strategy.

Share diagnosis with employer.

Share diagnosis with children and grandchildren.

Help change the face of Alzheimer's.

15. "Just Shoot Me" Is Not a Plan   TO DO BY   COMPLETED

Control incoming information from doctor.

Tap into religious and/or spiritual resources.

Create instructions in the event of incapacity.

Research palliative care options.

Research hospice options.

Research DNR.

Research DNH.

Research Aid in Dying options.

Create end-of-life bedside companions.

16. Places to Go and Things to Do	TO DO BY	COMPLETED

Make plans to leave a legacy.

Create an ethical will.

Give away special belongings.

Consider taking life at a slower pace.

Complete the Tie Up Loose Ends Worksheet.

Determine destiny of your remains.

Create celebration ceremony.

Fulfill final wish.

Create death-services written instructions.

Worksheets and Checklists

Websites

General Interest

Facebook: www.facebook.com
Twitter: www.twitter.com
Pinterest: www.pinterest.com

Joy Loverde's Social Media

Website: www.elderindustry.com
Facebook: www.facebook.com/joy.loverde
Twitter: https://twitter.com/joyloverde
Pinterest: http://pinterest.com/joyloverde
LinkedIn: www.linkedin.com/in/joyloverde

1. Meet Your Future Self

Aging 2.0: www.aging2.com
Blue Zones: www.bluezones.com
The Center for Conscious Eldering: www.centerforconsciouseldering.com
Encore: www.encore.org
Inventure: The Purpose Company: http://richardleider.com
Karen Sands, GeroFuturist: www.karensands.com
Life Reimagined: https://lifereimagined.aarp.org
The Longevity Project: www.howardsfriedman.com/longevityproject
Over 60: www.over60.com.au
Sixty and Me: http://sixtyandme.com
Values: www.values.com

2. Good-bye Change, Hello Transition

National Sleep Foundation: https://sleepfoundation.org

3. Think Like a Strategist

Abraham-Hicks: www.abraham-hicks.com
American Philosophical Association: www.apaonline.org
Dropbox: www.dropbox.com
Foundation and Center for Critical Thinking: www.criticalthinking.org
Frameworks Institute: www.frameworksinstitute.org
Google Drive: www.google.com/drive
Make a Vision Board: http://makeavisionboard.com
Mind Tools: www.mindtools.com
Pinterest: www.pinterest.com
The Progress Principle: http://progressprinciple.com
Psych Wisdom: www.psychwisdom.com
Srini Pillay, MD: http://drsrinipillay.com

4. You Are Tougher Than You Look

Boomer Living: www.boomer-living.com
Growing Bolder: www.growingbolder.com
Project Resilience: www.projectresilience.com

5. The Fierce Urgency of Money

AARP: www.aarp.org
Age UK: www.ageuk.org.uk
Aid and Attendance Veteran Pension: www.VeteranAid.org
American Association of Daily Money Managers: www.aadmm.com
American Grandparents Association: https://aga.grandparents.com
American Institute of CPAs: www.aicpa.org
American Institute of Financial Gerontology: www.aifg.org
Benefits Checkup: www.benefits.gov
Canadian Securities Institute: www.csi.ca
Care.com: www.care.com
Celebrant Foundation and Institute: www.celebrantinstitute.org
Certified Financial Planner Board of Standards: www.cfp.net
Children's Health Insurance Program (CHIP): www.healthcare.gov

Christmas in April: www.christmasinapril.org

Dental Lifeline Network: https://dentallifeline.org

Department of Veterans Affairs: www.va.gov

Easterseals: www.easterseals.com

Eldercare Locator: www.eldercare.gov

Elder Law Answers: www.elderlawanswers.com

Everything Zoomer: www.everythingzoomer.com

Feeding America: www.feedingamerica.org

Financial Industry Regulatory Authority: www.finra.org

Free Medical Camps: www.freemedicalcamps.com

Funeral Consumer Alliance: www.funerals.org

The Funeral Site: www.thefuneralsite.com

Generations United: www.gu.org

Give Forward: www.GiveForward.com

Go Fund Me: www.GoFundMe.com

Grandfamilies: www.grandfamilies.org

Grandfamilies of America: www.grandfamiliesofamerica.com

Grand Magazine: www.grandmagazine.com

The Grandparent Effect: www.grandparenteffect.com

Grandparents Association: www.grandparents-association.org.uk

Grandparents Rights Organization: www.grandparentsrights.org

Help for Aging Veterans: www.helpforagingveterans.com

Help Hope Live: www.HelpHopeLive.org

I'm Sorry to Hear: www.imsorrytohear.com

Institute of Financial Planning (UK): www.financialplanning.org.uk

Internal Revenue Service: www.irs.gov

International Coach Federation: http://coachfederation.org

International End of Life Doula Association: www.inelda.org

International Virtual Assistants Association: http://ivaa.org

Justice in Aging: www.justiceinaging.org

Kiwanis: www.kiwanis.org

LegalShield: www.legalshield.com

Lemonade: www.lemonade.com

Lions: www.lionsclubs.org

Long Term Care Clearinghouse: www.longtermcare.gov

Medical Tourism Association: www.medicaltourismassociation.com

Medicaid: www.medicaid.gov

Medicare: www.medicare.gov

Michigan State University School of Social Work Kinship Care Resource Center: www
.kinship.msu.edu

Money Advice Service: www.moneyadviceservice.org.uk

National Able Network: www.nationalable.org

National Academy of Elder Law Attorneys: www.naela.org

National Association of Personal Financial Advisors: www.napfa.org

National Association of Realtors: www.realtor.org

National Association to Stop Guardian Abuse: http://stopguardianabuse.org

National Council on Aging: www.ncoa.org

National LGBT Legal Aid Forum: www.nclrights.org

Oregon State University Extension: http://extension.oregonstate.edu

Parting: www.parting.com

Persons with Disabilities: www.disability.gov

Pharmaceutical Assistance Programs: www.medicare.gov/pharmaceutical-assistance-program

Programs4People: www.invisibledisabilities.org

Rotary: www.rotary.org

SAGE (Services and Advocacy for Gay, Lesbian, Bisexual, and Transgender Elders): www
.sageusa.org

Senior Service America: www.seniorserviceamerica.org

Social Security: www.socialsecurity.gov

State Health Assistance Insurance Program: www.shiptacenter.org

Stuff Seniors Need: http://stuffseniorsneed.com

Supplemental Security Income (SSI): www.ssa.gov

Temporary Assistance for Needy Families (TANF): www.benefits.gov

Tooth Wisdom: www.toothwisdom.org

University of Florida Extension: http://edis.ifas.ufl.edu

University of Georgia Cooperative Extension Family and Consumer Sciences: www.fcs.uga
.edu

University of Wisconsin–Extension Family Living Programs: http://fyi.uwex.edu

USA.gov: www.usa.gov/child-care

US Department of Education: www.ed.gov

US Funerals Online: www.us-funerals.com

Veterans Benefits Administration: www.benefits.va.gov

Western Michigan University: https://wmich.edu

Why Hunger: www.whyhunger.org

6. Aging in Place Alone—What You Need to Know

AARP: www.aarp.org

ACT on Alzheimer's: www.actonalz.org

Aging Life Care Professional: www.aginglifecare.org

American Planning Association: www.planning.org

Alzheimer's Association: www.alz.org

Alzheimer's Australia National: www.fightdementia.org.au

Alzheimer's Disease International: www.alz.co.uk

Alzheimer's Reading Room: www.alzheimersreadingroom.com

Alzheimer's Society: www.alzheimers.org.uk

American Council on Aging: www.medicaidplanningassistance.org/find-a-medicaid-planner

American Seniors Housing Association: www.seniorshousing.org

American Society on Aging: www.asaaging.org

CenterLink: www.lgbtcenters.org

Certified Eden at Home Associate: www.edenalt.org

Certified Senior Advisor: www.csa.us

Certified Senior Housing Professional: www.seniorsrealestateinstitute.com

Dementia Action Alliance: http://daanow.org

Dementia Friendly America: www.dfamerica.org

Dementia Friends USA: www.dementiafriendsusa.org

Gay and Lesbian Medical Association: www.glma.org

Human Rights Campaign: www.hrc.org

LeadingAge: www.leadingage.org

Life Plan Community: www.lifeplancommunity.org

Medicaid: www.medicaid.gov

Medicare: www.mcdicarc.gov

National Aging in Place Council: www.naipc.org

National Association of Home Builders: www.nahb.org

National Center for Lesbian Rights: www.nclrights.org

National Center on Elder Abuse: www.ncea.aoa.gov

National Gay and Lesbian Chamber of Commerce: www.nglcc.org

National LGBT Elder Housing: http://sageusa.org/lgbthousing

National Resource Center on L.G.B.T. Aging: www.lgbtagingcenter.org

NextAvenue: www.nextavenue.org
LGBT National Help Center: www.glbthotline.org
LGBTQ Aging Pinterest: www.pinterest.com/joyloverde
Old Women's Project: www.oldwomensproject.org
Opening Doors London: http://openingdoorslondon.org.uk
PrideNet: www.pridenet.com
SAGE: www.sageusa.org
World Health Organization: www.who.int

7. Bring Livability Home

AARP: www.aarp.org
AARP Driver Safety Program: www.aarpdriversafety.org
Age in Place Tech: www.ageinplacetech.com
The Age of No Retirement: www.ageofnoretirement.org
Aging in Place: http://aginginplace.com
Alzheimer's Association: www.alz.org
American Academy of Home Care Medicine: www.aahcm.org
American Automobile Association (AAA): www.aaa.com
American Public Transportation Association: www.apta.com
Area Vibes: www.areavibes.com
Benefits Checkup: www.benefitscheckup.org
Canadian Automobile Association: www.caa.ca
Center for Research and Education on Aging and Technology Enhancement: www.create
    -center.org
CityLab: www.citylab.com
Community Transportation Association of America: www.ctaa.org
Corporation for National and Community Service: www.nationalservice.gov
Eldercare Locator: www.eldercare.gov
GoGo Grandparent: https://gogograndparent.com
Good Life Project: www.goodlifeproject.com
Grantmakers in Aging: www.giaging.org
GreatCall: www.greatcall.com
Home Healthcare Agencies: www.homehealthcareagencies.com
Independent Transportation Network of America: www.itnamerica.org
Keeping Us Safe: www.keepingussafe.org
LeadingAge Center for Aging Services Technologies: www.leadingage.org/cast

Lifecare Innovations: www.lcius.com

Life Planning Network: www.lifeplanningnetwork.org

Livability: www.livability.com

Meals on Wheels America: www.mowaa.org

Medicaid: www.medicaid.gov

Medicare: www.medicare.gov

Milken Institute: http://aging.milkeninstitute.org

National Aging and Disability Transportation Center: www.nadtc.org

National Association of Letter Carriers: www.nalc.org

National Council on Aging: www.ncoa.org

National Veteran's Foundation: http://nvf.org

Naturally Occurring Retirement Community: www.norc.org

Never Leave the Playground: www.neverleavetheplayground.com

Pass It On Network: http://passitonnetwork.org

Prevention Institute: www.preventioninstitute.org

Project Action: www.projectaction.com

Redstring: www.myredstring.com

Senior Care: www.seniorcare.com

Shared-Use Mobility Center: http://sharedusemobilitycenter.org

Silver Line: www.thesilverline.org.uk

Silvert's Adaptive Clothing and Footwear: www.silverts.com

Smart Growth Network: http://smartgrowth.org

TeleConnect Senior Services: www.teleconnect4seniors.com

Transportation for America: www.t4america.org

Village to Village Network: www.vtvnetwork.org

Volunteers of America: www.voa.org

The Wright Stuff: www.thewright-stuff.com

8. Moving On

55 Places: www.55places.com

Action with Communities in Rural England: www.acre.org.uk

Administration for Community Living: www.acl.gov

Airbnb: www.airbnb.com

American Automobile Association (AAA): www.aaa.com

American Seniors Housing Association: www.seniorshousing.org

Association of Professional Declutterers and Organizers: www.apdo.co.uk

Australasian Association of Professional Organizers: www.aapo.org.au

Bed and Breakfast: www.bedandbreakfast.com

BOOND: www.boond.de/home.html

Camping World: www.campingworld.com

Canada Seniors: www.seniors.gc.ca

Cohousing Association of the United States: www.cohousing.org

Coliving: http://coliving.org

The Earth Awaits: www.theearthawaits.com

Escapees CARE: www.escapeescare.org

Escapees Club's RV-Alliance America: www.escapees.com

Estate Inventory Services: www.estateinventoryservices.com

Federal Office of Rural Health Policy: www.hrsa.gov/ruralhealth

The Fellowship for Intentional Community: www.ic.org/directory

Global Ecovillage Network: http://gen.ecovillage.org

Good Sam Club: www.goodsamclub.com

Group Homes Online: www.grouphomesonline.com

Japan Association of Life Organizers: http://jalo.jp

Just Landed: www.justlanded.com

LeadingAge: www.leadingage.org

Life Plan Community: www.lifeplancommunity.org

National Association of Home Inventory Professionals: http://nahip.com

National Association of Professional Organizers: www.napo.net

National Association of Senior Move Managers: www.nasmm.org

National Center of Veteran Homelessness: www.va.gov/homeless

National Rural Health Association: www.ruralhealthweb.org

National Shared Housing Resource Center: http://nationalsharedhousing.org

Naturally Occurring Retirement Communities: www.norc.org

NBPO: www.nbpo.nl

Peace Corps: www.peacecorps.gov

Professional Organiser Association Africa: http://podirectory.com

Professional Organizers in Canada: www.organizersincanada.com

Programs for Elderly: www.programsforelderly.com

Rural Health Information Hub: www.ruralhealthinfo.org

Senior Housing Checklist: www.elderindustry.com

Shared Lives: http://sharedlivesplus.org.uk

Silvernest: www.silvernest.com

Sustainable Ecovillages Forum: www.sustainableecovillages.net

Transitions Abroad: www.transitionsabroad.com

TravelSure: www.travelsure.co.uk

UK Cohousing Network: http://cohousing.org.uk

USA.gov: www.usa.gov/housing

US Department of Agriculture Rural Housing Service: www.rd.usda.gov

Village to Village Network: www.vtvnetwork.org

Women Living in Community: www.womenlivingincommunity.com

9. The Broken Hearts Club

About (Grandparents): http://grandparents.about.com

Alienated Grandparents Anonymous Incorporated: http://www.aga-fl.org

Department of Veterans Affairs: www.veterans.gov

Disinherited: www.disinherited.com

Dr. Joshua Coleman: www.drjoshuacoleman.com

Empowering Parents: www.empoweringparents.com

Estranged Parents Speak Up: http://peacefulparents.proboards.com

Estranged Stories: www.estrangedstories.com

Estrangements: www.estrangements.com

Facebook: www.facebook.com

Family Caregiver Alliance: www.caregiver.org

Human Rights Campaign: www.hrc.org

Lambda Legal: www.lambdalegal.org

Legacy Connect: http://connect.legacy.com

The Lilac Tree: www.thelilactree.org

National Center for Lesbian Rights: www.nclrights.org

National Family Caregiver Support Program: www.aoa.acl.gov

National LGBT Aging Resource Center: www.lgbtagingcenter.org

Parents, Families, Friends, and Allies United with LGBTQ (PFLAG): http://home.pflag.org

Rejected Parents: www.rejectedparents.net

SAGE: www.sageusa.org

Social Security: www.socialsecurity.gov

Splitsville: www.splitsville.com

Stand Alone: www.standalone.org.uk

Widows Hope: www.widowshope.org

10. Zero Isolation

Ageing Without Children: https://awoc.org

American Association for Marriage and Family Therapy: www.aamft.org

Big Brothers Big Sisters of America: www.bbbs.org

Campaign to End Loneliness: www.campaigntoendloneliness.org

Cards 4X: www.cards4x.com

Childfree: www.childfree.net

Circle of Care: www.circleofcareproject.org

Connect2Affect: http://connect2affect.org

Contact the Elderly: www.contact-the-elderly.org.uk

Council on Contemporary Families: https://contemporaryfamilies.org

Experience Corps: www.experiencecorps.org

Find a Grandparent: www.findagrandparent.org.au

The Freebird Club: www.thefreebirdclub.com

Lauren Mackler: http://laurenmackler.com

Meetup: www.meetup.com

Mentor: The National Mentoring Partnership: www.mentoring.org

The Mentoring Project: www.thementoringproject.org

My Mentor Advisor: www.mymentoradvisor.com

National and Community Service: www.nationalservice.gov

National Coloring Book Day: www.coloringbookday.com

Nextdoor: www.nextdoor.com

Royal Voluntary Service: www.royalvoluntaryservice.org.uk

RSVP: www.nationalservice.gov

San Pasqual Academy: www.sanpasqualacademy.org

Senior Center Directory: www.seniorcenterdirectory.com

Senior Corps: www.seniorcorps.gov

Share the Care: www.sharethecare.org

Stephanie Coontz: www.stephaniecoontz.com

Susan RoAne: www.susanroane.com

The Transition Network: www.thetransitionnetwork.org

Wikipedia: https://en.wikipedia.org

Work Hard Anywhere: http://workhardanywhere.com.

11. Love Is Love: Pets Are Family, Too

American Society for the Prevention of Cruelty to Animals: www.aspca.org

Best Friends: http://bestfriends.org

Care.com: www.care.com

CareGuide: www.careguide.com

Cat Lovers Only: www.cat-lovers-only.com

Cesar's Way: www.cesarsway.com

Eden Alternative: www.edenalt.org

The Grey Muzzle: www.greymuzzle.org

Humane Society: www.humanesociety.org

The International Association of Animal Hospice and Palliative Care: www.iaahpc.org

International Boarding and Pet Services Association: www.ibpsa.com

National Association of Professional Pet Sitters: www.petsitters.org

Paws: www.paws.org

Pet Finder: www.petfinder.com

Pet Health Information: www.pethealthinfo.org.uk

Pet Partners: https://petpartners.org

Pet Sitters International: www.petsit.com

Pet University: www.petuniversity.com

Pets for Vets: www.petsforvets.com

Pets WebMD: www.pets.webmd.com

Serenity Park Parrot Sanctuary: http://parrotcare.org/serenity-park

Service Dog Central: www.servicedogcentral.org

Service Dogs, Inc.: www.servicedogs.org

The Shelter Pet Project: www.theshelterpetproject.org

Volunteers of America: www.voa.org

Web Vet: www.webvet.com

12. Doctor Me

Academy of Nutrition and Dietetics: www.eatright.org

Age Brilliantly: www.agebrilliantly.org

AIM Doc Finder: www.docboard.org

Alive Inside Foundation: www.aliveinside.org

Alzheimer's Association: Early-Stage Advisory Group: www.alz.org/about_us_early_stage_advisory_group.asp

American Academy of Pain Medicine: www.painmed.org

American Association of Acupuncture and Oriental Medicine: www.aaaomonline.org

American Association of Naturopathic Physicians: www.naturopathic.org

American Board of Medical Specialties: www.abms.org

American Massage Therapy Association: www.amtamassage.org

American Medical Association: www.ama-assn.org

Association of Nature and Forest Therapy Guides and Programs: www.natureandforesttherapy.org

Best Doctors: www.bestdoctors.com

Center for Preventive Cardiology: http://medschool.umaryland.edu

Center for Technology and Aging: www.techandaging.org

Centers for Disease Control and Prevention: http://www.cdc.gov

Centers for Medicare and Medicaid Services: www.cms.gov

Changing Aging: www.changingaging.org

Conductorcise: www.conductorcise.com

Drugs.com: www.drugs.com

Federal Trade Commission: www.ftc.gov

Federation of State Medical Boards: www.docinfo.org

Fisher Institute for Wellness and Gerontology: http://cms.bsu.edu/academics/centersandinstitutes/wellness

Genome: www.genomemag.com

HealthCare Trip: www.healthcaretrip.org

Health Grades: www.healthgrades.com

Health in Aging: www.healthinaging.org

Health Insurance Portability and Accountability Act: www.hhs.gov/hipaa

Health IT: www.healthit.gov

Hopkins Medicine: www.hopkinsmedicine.org

International Association of Professional Life Coaches: www.iaplifecoaches.org

International Coach Federation: www.coachfederation.org/ICF

International Council on Active Aging: www.icaa.cc

International Medical Travel Journal: www.imtj.com/medical-tourism-associations

Laughter Yoga: www.laughteryoga.org

Mayo Clinic: www.mayoclinic.org

Medical Tourism Association: www.medicaltourismassociation.com

Medivizor: www.medivizor.com

Medline Plus: https://medlineplus.gov

Montessori for Dementia: http://montessorifordementia.com.au

Mouth Healthy: www.mouthhealthy.org/en/adults-over-60

National Association for Continence: www.nafc.org

National Center for Complementary and Integrative Health: https://nccih.nih.gov

National Center for Creative Aging: www.creativeaging.org

National Center for Homeopathy: www.homeopathycenter.org

National Institutes of Health: www.nih.gov/health-information

Patients Beyond Borders: www.patientsbeyondborders.com

Pharmacy Checker: www.pharmacychecker.com

Philips Breathless Choir: http://philips.to/breathless-choir

Physician's Practice: www.physicianspractice.com

Planetree: www.planetree.org

Rock Steady Boxing: www.rocksteadyboxing.org

The SCAN Foundation: www.thescanfoundation.org/learn-more-about-person-centered-care

Surgeon Scorecard: https://projects.propublica.org/surgeons

TapCloud: www.tapcloud.com

Upside Edibles: www.upsideedibles.com

US Department of Health and Human Service: www.hhs.gov

US Travel Insurance Association: www.ustia.org

WebMD: www.webmd.com

Women's Healthy Aging: www.womenshealth.gov/aging

13. Chronic Illness: The Game Changer

AdvoConnection: http://advoconnection.com

Aging Life Care Association: www.aginglifecare.org

Alliance of Professional Health Advocates: www.aphadvocates.org

American Diabetes Association: www.diabetes.org

Argentum: www.argentum.org/alfa

Beneficiary and Family Centered Care Quality Improvement Organization: www.medicare
    .gov/claims-and-appeals

Center for Excellence in Assisted Living: www.theceal.org

Center for Patient Partnerships: www.patientpartnerships.org

ChoiceWorks: www.choiceworks.com

Eden Alternative: www.edenalt.org

Eldercare Locator: www.eldercare.gov

Governed Advocacy Information Network: www.gain.org.uk

Green House Project: www.thegreenhouseproject.org

Kind Ethics: http://kindethics.com

The King's Fund: www.kingsfund.org.uk

Long-Term Care Ombudsman: www.ltcombudsman.org

Marguerite Casey Foundation: www.caseygrants.org

Medicaid: www.medicaid.gov

Medicare Nursing Home Guide: www.medicare.gov

My Elder Advocate: www. http://myelderadvocate.com

National Association of Healthcare Advocacy Consultants: http://nahac.memberlodge.com

National Care Planning Council: www.longtermcarelink.net

National Center for Assisted Living: www.ahcancal.org/ncal

National Consumer Voice for Quality Long-Term Care: http://theconsumervoice.org

National Domestic Workers Alliance: www.domesticworkers.org

National Parkinson Foundation: www.parkinson.org

Patient Advocate Foundation: www.patientadvocate.org

Patient Navigator: http://patientnavigator.com

Senior Housing Forum: www.seniorhousingforum.net

Seniorly: www.seniorly.com

US Department of Health and Human Services: www.hhs.gov

Veterans Health Administration Patient Advocate: www.va.gov/health/patientadvocate

Who Will Take Care of Me When I'm Old?: www.elderindustry.com

14. Early-Onset Alzheimer's: The Value of Knowing

Alive Inside: www.aliveinside.us

Alzheimer's Association: www.alz.org

Alzheimer's Association Green-Field Library: www.alz.org/library

Alzheimer's Reading Room: www.alzheimersreadingroom.com

Best Friends Approach to Alzheimer's Care: http://bestfriendsapproach.com

Better Business Bureau Wise Giving Alliance: http://give.org

Charity Navigator: www.charitynavigator.org

Charity Watch: www.charitywatch.org

Dementia Action Alliance: http://daanow.org

Dementia Alliance International: www.dementiaallianceinternational.org

Disrupt Dementia: https://drbillthomas.org/local/disrupt-dementia

Federal Trade Commission Charity Scams: www.consumer.ftc.gov

Giving Voice Chorus: www.givingvoicechorus.org

GuideStar: www.guidestar.org

Instagram: www.instagram.com

Internal Revenue Service: www.irs.gov/charities

National Association of State Charity Officials: www.nasconet.org

National Council of Certified Dementia Practitioners: www.nccdp.org

National Institute on Aging: www.nia.nih.gov

Pinterest, "Early-Stage Alzheimer's Disease": www.pinterest.com/joyloverde

Purple Angel Dementia Awareness Campaign: www.purpleangel-global.com

Teepa Snow: http://teepasnow.com/resources/for-kids-teens

Together in This: http://togetherinthis.com

To Whom I May Concern: www.towhomimayconcern.info

WikiHow: www.wikihow.com

Young Dementia UK: www.youngdementiauk.org

YouTube: www.youtube.com

15. "Just Shoot Me" Is Not a Plan

Aging Life Care Association: www.aginglifecare.org

American Bar Association: www.americanbar.org

Americans for Better Care of the Dying: www.abcd-caring.org

Axiom Action: http://axiomaction.com

Because Hope Matters: http://becausehopematters.com

Best Endings: www.bestendings.com

Betsy Trapasso: www.betsytrapasso.com

Caring.com: www.caring.com/end-of-life

CaringBridge: www.caringbridge.org

Compassion and Choices: www.compassionandchoices.org

The Conversation Project: www.theconversationproject.org

Death Café: http://deathcafe.com

Death with Dignity: www.deathwithdignity.org

Dying Matters: www.dyingmatters.org

Eldercare Locator: www.eldercare.gov

End of Life University: www.eoluniversity.com

Exit International: https://exitinternational.net

Final Exit Network: www.finalexitnetwork.org

Five Wishes: www.agingwithdignity.org/five-wishes

The GroundSwell Project: https://thegroundswellproject.squarespace.com

Growth House: www.growthhouse.org

Hospice Foundation of America: www.hospicefoundation.org

Hospice Net: www.hospicenet.org

Impermanence: http://impermanenceatwork.org

International End of Life Doula Association: www.inelda.org

Let's Have Dinner and Talk About Death: http://deathoverdinner.org

Life. Death. Whatever.: www.lifedeathwhatever.com

Living and Dying Consciously Project: www.livinganddyingconsciouslyproject.org

The Metta Institute: www.mettainstitute.org

Music-Thanatology Association International: www.mtai.org

National Association for Home Care and Hospice: www.nahc.org

National Association of Area Agencies on Aging: www.n4a.org

National Home Funeral Alliance: www.homefuneralalliance.org

National Hospice and Palliative Care Organization: www.nhpco.org

National Social Worker Finder: www.helpstartshere.org

No One Dies Alone: www.peacehealth.org

The Peaceful Pill Handbook: www.peacefulpillhandbook.com

Physician Orders for Life-Sustaining Treatments (POLST): www.polst.org

Slow Medicine: www.facebook.com

Soul Care Project: http://soulcareproject.org

Spiritual MD: www.karenwyattmd.com

Suicide Prevention Lifeline: https://suicidepreventionlifeline.org

A Traveler's View: www.atravelersview.org

Veriditas: www.veriditas.org

World Federation of Right to Die Societies: www.worldrtd.net

Yellow Dot: www.nationalyellowdot.org

You're Going to Die: www.yg2d.com

16. Places to Go and Things to Do

Angels Flight: www.angels-flight.net

Body Worlds: www.bodyworlds.com

Celebrations of Life: https://celebrationsoflife.net/ethicalwills

Confessions of a Funeral Director: www.calebwilde.com

Cryonics: www.cryonics.org

Dream Foundation: www.dreamfoundation.org

ePassing: www.epassing.org
Eternal Ascent Society: www.eternalascent.com
Eternal Reef: www.eternalreefs.com
Fra Noi: www.franoi.com
Green Burial Council: https://greenburialcouncil.org
The History Project: www.thehistoryproject.com
Legacy: www.legacy.com
National Funeral Directors Association: www.nfda.org
National Handwriting Association: www.nha-handwriting.org.uk
Personal Legacy Advisors: www.personallegacyadvisors.com
Second Wind Dreams: www.secondwind.org
StoryCorps: www.storycorps.org
Twilight Wish: www.twilightwish.org

Recommended Reading

1. Meet Your Future Self: *The Complete Eldercare Planner: Where to Start, Which Questions to Ask, and How to Find Help* (2009) by Joy Loverde

2. Good-bye Change, Hello Transition: *Managing Transitions, 25th Anniversary Edition: Making the Most of Change* (2017) by William Bridges and Susan Bridges

3. Think Like a Strategist: *Leadership Simple: Leading People to Lead Themselves* (2003) by Steve Morris and Jill Morris

4. You Are Tougher Than You Look: *The Untethered Soul: The Journey Beyond Yourself* (2007) by Michael A. Singer

5. The Fierce Urgency of Money: *Affluence Intelligence: Earn More, Worry Less, and Live a Happy and Balanced Life* (2011) by Stephen Goldbart and Joan Indursky DiFuria

6. Aging in Place Alone—What You Need to Know: *Going Solo: The Extraordinary Rise and Surprising Appeal of Living Alone* (2013) by Eric Klinenberg

7. Bring Livability Home: *The Berenstain Bears Lend a Helping Hand* (1998) by Stan and Jan Berenstain

8. Moving On: *Big Magic: Creative Living Beyond Fear* (2016) by Elizabeth Gilbert

9. The Broken Hearts Club: *Conscious Living, Conscious Aging: Embrace & Savor Your Next Chapter* (2014) by Ron Pevny

10. Zero Isolation: *How to Be an Adult in Relationships: The Five Keys to Mindful Loving* (2002) by David Richo

11. Love Is Love: Pets Are Family, Too: *What Pet Should I Get?* (2015) by Dr. Seuss

12. Doctor Me: *The Four Things That Matter Most—10th Anniversary Edition: A Book About Living* (2014) by Ira Byock, MD

13. Chronic Illness: The Game Changer: *29 Gifts: How a Month of Giving Can Change Your Life* (2010) by Cami Walker

14. Early-Onset Alzheimer's: The Value of Knowing: *Alzheimer's Early Stages: First Steps for Family, Friends, and Caregivers,* updated edition (2013) by Daniel Kuhn

15. "Just Shoot Me" Is Not a Plan: *Too Soon Old, Too Late Smart: Thirty True Things You Need to Know Now* (2008) by Gordon Livingston

16. Places to Go and Things to Do: *Modern Death: How Medicine Changed the End of Life* (2017) by Haider Warraich

Recommended Movies

1. Meet Your Future Self: *The Big Chill* (1983)

2. Good-bye Change, Hello Transition: *Life Is Beautiful* (1997)

3. Think Like a Strategist: *Inside Out* (2015)

4. You Are Tougher Than You Look: *Little Miss Sunshine* (2006)

5. The Fierce Urgency of Money: *The Pursuit of Happyness* (2006)

6. Aging in Place Alone—What You Need to Know: *Wings of Desire* (1998)

7. Bring Livability Home: *St. Vincent* (2014)

8. Moving On: *Life as a House* (2001)

9. The Broken Hearts Club: *Griefwalker* (2008)

10. Zero Isolation: *The Lonely Guy* (1984)

11. Love Is Love: Pets Are Family, Too: *The Secret Life of Pets* (2016)

12. Doctor Me: *Awakenings* (1990)

13. Chronic Illness: The Game Changer: *The Sessions* (2012)

14. Early-Onset Alzheimer's: The Value of Knowing: *Still Alice* (2014)

15. "Just Shoot Me" Is Not a Plan: *Up* (2009)

16. Places to Go and Things to Do: *Two Weeks* (2006)

Recommended YouTube

1. Meet Your Future Self: *100 Years of Beauty: Aging Cut Has a Field Day*, published May 14, 2015

2. Good-bye Change, Hello Transition: Eckhart Tolle, *I'm Aware of Fear That Is Almost Continually in Me*, published May 10, 2016

3. Think Like a Strategist: *5 Tips To Improve Your Critical Thinking* by Samantha Agoos, published March 15, 2016

4. You Are Tougher Than You Look: Pharrell Williams, *Happy* (Official Music Video), published November 21, 2013

5. The Fierce Urgency of Money: Pink Floyd, *Money* (Official Music Video), published June 25, 2014

6. Aging in Place Alone—What You Need to Know: *How I Love My House* (from *The Wubbulous World of Dr. Seuss*)

7. Bring Livability Home: Gil Penalosa, *Mobility as a Force for Health, Wealth, and Happiness*, published December 12, 2014

8. Moving On: *Somewhere over the Rainbow*, Judy Garland 1939, uploaded March 27, 2010

9. The Broken Hearts Club: *Somebody That I Used to Know*, performed by Gotye, written by Walter Andre De Backer

10. Zero Isolation: *You've Got a Friend in Me*, Randy Newman (*Toy Story* edition), published March 25, 2015

11. Love Is Love: Pets Are Family, Too: *Ultimate Dog Tease*, uploaded May 1, 2011; *Ultimate Cat Tease*, published April 12, 2012

12. Doctor Me: Subscribe to *Attitude Is Altitude*. Type "attitude is altitude" into the YouTube search engine.

13. Chronic Illness: The Game Changer: *What Is Social Justice?* published by PragerU, March 24, 2014

14. Early-Onset Alzheimer's: The Value of Knowing: Subscribe to the Alzheimer's Society YouTube channel. Type "Alzheimer's Society" into the YouTube search engine. Also type "I have Alzheimer's" into the YouTube search engine to access many excellent videos on the topic of early-onset dementia.

15. "Just Shoot Me" Is Not a Plan: *Ask a Mortician* video series

16. Places to Go and Things to Do: Amy Krouse Rosenthal's Thought Bubble: *Kindness Thought Café*, uploaded April 16, 2010

Recommended Television Shows

7. Bring Livability Home: *Seinfeld*

10. Zero Isolation: *The Golden Girls*

Recommended Songs

1. Meet Your Future Self: "My Way," performed by Frank Sinatra, written by Thibault, Anka, Revaux, and François

2. Good-bye Change, Hello Transition: "Does Anybody Really Know What Time It Is?" by Chicago

3. Think Like a Strategist: "Ironic" by Alanis Morissette

4. You Are Tougher Than You Look: "I Hope You Dance" by Tia Sillers and Mark Sanders

5. The Fierce Urgency of Money: "Spinning Wheel" by Blood, Sweat, and Tears

6. Aging in Place Alone—What You Need to Know: "What a Wonderful World," performed by Louis Armstrong, written by George David Weiss and Robert Thiele

7. Bring Livability Home: "Lean on Me" by Bill Withers

8. Moving On: "Right Place, Wrong Time" by Dr. John

9. The Broken Hearts Club: "This Is It," performed by Kenny Loggins, written by Kenneth Clark Loggins and Michael McDonald

10. Zero Isolation: "While You See a Chance" by Steve Winwood

11. Love Is Love: Pets Are Family, Too: "No One" performed by Alicia Keys

12. Doctor Me: "Stayin' Alive" by the Bee Gees

13. Chronic Illness: The Game Changer: "We Gotta Get Out of This Place," written by Barry Mann and Cynthia Weil, recorded by the Animals

14. Early-Onset Alzheimer's: The Value of Knowing: "Both Sides Now" by Joni Mitchell

15. "Just Shoot Me" Is Not a Plan: "Softly As I Leave You," sung by Andy Williams, composed by Giorgio Calabrese and Tony De Vita

16. Places to Go and Things to Do: "Instant Karma! (We All Shine On)" by John Lennon

Recommended TED Talks

1. Meet Your Future Self: "The Psychology of Your Future Self," presented by Dan Gilbert, psychologist and happiness expert, filmed March 2014

2. Good-bye Change, Hello Transition: "The Art of Being Yourself," presented by Caroline McHugh, chief idologist, filmed February 18, 2013

3. Think Like a Strategist: "The Surprising Habits of Original Thinkers," presented by Adam Grant, filmed February 2016

4. You Are Tougher Than You Look: "How to Stop Screwing Yourself Over," presented by Mel Robbins, career and relationship expert, filmed June 11, 2011

5. The Fierce Urgency of Money: "How a Penny Made Me Feel like a Millionaire," presented by Tania Luna, surprisologist, filmed July 2012

6. Aging in Place Alone—What You Need to Know: "The Power of Introverts," presented by Susan Cain, filmed February 2012

7. Bring Livability Home: "The World's Largest Family Reunion. We're All Invited!" presented by AJ Jacobs, author, filmed June 9, 2011

8. Moving On: "Where Is Home?" presented by Pico Iyer, global author, filmed January 2010

9. The Broken Hearts Club: "On Being Wrong," presented by Kathryn Schulz, wrongologist, filmed March 2011

10. Zero Isolation: "Why You Should Talk to Strangers" presented by Kio Stark, stranger enthusiast, filmed February 2016

11. Love Is Love: Pets Are Family, Too: "Four Legged Citizens," presented by Francis Battista, one of the founders of Best Friends Animal Society, filmed September 10, 2014

12. Doctor Me: "What Makes a Good Life? Lessons from the Longest Study on Happiness," presented by Robert Waldinger, psychiatrist, psychoanalyst and Zen priest, filmed November 2015

13. Chronic Illness: The Game Changer: "How Frustration Can Make Us More Creative," presented by Tim Harford, economist, journalist, and broadcaster, filmed September 2015

14. Early-Onset Alzheimer's: The Value of Knowing: "How I'm Preparing to Get Alzheimer's," presented by Alanna Shaikh, filmed June 2012

15. "Just Shoot Me" Is Not a Plan: "What Really Matters at the End of Life," presented by BJ Miller, palliative care physician, filmed March 2015

16. Places to Go and Things to Do: "Before I Die I Want to . . . ," presented by Candy Chang, artist, designer, urban planner, filmed July 2012

Gratitudes

There have been many caring people in my life who I am grateful for, beginning with my grandparents, Pellegro and Maria Marsalli Nesti and Frank and Marie Wherry Loverde.

To my parents, Charles Loverde and Alba Loverde Wright—who helped me succeed in chasing my dreams. I am especially thankful that you showed me the value of working hard. Without you, I'd be nowhere near the person I am and the woman I continue to become.

To my siblings, Jimmy, Carol, Peter, and Linda—I cannot imagine living in this world without your closeness, guidance, and loyalty. Thank you for coaching me from the sidelines, and especially for the gift of your families—Dominic, Pasquale, Orasa, Angelina, Maria, Lou, Louis, and Nic.

To Bonnie, my daughter—thank you for teaching me the true meaning of commitment to family, especially the loving care you gave to Paul. My words of gratitude barely scratch the surface when it comes to the many precious gifts you have given me, especially Joe, Lanea, Henry, Siena, Ivy, Jacqueline, Trinity, Emily, Michael, Evie, and Willow.

To my husband, David Schultz, who gets me like no other—your support of my writing and work schedule and your brilliant editing gave us a partnership made in heaven. Thank you for being my forever bleacher buddy and baseball fanatic, voice of reason, personal shopper, chauffeur, humorist, chef, and best friend. I will always love you.

To the Schultz clan—thank you for bringing never-ending joy to my heart—Jeff, Amy, Garrett, Greg, Kim, Sam, Ellie, Jack, Ben, Lucy, Max, Lexi, Gardner, Herb, Sharon, Devin, Nancy, and Jim.

To my loving aunts and uncles—Natalino, Graziella, Graziano, Ilide, Oreste, Vittorio, Guglielmo, Guy, Leo, Sergio, Iola, Frank, Bernice, Frank, Margaret, Robert, and Ethel— thank you for the family gatherings and the memories that I will forever and always hold in my heart. Also, a thank-you to my special aunts, Lisa and Laura.

To my fun and fabulous cousins—Carla, Raul, Teri, Bill, Laura, Glen, Martha, John, Rita, Sergio, Patti, Michelle, Peter, Nancy, Rachel, Frankie, Francine, Maya, Joe, Paul, Marie, Emmett, Troy, Gianna, Bridie, Bill, Bobby, Donna, Michael, Karen, Pati, Chuck, Margaret, Jack, Barbara, Mary Beth, Jim, Claudio, Antonella, Fabbio, Marilù, and Linda. Thank you for being my lifeline and playmates. I love all of you dearly.

To my forever-loving friends—I am grateful that we have chosen to experience life together. As the saying goes . . . *A friend is someone who will bail you out of jail. A best friend is the one sitting next to you, saying, "Boy, was that fun."*

The opportunity for this book would never have come my way if it were not for three special people—Angie Thoburn, who woke me up; Jill Morris, who keeps me moving forward; and Lisa Hudson, who recognized my mission early on. How can I ever thank you?

To you, Joe Durepos, literary agent—in the wee hours of the morning during writing time, bleary-eyed, and surrounded by stacks of research and umpteen empty coffee mugs, I hear your soothing voice and gentle laugh. It is then that I see the light at the end of the tunnel. Thank you for your unwavering and unflinching faith and support.

And finally, to my incredible team at Da Capo Press—Claire Schulz, Raquel Hitt, Matthew Weston, Amber Morris, and Iris Bass. Thank you for thinking through each and every word in this book, for deeply caring about the subject of aging solo, and for believing in me. No one stands alone in the publishing process and I am forever grateful that you chose to join me on this journey of a lifetime.

Notes

GET REAL

1. Susan L. Brown and I-Fen Lin, "The Gray Divorce Revolution: Rising Divorce Among Middle-Aged and Older Adults, 1990–2010," *Journals of Gerontology, Series B: Psychological Sciences and Social Sciences* 67, no. 6 (2012): 731–741.

2. GOOD-BYE CHANGE, HELLO TRANSITION

1. James W. Pennebaker, "Writing About Emotional Experiences as a Therapeutic Process," *Psychological Science* 8, no. 3 (May 1997): 162–166, http://dx.doi.org/10.1111/j.467-9280.1997.tb00403.x, http://psyc-net.apa.org/psycinfo/1997-06306-006.
2. John Wallis Rowe, MD, and Robert L. Kahn, *Successful Aging* (Pantheon, 1998).
3. Stephanie Silberman and Charles Morin, *The Insomnia Workbook: A Comprehensive Guide to Getting the Sleep You Need* (New Harbinger Publications, 2009).

3. THINK LIKE A STRATEGIST

1. Srini Pillay, MD, "To Reach Your Goals, Make a Mental Movie," *Harvard Business Review*, March 5, 2014, https://hbr.org/2014/03/to-reach-your-goals-make-a-mental-movie.
2. Demis Hassabis and Eleanor A. Maguire, "The Construction System of the Brain," published March 30, 2009, doi: 10.1098/rstb.2008.0296, Wellcome Trust Centre for Neuroimaging, Institute of Neurology, University College London, London, UK, http://rstb.royalsocietypublishing.org/content/364/1521/1263.
3. L. Sapadin, "Talking to Yourself: A Sign of Sanity," Psych Central (2009), http://psychcentral.com/blog/archives/2012/12/07/talking-to-yourself-a-sign-of-sanity.

4. YOU ARE TOUGHER THAN YOU LOOK

1. Susan Nolen-Hoeksema, Louise E. Parker, and Judith Larson, "Ruminative Coping with Depressed Mood Following Loss," *Journal of Personality and Social Psychology* 67, no. 1 (July 1994): 92–104, http://psycnet.apa.org/journals/psp/67/1/92.

5. THE FIERCE URGENCY OF MONEY

1. Genworth Financial, Inc., "Genworth 2015 Cost of Care Survey. Home Care Providers, Adult Day Health Care Facilities, Assisted Living Facilities and Nursing Homes," https://www.genworth.com/dam/Americas/US/PDFs/Consumer/corporate/130568_040115_gnw.pdf.

2. https://www.consumer.ftc.gov/articles/0301-funeral-costs-and-pricing-checklist.

3. Amy Goyer, "More Grandparents Raising Grandkids: New Census Data Shows an Increase in Children Being Raised by Extended Family," December 20, 2010, http://www.aarp.org/relationships/grandparenting/info-12-2010/more_grandparents_raising_grandchildren.html.

6. AGING IN PLACE ALONE—WHAT YOU NEED TO KNOW

1. Centers for Disease Control and Prevention, "Heat-Related Mortality—Chicago, July 1995," *Morbidity and Mortality Weekly Report*, 44, no. 31 (August 11, 1995): 577–579, http://www.cdc.gov/mmwr/preview/mmwrhtml/00038443.htm.

2. N. R. Kleinfeld, "The Lonely Death of George Bell," *New York Times*, October 17, 2015, http://www.nytimes.com/2015/10/18/nyregion/dying-alone-in-new-york-city.html.

3. Elizabeth Day, "Nobody Cared When They Were Alive or Mourned When They Died Alone," *Guardian*, August 16, 2008, https://www.theguardian.com/society/2008/aug/17/communities.socialexclusion.

4. Linda Poon, "Why Won't You Be My Neighbor?" August 19, 2015, http://www.citylab.com/housing/2015/08/why-wont-you-be-my-neighbor/401762/.

5. The Global Age-Friendly Cities Guide, 2006, http://www.who.int/ageing/publications.

6. Ashton Applewhite, *This Chair Rocks: A Manifesto Against Ageism* (Networked Books, 2016).

7. BRING LIVABILITY HOME

1. Economist Intelligence Unit, 2016, http://www.economist.com/blogs/graphicdetail/2016/08/daily-chart-14.

2. Alok Jha, "How Facial Recognition Could Be Key to Maintaining Independence of Elderly," ITV, February 17, 2017, http://www.itv.com/news/2017–02–17/technology-could-be-key-to-maintaining-independence-of-elderly/.

8. MOVING ON

1. "Housing Options for Adults with Special Needs," February 1, 2015, Special Needs Answers, http://specialneedsanswers.com/housing-options-for-adults-with-special-needs-14975.

2. New York City Department for the Aging, http://www.nyc.gov/html/dfta/html/services/retirement.shtml.

3. Erin G. Roth, MA, J. Kevin Eckert, PhD, and Leslie A. Morgan, PhD, "Stigma and Discontinuity in Multilevel Senior Housing's Continuum of Care," Department of Sociology and Anthropology, Center for Aging Studies, UMBC, Baltimore, MD, January 29, 2015, accepted March 29, 2015, http://gerontologist.oxfordjournals.org/content/early/2015/05/04/geront.gnv055.full.pdf+html.

9. THE BROKEN HEARTS CLUB

1. Kathleen McGarry and Robert F. Schoeni, "Medicare Gaps and Widow Poverty," *Social Security Bulletin* 66, no. 1 (2005): 58.

2. Susan L. Brown and I-Fen Lin, "The Gray Divorce Revolution: Rising Divorce Among Middle-Aged and Older Adults, 1990–2010," Bowling Green State University, National Center for Family and Marriage Research Working Paper Series WP-13–03, March 2013, https://www.bgsu.edu/content/dam/BGSU/college -of-arts-and-sciences/NCFMR/documents/Lin/The-Gray-Divorce.pdf.

3. Abby Ellin, "After Full Lives Together, More Older Couples Are Divorcing," *New York Times*, October 20, 2015, http://www.nytimes.com/2015/10/31/your-money/after-full-lives-together-more-older-couples-are -divorcing.html?_r=0.

4. Ibid.

5. 2016 Merriam-Webster, Incorporated, https://www.merriam-webster.com/dictionary/estrange.

6. 2016 Merriam-Webster, Incorporated, https://www.merriam-webster.com/dictionary/alienate.

7. Trevor Todd, "Dysfunctional Families: The Estrangement Epidemic," February 19, 2014, http://dis inherited.com/family-estrangement-a-silent-epidemic/.

8. Lawrence Kutner, "Parent and Child," *New York Times*, March 1, 1990, http://www.nytimes.com/1990 /03/01/garden/parent-child.html.

9. Lena Etuk, "How Family Structure Has Changed," Oregon State University Extension Service, 2008, http://oregonexplorer.info/content/how-family-structure-has-changed.

10. ZERO ISOLATION

1. Ephrat Livni, "A Wildly Popular Japanese Restaurant Chain Where Diners Eat Alone in Meditation Opened Its First US Location," www.qz.com, November 1, 2016, https://qz.com/823754/ichiran-ramen -meditation/.

2. Stephanie Coontz, "How to Stay Married," *Times* (London), November 30, 2006, http://www.stephanie coontz.com/articles/article34.htm.

3. Vikki Ortiz Healy, "After 80 Christmases Apart, Reunion Is Gift for Birth Mother and Daughter," *Chicago Tribune*, December 24, 2016, http://www.chicagotribune.com/news/ct-mother-daughter-reunited-update -met-20161224-story.html.

11. LOVE IS LOVE: PETS ARE FAMILY, TOO

1. P. Raina, D. Waltner-Toews, B. Bonnett, C. Woodward, and T. Abernathy, "Influence of Companion Animals on the Physical and Psychological Health of Older People: An Analysis of a One-Year Longitudinal Study," *Journal of the American Geriatric Society* 47, no. 3 (March 1999): 323–329, http://center 4research.org/healthy-living-prevention/pets-and-health-the-impact-of-companion-animals/#wsa-endnote-10.

2. Glenn N. Levine, Karen Allen, Lynne T. Braun, Hayley E. Christian, Erika Friedmann, Kathryn A. Taubert, Sue Ann Thomas, Deborah L. Wells, Richard A. Lange, "Pet Ownership and Cardiovascular Risk: Scientific Statement from the American Heart Association," *Circulation* (May 9, 2013), https://doi.org /10.1161/CIR.0b013e31829201e1.

3. Maureen McKinney, "Why More Hospitals Are Letting Pets Visit Their Sick Owners," March 20, 2014, http://www.vetstreet.com/our-pet-experts/why-more-hospitals-are-letting-pets-visit-their-sick-owners.

12. DOCTOR ME

1. http://www.patientsbeyondborders.com/medical-tourism-statistics-facts.

2. Age Without Borders Virtual Summit, March 4, 2017, www.agewithoutborders.net.

3. "Music Therapy and Medicine," Music Therapy, Silver Spring, MD, http://www.musictherapy.org/assets/1/7/MT_Medicine_2006.pdf.

14. EARLY-ONSET ALZHEIMER'S: THE VALUE OF KNOWING

1. Stephanie Watson, "Expert Panel Says 'No' to Widespread Testing for Alzheimer's, Dementia," Harvard Women's Health Watch, March 28, 2014, http://www.health.harvard.edu/blog/expert-panel-says-widespread-testing-alzheimers-dementia-201403257090.

15. "JUST SHOOT ME" IS NOT A PLAN

1. Anna Hodgekiss, "The Dying Have a Right NOT to Know They Are Terminally Ill: Couple Launch Campaign to Keep Bad News a Secret After Their Daughter with Cancer 'Gave Up Hope,'" *Daily Mail*, April 7, 2014, http://www.dailymail.co.uk/health/article-2598877/The-dying-right-NOT-know-terminally-ill-Couple-launch-campaign-bad-news-secret-daughter-cancer-gave-hope.html.

2. Peter Whoriskey and Dan Keating, "Terminal Neglect? How Some Hospices Decline to Treat the Dying," *Washington Post*, May 3, 2014, https://www.washingtonpost.com/business/economy/terminal-neglect-how-some-hospices-fail-the-dying/2014/05/03/7d3ac8ce-b8ef-11e3–96ae-f2c36d2b1245_story.html?utm_term=.b9c23aec3de1.

3. Ibid.

16. PLACES TO GO AND THINGS TO DO

1. Heidi Stevens, "Baking with Kids a Reminder That Quick Isn't Always the Best Fix," *Chicago Tribune*, November 23, 2016, http://www.chicagotribune.com/lifestyles/stevens/ct-reminders-to-slow-down-balancing-1127-20161122-column.html.

Index

About the Author

Consultant by day and a writer by night, Joy Loverde has been advocating and troubleshooting the causes, concepts, and needs of an aging population since 1989. Joy is the author of the best seller *The Complete Eldercare Planner: Where to Start, Questions to Ask, and How to Find Help*. In addition to sharing her life's work on the *Today Show* and National Public Radio, and in *Time* and the *Wall Street Journal*, among numerous other major media, she is a popular keynote speaker and blogger. Joy was born and raised in Chicago. You will find Joy here: www.elderindustry.com, on social media—and, on warm summer afternoons, sitting in the right-field bleachers at Wrigley Field.